KV-478-649

CHRIST'S COLLEGE
LIBRARY

REALITY AND CREATIVE VISION
IN GERMAN LYRICAL POETRY

ENGLAND: BUTTERWORTH & CO. (PUBLISHERS) LTD.
                  LONDON: 88 Kingsway, W.C.2

AFRICA: BUTTERWORTH & CO. (AFRICA) LTD.
                  DURBAN: 33/35 Beach Grove

AUSTRALIA: BUTTERWORTH & CO. (AUSTRALIA) LTD.
                  SYDNEY: 6-8 O'Connell Street
                  MELBOURNE: 473 Bourke Street
                  BRISBANE: 240 Queen Street

CANADA: BUTTERWORTH & CO. (CANADA) LTD.
                  TORONTO: 1367 Danworth Avenue, 6

NEW ZEALAND: BUTTERWORTH & CO. (NEW ZEALAND) LTD.
                  WELLINGTON: 49/51 Ballance Street
                  AUCKLAND: 35 High Street

U.S.A.:   BUTTERWORTH INC.
                  WASHINGTON, D.C.: 7235 Wisconsin Avenue, 14

December, 1963

©

The Colston Research Society

1963

Made and printed in Great Britain by
J. W. Arrowsmith Ltd., Bristol

REALITY AND CREATIVE VISION

IN GERMAN LYRICAL POETRY

Edited by

A. CLOSS

Proceedings of the
Fifteenth Symposium of the Colston Research Society
held in the University of Bristol

April 1st–4th, 1963

LONDON

BUTTERWORTHS

1963

This book is Volume XV of the Colston Papers. Permission must be obtained from the Colston Research Society, 71 Winterstoke Road, Bristol 3, England, and from the Publishers, before any part of the contents may be reproduced.

CHRIST'S COLLEGE
LIBRARY

Accession No. 32021

Class No. Quarto
831.04

Catal.
19-3-71

Foreword

THE name of Edward Colston, the great seventeenth-century philanthropist and educationalist, is associated in Bristol with a number of scholastic and charitable institutions. It was adopted by a group of public-spirited citizens when, in 1899, they established the 'University College Colston Society', with the aim of fostering the young and struggling University College. For a decade it played a part in the movement which culminated in the institution of the University of Bristol in 1909.

The Society then changed its name and made its object more precise: it became the 'Colston Research Society', and devoted itself to the encouragement of original work in the University. It made grants for the purpose of apparatus and for the other expenses of research. As resources increased activities expanded and, notably, in the later 'thirties the Society financed a full-scale Social Survey of Bristol.

After the war a new reconsideration of policy led to the decision to devote the major part of the Society's efforts to the promotion of an annual symposium, the first being held in 1948. The rapid growth of the symposium as a means for the advancement of knowledge is one of the remarkable features of the intellectual life of recent years. Usually such meetings are fostered by bodies interested in one particular field of learning. As the list of titles (on the page opposite) shows, no such limitation applies to the symposia of the Colston Research Society. That the subject should be one at an interesting and active stage of development is the main factor in making a choice. The fact that the symposium is held in one of the younger seats of learning, with its home in an historic city, is a stimulus not only to the University but also, we believe, to the visiting guests who have come from many countries. The publication of the proceedings ensures the communication of the papers and discussions to wider circles.

It has been my privilege to have been President of the Colston Research Society for the year 1962–63, during which the fifteenth symposium was promoted by the Society. Its subject was entitled 'Reality and Creative Vision in German Lyrical Poetry', but the difficulties of the subject were not as profound as this somewhat daunting title might suggest. The papers proved an inspiration to many who are called upon to study German literature at academic level and thereby to improve the standard of teaching of this important language.

W. R. S. Bathurst

Introduction

Astraddle on the dolphin's mire and blood,
Spirit after spirit! The smithies break the flood,
.... Those images that yet
Fresh images beget,
That dolphin-torn, that gong-tormented sea.

W. B. Yeats: Byzantium.

THE purpose of the present Colston Research Society Symposium on 'Reality and Creative Vision in German Lyrical Poetry' is an enquiry into the secret which underlies the limitless flux and the process of condensation in lyrical poetry, and into the interrelationship between the universal and the individual, and between matter and artistic presentation. If German poetry has been selected as a test case, our Symposium is by no means narrowly restricted to *one* language in our search for the interrelationship between reality and vision. The poet, according to Goethe, gives permanence to the fleeting moments of life. He can harmonize the sensuous and the intellectual chaos of our world, and secure the very continuity of man's spiritual existence.

The poet's universe is not merely a verbal universe. A true study of poetry is by no means simply a linguistic exercise; its research probes the secrets which underlie the interrelationship between substance and creative activity, and those mysterious depths where intuitive and conceptual knowledge are joined. Thus poetry, as an artistic expression of human feelings, thoughts and dreams, concerns us all. Moreover, our Symposium also looks at the poet in a changing world. Every creative writer is to some extent a mirror of his own time. What is the poet's situation in the time of our spiritual and artistic crisis? Just ten years ago, in a literary prognosis, the following three criteria of the artistic and intellectual situation of our day were singled out (cf. *Monatshefte für Weltliteratur*, I, 1953):

(a) The inclination towards *refinement*, e.g. in the works of Rilke, Valéry, T. S. Eliot. It seems as if there was no way back to the direct expression of personal emotion and commitment. Modern poetry, being predominantly intellectual, is symptomatic of our contemporary predicament;

(b) The rediscovery of the *immense realm of the Unconscious* opened up again by authors such as Nietzsche, Dostoevsky, Yeats, Freud, C. G. Jung, Kafka and others;

(c) The tendency towards *inwardness*. In addition to the above three criteria one could perhaps add (though it is already implied) the predilection for the search into the archaic strata of our existence.

In the *Ptolemäer*, 1949 (in the year when G. Orwell's *1984* appeared) Gottfried Benn states his nihilistic view in unmistakable terms: History is seen as a justification of mass-murder, and European civilization as a stage of disintegration; modern man is depicted as a creature without a past or future. Only the artist (as already expounded in Nietzsche's *Birth of Tragedy*) can still cope with matter and give it sense and shape. Benn advocates pure artistry. Accordingly, the absolute poem is that which is left of a poem when through a process of distillation the artist has purified and cleared it of all dregs such as mood—atmosphere—'profundity'. Such poetry does not concern one privately, but it is a matter of highly specialized and sophisticated enterprise. We have, of course (cf. particularly Enzensberger, Celan etc.) already moved again far away from Benn's 'pure' poetry to highly committed utterances. But one of the most characteristic points about contemporary German and European form of expression lies in the use of words which free themselves from the object and become a law to themselves. This seems to be true of a great number of poems now. There is the mere *language of logic*, unable to bridge the division of the inward and outward; on the other hand there is the *magic of otherness* as the language of disguises, e.g. the favoured themes are: the merry-go-round, kaleidoscope, fish, bird, tree etc.; there is, moreover, the language of *personal withdrawal* because of the bitter edge of love, and the language of *alienation from the natural scene*. But non-representational poetry is, paradoxically, often highly personal: it conceals its depth under an apparently thin layer of baffling tissues. Such poetry deliberately hides the image of the soul and aims at being or appearing depersonalized, antihuman and inorganic. Thus the preoccupation with language has become an end in itself. But as the Symposium will, I feel sure, make abundantly clear, the living springs of German lyrical heritage prove to be inexhaustible, and the forces of tradition and non-representational innovation hold a balance.

Nobody can deny the fact that literature, as mentioned above, reflects the predicaments of our time. Yet literature in its noblest representations is not just a mirror of physical and mental disturbances. The artist is not necessarily a neurotic, but, according to C. G. Jung, a collective man, 'the carrier and former of the unconsciously active soul of mankind' who is able to experience and shape the eternal basic human themes rooted in mysterious depths where feeling and thinking are still one, as for instance in archetypical creations such as *Prometheus, Ödipus, Antigone, Tristan, Parzival, Lear, Hamlet* and *Faust*.

Today, we are embarking on an enterprise which reflects the ultimate endeavour of all university work, i.e. unbiased research. Moreover, our Symposium, as is clear from its programme, stresses the universal character of our academic pursuits. All scientific research belongs to the World, not to a special country, age or university, but at the same time it is rooted in its own sphere and must not be divorced from specialization. The balance of both, universality and specialization, remains the ideal of all true culture. It is my profound belief that this is also the inspiring aim of our own activities which were made possible by the Colston Research Society.

Here I should like to take the opportunity of thanking all those who have made this Symposium possible: above all the Colston Research Society's Honorary Secretary, Mr. R. H. Brown; Professor J. E. Harris, F.R.S., of Bristol University, and my own colleagues who offered me their valuable help unstintingly: Dr. Estelle Morgan as the Academic Secretary, and Miss Margaret Goodbody and Mr. S. Radcliffe as the two Recorders, who most kindly helped me in extracting from the verbatim records the essential points of discussion for publication in the present volume. Mr. M. R. Townson most generously helped me in reading the page-proofs. My profound thanks also go to the contributors who generously responded to the invitations and made this Symposium a unique occasion.

DIRECTOR OF THE SYMPOSIUM   A. CLOSS

Contents

FIFTH SESSION

Chairman: Professor W. I. Lucas

Chairman: The Hon. W. R. S. Bathurst

President of the Colston Research Society

The University was represented by the Pro-Vice-Chancellor, Sir Alfred Pugsley

SIXTH SESSION

Chairman: Professor W. McC. Stewart

Chairman: Professor S. Körner

SEVENTH SESSION

Chairman: Professor L. C. Knights

Illustrations

Speakers

Professor Dr. Jan Aler, Professor of German, University of Leiden, Netherlands.

Professor Beda Allemann, University of Kiel, Germany.

Professor Dr. Paul Böckmann, University of Cologne, Germany.

Richard Thomas Church, C.B.E., F.R.S.L., poet, novelist and literary critic, was the Guest Speaker at the Annual Reception of the Society on Wednesday, 3 April.

Professor A. Closs, M.A., D.Phil., Director of the Symposium, Professor of German, University of Bristol.

Professor H. B. Garland, J.P., M.A., Ph.D., Professor of German, University of Exeter.

Professor L. C. Knights, M.A., D.Phil., Winterstoke Professor of English, University of Bristol.

Professor W. F. Mainland, M.A., Professor of German, University of Sheffield.

Professor R. Peacock, M.A., D.Phil., Litt.D., Professor of German, Bedford College, University of London.

S. S. Prawer, M.A., Ph.D., Litt.D., Senior Lecturer in German, University of Birmingham.

Professor H. Salinger, Chairman and Professor of German, Duke University, North Carolina, U.S.A.

Professor G. C. Schoolfield, Chairman and Professor of Germanic Languages and Literatures, Cincinnati University, Ohio, U.S.A.

Professor W. D. Williams, M.A., D.Phil., Professor of German, University of Liverpool.

List of Members

apart from the speakers

Auerbach, Miss Hilde, Bath.

Bacarisse, S., Department of Spanish, University of Bristol.

Bednall, J. B., Department of German, University College of North Wales, Bangor.

Bridgwater, W. P., Department of German, University of Leicester.

Brooke, Professor K., Department of Modern Languages, University of Keele.

Engel, Dr. Eva J., Department of Modern Languages, University of Keele.

Fowler, Dr. F. M., Department of German, King's College, Aberdeen.

Fox, W. H., Department of German, University of Liverpool.

Gaskell, R. W., Department of English, University of Bristol.

Gifford, Professor C. H., Department of English, University of Bristol.

Goodbody, Miss Margaret L., Department of German, University of Bristol.

Harper, A. J., Department of German, University of Edinburgh.

Hilton, Dr. Ian, Department of German, University College of North Wales, Bangor.

Holmes, F. A., Department of Modern Languages, University of Keele.

Jury, Miss Margaret, Brighton.

Keith-Smith, B., Department of German, University of Bristol.

Körner, Professor S., Department of Philosophy, University of Bristol.

Leighton, J., Department of German, University of Bristol.

Low, D. S., Department of German, University College of Wales, Aberystwyth.

Lucas, Professor W. I., Department of German, University of Southampton.

Morgan, Dr. Estelle, Department of German, University of Bristol.

O'Boyle, Miss Ita, Department of German, Trinity College, Dublin.

Ockenden, R. C., Department of German, University of London (Bedford College).

Peace, R. A., Department of English, University of Bristol.

Popper, Dr. H., Department of German, University College of Swansea.

Prochnick, P., Department of German, University College of Wales, Aberystwyth.

Radcliffe, S., Department of German, University of Bristol.

Van Rest, Miss Hazel, Department of German, University of Exeter.

Reynolds, A. B., Department of English, University of Bristol.

Rowley, Dr. B. A., Department of German, University of London (University College).

Schatzky, Miss Brigitte, Department of Modern Languages, London School of Economics.

Smith, N. Horton, Department of German, University of Nottingham.

Steer, Mrs. Rona M., Edinburgh.

Stewart, Professor W. McC., Department of French, University of Bristol.

Thomas, Dr. L. H. C., Department of German, Trinity College, Dublin.

Tucker, Miss Susie I., Department of English, University of Bristol.

Waidson, Professor H. M., Department of German, University College of Swansea.

Walker, C. A. S., Department of German, University of Bristol.

Walker, R. M., Department of Spanish, University of Bristol.

Warren, J. D. A., Dover College.

Wirtz, Miss Erika A., Department of German, University of Liverpool.

FIRST SESSION

Chairman: Professor A. CLOSS

Professor L. C. KNIGHTS: Poetry as discovery.

Chairman: Professor R. PEACOCK

Professor H. SALINGER: On translating poetry.

Poetry as discovery

by

L. C. KNIGHTS

Lord Clarendon, the great historian of the English Revolution of the Seventeenth Century, says somewhere that the benefit of general councils lies in the fact that they draw contributions from men of very varied aptitudes and abilities: 'And, no question, all great enterprises and designs . . . have many parts . . . fit for the survey and disquisition of several faculties and abilities, and equally for the decision of sharper and more phlegmatic understandings'. As one whose part in these proceedings will necessarily display more phlegm than sharpness, I draw comfort from the thought. I do not know German; neither can I bring to the discussion of Reality and Creative Vision in lyrical poetry the insight of the creative writer; and if, in this meeting, I am not the sole possessor of the second of these disqualifications, I must surely be alone in my claim to the first. My function here can only be to remind you that the problems you are going to discuss are problems of poetry in any language, and that sometimes light can be shed from the understanding of poetry in one language to the understanding of poetry in another.

I wish to begin by citing the testimony of poets to the element of the unplanned, of the virtually *unknown*, that enters into poetic composition. Older poets spoke of inspiration by the Muses; and Blake, who surely worked at his compositions once they had come to him as hard and deliberately as any man, said of his poems, 'The authors are in Eternity'. Modern poets prefer a different language, but what they tell us of the conception of their poems likewise points to an origin beyond deliberate and conscious control. T. S. Eliot says in his essay, 'The Music of Poetry':

> It is a commonplace to observe that the meaning of a poem may wholly escape paraphrase. It is not quite so commonplace to observe that the meaning of a poem may be something larger than its author's conscious purpose, and something remote from its origins (*On Poetry and Poets*, p. 30).

And again:

> If, as we are aware, only a part of the meaning can be conveyed by paraphrase, that is because the poet is occupied with frontiers of consciousness beyond which words fail, though meanings still exist (*ibid.*).

So, too, Wallace Stevens, writing on 'The Irrational Element in Poetry', says of one of his poems:

> While there is nothing automatic about the poem, nevertheless it has an automatic aspect in the sense that it is what I wanted it to be without knowing before

3

it was written what I wanted it to be, even though I knew before it was written what I wanted to do . . . One is always writing about two things at the same time in poetry and it is this that produces the tension characteristic of poetry. One is the true subject and the other is the poetry of the subject (*Opus Posthumous*, ed. Samuel French Morse, pp. 219–221).[1]

The testimony of Valéry is to the same effect. In an essay 'Au Sujet du *Cimetière marin*' he writes of Gustave Cohen's exposition of his poem:

Parmi cette diversité de sensations et de réflexions qui me composaient cette heure de Sorbonne, la dominante était bien la sensation du contraste entre le souvenir de mon travail, qui se ravivait, et la figure finie, l'ouvrage déterminé et arrêté auquel l'exégèse et l'analyse de M. Gustave Cohen s'appliquaient. C'était là ressentir comme notre *être* s'oppose à notre *paraître*. D'une part, mon poème étudié comme un fait accompli, révélant à l'examen de l'expert sa composition, ses intentions, ses moyens d'action, sa situation dans le système de l'histoire littéraire; ses attaches, et l'état probable de l'esprit de son auteur . . . D'autre part, la mémoire de mes essais, de mes tâtonnements, des déchiffrements intérieurs, de ces illuminations verbales très impérieuses qui imposent tout à coup une certaine combinaison de mots,—comme si tel groupe possédât je ne sais quelle force intrinsèque . . . j'allais dire: je ne sais quelle *volonté* d'existence, tout opposée à la 'liberté' ou au chaos de l'esprit, et qui peut quelquefois contraindre l'esprit à dévier de son dessein, et le poème à devenir tout autre qu'il n'allait être, et qu'on ne songeait qu'il dût être.

(On voit par là que la notion d'*Auteur* n'est pas simple: elle ne l'est qu'au *regard des tiers*.)

And of the 'world', or 'mode of existence', of a poem, which is something quite other than its prose summary:

Si donc l'on m'interroge; si l'on s'inquiète, (comme il arrive, et parfois assez vivement) de ce que j'ai 'voulu dire' dans tel poème, je réponds que je n'ai pas *voulu dire*, mais *voulu faire*, et que ce fut l'intention de *faire* qui *a voulu* ce que j'ai dit.

Quant au '*Cimetière marin*', cette intention ne fut d'abord qu'une figure rythmique vide, ou remplie de syllabes vaines, qui me vint obséder quelque temps.

What seems to be agreed is that poetry comes from below, or beyond, the level of deliberate and conscious control: the poet does not 'have a thought'—or 'a perception'—and then proceed to clothe it in poetry; his task is rather—and the phrase comes from, of all people, John Dryden—that of 'moving the sleeping images of things towards the light'. This does not mean that poetry is innocent of thought or that poetic thought is radically different from all other kinds. It means that the poet is abnormally sensitive to normal processes, and that what he finally produces still retains a charge of pre-conceptual meanings that are discarded in discursive prose.

4

In a subtle and suggestive paper contributed to the Twelfth Colston Symposium, D. W. Harding discussed the way in which all thought—except perhaps in its more rigidly disciplined forms—emerges from an obscure and complex hinterland of promptings, feelings, interests and attitudes that normally remain below the level of consciousness.[2] What makes a man a poet—and Harding's paper brought this out very clearly—is not only his receptiveness to normally elusive promptings, but his ability to construct a symbolic form in which meanings that elude the firm grasp of the mind are still somehow actively present. Perhaps this is what Wallace Stevens meant when he said that 'The poem must resist the intelligence / Almost successfully'.

From this various things follow. One, in Harding's words, is that 'a writer, especially a poet, using words, images and incidents with evaluative or symbolic overtones is likely very often to convey meanings which he can't be said to have intended before writing and which he may not observe even when he reads over what he has written'—which is a slightly extended version of 'How can I know what I mean till I see what I say?'[3] Another, unless this is simply a different way of saying the same thing, is that there is an element of *discovery* in all good poetry (I mean for the poet as well as for the reader); and sometimes this takes so entirely unexpected a form, seems so contrary to the *données* of the poem, so against the direction in which the poem promises to move, that we can see with unusual clarity how poetry becomes a new thought. When this happens it is not necessarily by any determined attack on the unknown, but by the poet's simply being faithful to the 'feel' of what lies behind his more or less deliberate intention, of those subliminal promptings that 'thought', proceeding in a straight line ('reason's click-clack'), would necessarily ignore. What I mean by discovery I must now attempt to define by some examples.

My first example is Keats's 'Ode on a Grecian Urn'. You will remember how, in contemplating the urn, Keats sees it as the embodiment of an ideal beauty that transcends the conflicts and thwartings of life as we know it ('All breathing human passion far above . . .'), whilst at the same time he projects onto the depicted figures a pulsing sensuous vitality ('more happy, happy love! For ever warm and still to be enjoy'd . . .'). The question imposes itself therefore whether the poem—for all its obvious power—is anything more than the indulgence of a day-dream. 'Getting it both ways', says F. R. Leavis, '—the poem essentially *is* that . . . Clearly (he goes on), the urn for Keats is the incitement and support to a day-dream; the dream of a life that, without any drawbacks, shall give him all he desires—shall be for ever warm and still be enjoyed' (*Revaluation: Tradition and Development in English Poetry*, p. 253). Leavis's masterly essay certainly helped to get recognition for aspects of Keats's genius hitherto obscured, and one remains grateful for it. But in the course of years I have come to feel that this particular judgement—'Clearly . . . the incitement and support to a day-dream'—ignores disturbing powers of growth that, present and working in the poem, give a decisive turn to the current of the poet's thought.

Everything of course depends on how we take—on how we are intended to take—the final stanza, where Keats stands back from the scenes into which he has imaginatively entered and again, as at the beginning of the poem, addresses the urn as a whole:

5

> O Attic shape! Fair attitude! with brede
>   Of marble men and maidens overwrought,
> With forest branches and the trodden weed;
>   Thou, silent form, dost tease us out of thought
> As doth eternity: Cold Pastoral!
>   When old age shall this generation waste,
>   Thou shalt remain, in midst of other woe
> Than ours, a friend to man, to whom thou say'st,
>   'Beauty is truth, truth beauty,'—that is all
>   Ye know on earth, and all ye need to know.

In the last two lines, who is addressing whom? Clearly, 'Beauty is truth, truth beauty' is spoken by the urn, and there seems to be something like general agreement that in the last line and a bit Keats is exhorting his readers to accept the message of the urn—that 'beauty', with whatever meanings that word may take in the context of the poem, is the ultimate reality. But must it be with that unctuous lift that we read the last two lines of a poem that is clearly shaped by an energy that will not for long allow even the most vividly realized self-indulgence? Accept the suggestion made by an American critic[4] that '"Ye" means not everybody-in-time-to-come, but the *figures on the urn* (whose experience now *is* limited to the Beautiful as there depicted)', and different tones, and with them different meanings, impose themselves: in 'that is all Ye know on earth' the emphasis shifts from 'all' to 'Ye'—

> that is all
> *Ye* know on earth, and all *ye* need to know.

There is of course no question of substituting for a mere easy exaltation a mere bitter irony (as the crude notation of italics may suggest): all that is needed is the slightest change of stress to show that the poet is now pondering, distancing—a process that began with the hushed coolness of the beautiful fourth stanza, found a focus in 'desolate'

> —And, little town, thy streets for evermore
>   Will silent be; and not a soul to tell
>   Why thou art desolate, can e'er return—

and continued in the last stanza with 'silent form' and 'Cold Pastoral'. The poet now identifies himself not with the figures on the urn but with his readers ('Thou, silent form, dost tease us out of thought'), and what *we* know, subject as we are to 'old age' and 'woe', is very different from what *they* know, or are assumed to know.

It is the tenor of the poem's conclusion (beginning in the fourth stanza), therefore, that prevents us from taking the message of the urn as a simple unanalyzed assertion of beauty as somehow a higher reality. The urn of course says it is: it says that the ideal satisfactions imputed to the figures on the urn represent real possibilities of human living and are not the product of a cheating fancy. The poet who wrote those words for the urn to say had of course tried hard to endorse them; but—'the fancy cannot cheat so well As she is fam'd to do'—it is when he allows the urn to reverse the proposition—'Beauty is truth, truth beauty'—that the counter-balancing strains, present though subdued in the poem as a whole, assert themselves. The truth about human life (inevitably we think of the Induction to the revised *Hyperion*) is not 'beautiful'—not, that is, in any sense applicable to the urn's pronouncement. A complex symbol has been created and its meaning explored; the poet has tried to sum up that meaning in a simple sweeping assertion about the identity of truth and beauty; and the energy of his imagination, his honesty, has prevented him. It is the emergent recognition that what the urn says, taken as an affirmation about life as a whole, just will not do, that explains the final shift of tone in which the discovery—something the poet knows and the urn cannot know—is registered.

There is of course room for some variety of interpretation of Keats's Ode; some of you may feel that the poem's success is limited and precarious, or that the growing-point is below the surface of the verse rather than established in it. Of my next example—the second of five poems to which George Herbert gave the title, 'Affliction'—the success is, I think, assured, and we can give our attention to the way in which it is achieved.

> Broken in pieces all asunder,
>   Lord, hunt me not,
>   A thing forgot,
> Once a poore creature, now a wonder,
>   A wonder tortur'd in the space
>   Betwixt this world and that of grace.
>
> My thoughts are all a case of knives,
>   Wounding my heart
>   With scatter'd smart,
> As wat'ring pots give flowers their lives.
>   Nothing their furie can controll
>   While they do wound and pink my soul.
>
> All my attendants are at strife,
>   Quitting their place
>   Unto my face:
> Nothing performs the task of life:
>   The elements are let loose to fight,
>   And while I live, trie out their right.
>
> Oh help, my God! let not their plot
>   Kill them and me,
>   And also thee,
> Who art my life: dissolve the knot,
>   As the sunne scatters by his light
>   All the rebellions of the night.

7

Then shall those powers, which work for grief,
Enter thy pay,
And day by day
Labour thy praise, and my relief;
With care and courage building me,
Till I reach heav'n, and much more, thee.

The craftsmanship of this is superb, though the poem looks simple enough. In each stanza a line of four stresses is followed by two short rhyming lines, each of two beats; another four-stress line rhymes with the first; and then two more four-stress lines rhyme together and complete the stanza. Needless to say, this is only an approximation to what we find when we read the poem aloud: metrical feet are reversed and broken, and there is great variation in the weight of the stresses, so that the rather formal pattern of the verse in no way suggests artificiality: here, we feel, is a man speaking about something of urgent concern. Yet the formal patterning is important; for the verse structure—as in all good poems—is precisely shaped to reveal the intellectual and emotional structure of the experience behind or within it. Indeed, as so often with Herbert, the verse is so 'wrought', so clear in immediate impact, that one is surprised to find how much is going on underneath. There should however be no surprise: only poetic craftsmanship of a high order could give form to insights so complex and elusive and yet, once they are established, so assured.

In the first three stanzas the pattern repeats itself, with variations. Each stanza opens with an emphatic statement of disintegration and pain ('Broken in pieces all asunder', 'My thoughts are all a case of knives'); the short, almost staccato, couplet that follows hammers home the meaning and implications: in the first stanza

—Lord, hunt me not,
A thing forgot,—

the poet is not only 'broken'—aware of disintegrating stresses—he feels the panic of the hunted; in the fourth line of each stanza the rhythm smooths out as the poet stands back from his experience to make a more general, less directly personal, statement about it; but this leads back at once to the more poignantly direct evocation of his plight in the concluding lines. Now in all this, you are made to feel, there is something paradoxical, and what I especially want to call attention to is that at first sight odd metaphor within a metaphor of the second stanza:

My thoughts are all a case of knives,
Wounding my heart,
With scatter'd smart,
As wat'ring pots give flowers their lives.

His thoughts cut and pierce like knives ('pink', later, is a term from fencing and suggests the desperate bout he feels engaged in); that is plain enough, but the metaphor of the watering-pot complicates things. Herbert's knife-like thoughts wound 'with scatter'd smart', like water from the rose of a watering-pot, and the image admirably suggests the not easily localized misery (a sort of prickly heat) that goes with some forms of spiritual distress. But the image isn't only descriptive in this way: Herbert says, 'As wat'ring pots *give flowers their lives*'. The troublesome thoughts don't 'give life', of course—quite the reverse—but, the metaphor suggests, they ought to. And this, I think brings to a head something pervasive in these first three stanzas:—the sense that the disintegration from which the poet suffers is caused by the conflict or misdirection of something valuable in itself. The fourth stanza marks the climax: it is an urgent plea for help, and the precise form that it takes, the order of its appeals, is important.

> Oh help, my God! let not their plot
>   Kill them and me,
>   And also thee,
> Who art my life. . . .

The misdirected 'powers' are working against God, against life, against the poet's own integrity, and against themselves. Herbert, then, doesn't ask God to destroy or dismiss his unruly 'attendants', but only to release them and set them free for their proper 'task of life'—

> . . . dissolve the knot,
> As the sunne scatters by his light
> All the rebellions of the night.

This movement of reversal—as triumphant and natural as the sun-rise—is continued in the final stanza, where the assured rhythm and the clinching alliteration provide a firm contrast to the 'Broken in pieces . . .' of the opening:

> Then shall those powers, which work for grief,
>   Enter thy pay,
>   And day by day
> Labour thy praise, and my relief;
>   With care and courage building me,
>   Till I reach heav'n, and much more, thee.

The insight in which the poem culminates is clear enough: the 'powers which work for grief' can 'enter God's pay': properly directed, they are necessary for the active, constructive process which is life ('with care and courage building me'). What gives the insight depth and actuality is of course the activity of the poetic process. This poem, so intimately concerned with the self, has a tough impersonality: as the careful craftsmanship shows, there is no mere outpouring of emotion; and it is this quality—the purity of the attention directed towards the self—that is the condition of the poet's finding himself. Putting it another way, we may say that it is the poet's 'concentration upon a task'[5] that enables him to draw on resources of intuitive knowledge, made available to the imagination through the complex play of the imagery.

This last point is one that I should like to emphasize, for in preparing this paper I have come to feel more and more that it is the poet's 'concentration upon a task' that allows him to tap sources of significance otherwise inaccessible. Valéry, I believe, more than once implies a profound connexion between the poet's deliberate attention to form and that re-making of the self which, he says, is what every poem is.[6]

> En particulier, je me trouvai accoutumé, après quelque temps, à un singulier renversement des opérations de l'esprit qui compose: il m'arrivait souvent de déterminer ce que les philosophes appellent, bien ou mal, le 'contenu' de la pensée (il vaudrait mieux parler du contenu des expressions) par des considérations de forme. Je prenais, si l'on veut, la pensée pour 'inconnue' et, par autant d'approximations qu'il en fallait, je m'avançais de proche en proche vers 'elle'. ('Souvenirs', *Mélange*).

'Form' of course is a tricky word, and although it is useful for the critic to keep in mind the distinction (borrowed by Coleridge from A. W. Schlegel) between 'mechanical' and 'organic' form[7]—the latter being the only sense that matters—abstract definition doesn't much help: only a poet can give us hints of the subtle play between rhythms, images and so on—the form to which he so scrupulously attends—and 'the unknown' to which he seeks to approximate. For present purposes it may be sufficient to point to the early drafts of obviously successful poems—of Blake's 'London', for example, where we can see the successive discarding of first approximations until line-order, epithet, rhythm and image combine to reveal the striven for meaning with an explosive force.

A brief reference to Coleridge's 'Dejection: an Ode' will allow me to draw these observations to a conclusion. The first draft[8] is a long verse letter to Sara Hutchinson that Coleridge wrote on 4 April, 1802, in the depths of his personal miseries. It contains much that could only have been written by a gifted poet, but it is not a great poem; what Coleridge finally made of it is. The draft is more than twice as long as the completed poem. Between the two there has been a labour of excision, re-arranging, tautening, so that a firm structure emerges from the apparent irregularity of the Ode: the poem no longer trails, it concentrates; and with the jettisoning of self-pity, the same kind of absorbed but impersonal attention that is given to the outward scene

> —Though I should gaze for ever
> On that green light that lingers in the west—

appears also in the self-analysis. The storm, whose coming-on is noticed at the beginning of the poem, no longer appears mid-way but is transferred to near the end, with the effect of suggesting (it 'long has raved unnoticed') that it is an inner storm—a disturbance going on beneath the controlled surface of the verse—that matters. What is now at the centre of the poem is the recognition, at a deep level of awareness, of creative energy—of 'joy', 'my shaping spirit of imagination'—as life's primary and indispensable power. It is only an apparent paradox that a poem that sets out to deal with a numbing misery—'A stifled, drowsy, unimpassioned grief'—should end with the deeply felt injunction to 'rejoice'.

Coleridge wrote no more poems of that order, but it is here, it seems to me, that he really discovered and made his own what was to become the vital principle of his thought. The *Biographia Literaria* is, among other things, a handbook of the 'modes of intellectual energy' that poetry embodies and evokes; and although here his main concern is the energies of art and language, his principles of criticism are very much the same as the principles that guide his explorations in other spheres. Just as imagination 'calls the whole soul of man into activity', so both reason and faith enlist not some isolated faculty but the personality as a whole; and whether Coleridge is dealing with poetry, with religion, with the art of thought, with education, or with politics, he shows the same fundamental concern with life and growth and creativeness—'The passion and the life, whose fountains are within'.[9]

It is appropriate to end with Coleridge. What I have tried to suggest in this paper is that because poetry reaches down below the level of conceptual understanding it may result in radically new 'discovery'—a reorientation of the person that makes possible a new and perhaps unexpected insight; and that discovery is most likely to occur when the poet is centring his powers on the job in hand, on shaping his 'form' under the pressure of an intuition that has yet to be brought to consciousness. And although the few poems I have dealt with have been poems of radical discovery, they all, I think, illustrate the normal working of the poetic imagination. What may now be added is that this account of the processes of poetic thought (if, as I hope, it is true) has implications far beyond the bounds of 'poetry' as commonly understood. It was not by chance that Coleridge, our greatest literary critic, was throughout his life concerned with the conditions of valid thinking and that his thought in these respects has no rigid dividing-lines. If he knew that for some of our most important intellectual operations we need to free ourselves from the tyranny of the visual, he also knew 'the danger of thinking without images': images engage the mind and prevent it from slipping too easily through its abstractions.[10] He also knew that because reason—unlike the notional understanding—is not purely abstract, there can be no final separation between knowledge and activated being. As he said in a well-known letter to Poole, 'My opinion is this—that deep Thinking is attainable only by a man of deep Feeling, and that all Truth is a species of Revelation'.[11]

NOTES

1. I should like to say that I was directed to this essay by a quotation in Professor Frank Kermode's extremely helpful little book on Stevens in the 'Writers and Critics' series (Oliver and Boyd).

2. D. W. Harding, 'The Hinterland of Thought' (*Metaphor and Symbol*, ed. L. C. Knights and Basil Cottle).

3. So too Wallace Stevens: 'Now, just as the choice of subject is unpredictable at the outset, so its development, after it has been chosen, is unpredictable' (*Opus Posthumous*, p. 221).

4. H. St. Quentin, quoted by John Berryman in the New York *Nation*, August, 1947.

5. 'No artist produces great art by a deliberate attempt to express his personality. He expresses his personality indirectly through concentrating upon a task which is a task in the same sense as the making of an efficient engine or the turning of a jug or a table-leg'. (T. S. Eliot, 'Four Elizabethan Dramatists,' *Selected Essays*, p. 114).

6. See Elizabeth Sewell, *Paul Valéry* (Bowes and Bowes), pp. 49–50. Miss Sewell refers to the passage quoted from *Mélange*.

7. Coleridge, *Shakespearean Criticism*, ed. T. M. Raysor (Everyman Library), Vol. I, p. 198.

8. An account of the composition of the poem, together with the original draft, is given by Ernest de Selincourt in *Essays and Studies* of the English Association, Vol. XXII (1936), and in the same writer's *Wordsworthian and Other Studies* (pp. 57–76). The draft is also printed as an Appendix in Humphrey House's *Coleridge*.

9. For the close relation, in Coleridge's thought, of imagination, reason and faith, see F. J. A. Hort, 'Coleridge', *Cambridge Essays* (1856), pp. 323–24. 'Coleridge on the Growth of the Mind', by Dorothy M. Emmet (*Bulletin of the John Rylands Library*, Vol. 34, No. 2) is a fine account of the relation between Coleridge's poetry and his philosophy.

10. Coleridge, *Letters*, ed. E. L. Griggs, Vol. I, p. 646 (1 November, 1800). T. E. Hulme said of Imagist poetry that it 'always endeavours to arrest you, and to make you continuously see a physical thing, to prevent you gliding through an abstract process'—*Speculations*, p. 134 (quoted by Frank Kermode, *Wallace Stevens*, p. 26). Similarly Northrop Frye says of the Bible that it offers a 'resistance to abstract thought'—*Fearful Symmetry*, p. 317.

11. *Letters*, ed. Griggs, Vol. II, p. 709, 23 March 1801. See also Hort, *op. cit.*, p. 325.

Discussion

Closs wondered whether the speaker thought that this kind of discovery occurred in literary genres other than lyric poetry.

Knights answered that it did occur in other genres, such as drama, especially Shakespearean drama. He instanced *Othello*, Act III, Sc. iii, where Othello echoes words used by Iago, and vice versa, thus creating the impression of 'a mind in dialogue with itself' revealing unconscious ideas which do not emerge in any other way.

Salinger interpreted the lecture on 'Poetry as Discovery' as indicating that a poem has *to do* and not just *to be*, and that poems had a message *for the poet*, as well as for the reader.

Closs stated that, to a certain degree, every artistic work had an autonomous life.

Salinger asked if there was the same inner dialogue in *Faust* as in *Othello*; he had in mind the dialogue between the Earth Spirit and Faust, followed by that between Faust and Wagner, as examples of this phenomenon.

Knights replied that he was not thinking of the author putting a part of himself into two different characters, but of the emergence in a poet of a heightened awareness in the course of writing his poem, an awareness in which what had previously been felt intuitively became conscious. In lyric poetry there was nothing comparable to the dramatist's deliberate splitting of himself into different persons. Poets, by their own admission, were *not* masters of their thoughts; but they did not merely *record* intuitive ideas; on the contrary, they worked very hard in developing them.

On translating lyric poetry

by

HERMAN SALINGER

An old friend of mine, who owed his training to the German humanistic *gymnasium*, used to say: 'You can begin any speech with the words: "Schon die alten Römer…"' A passage from Cicero is my point of departure. In his oration *Pro Archia Poeta* occurs a sentence, recognizable I am sure to many of you, which has been my favourite Cicero passage since school days, probably because it is almost the only quotation from that worthy man which has stuck with me:

> Haec studia adulescentiam alunt, senectutem oblectant, secundas res ornant, adversis perfugium ac solatium praebent, delectant domi, non impediunt foris, pernoctant nobiscum, peregrinantur, rusticantur.

By 'these studies' Cicero probably meant rhetoric and poetry, since Archias (for whom Cicero was seeking the protection and privilege of Roman citizenship) was, I believe, not only a poet but also a tutor and teacher, mayhap somewhat of a translator and comparatist, too, between the fields of the Greek and Latin literatures. If I am right in these conjectures, then Archias deserved to be made *de jure* what he already was *de facto*: namely a citizen of the then known world. And, to argue somewhat in reverse, nothing could have entitled him more to this privilege than the vocation or avocation of a translator, for in his humble way it is the translator who has made possible the coming alive of world literature and the coming of that age of *Welt-literatur* predicted by Goethe in the closing years of his life, from 1827 on. Cicero had, it would seem, no such internationalist ideas of 'these studies' when he wrote that 'these studies nourish adolescence, are a diversion to old age, adorn success, offer a refuge and a solace in adversity, delight at home and do not impede abroad; they spend the nights with us, they go on journeys with us, they go out into the country-side and rusticate with us'.

Therefore without hesitancy I offer you a journey into the lyric and at times linguistic countryside, in the pursuit of that elusive quintessence: the essential ingredients of a translator of lyric poetry, examining some of his procedures in reproducing a lyric in another language.

It was just as well that we started in the Latin classroom, since it was there that most of us first learned the process of translation. This was—undoubtedly for all—at first a chore; later it may have developed for a few into a 'delight at home', in the form of homework, and finally into a companionable habit. This habit of *nearly*-simultaneous thinking in two languages easily lent itself (a year or two later) to transition from a Latin-to-English process into a French-into-English or German-into-English process, while the time required to slip mentally from one tongue into the other grew less and less and the action became steadily *more nearly* simultaneous, approximating 'thinking in a foreign language'.

When, however, we come to examine the genesis of a lyric translator, I think we find the procedure consciously reversing itself. Having acquired this ability—to think simultaneously bilingually, at least to some extent—the budding translator of poetry, reading over and memorizing the original (be it a poem of Alfred de Musset or Francis Jammes or Rilke) is aware of a rising desire to think this poem *out* of its original French or German and into that English poem which already stands beside it in a blurred, ghost-like aura, like a double film exposure. Precisely *how* this happens, why it should happen at all, remains a mystery—perhaps the central mystery of this entire strange phenomenon. And I am inclined to believe that the desire to rethink the poem in one's own mother tongue, to recast this statue, as it were, in another medium, is and remains so mysterious because it is allied closely to the *malheur d'être poète*. We should, in fact, have to coin a new phrase for it: *le malheur d'être traducteur*. The disease has been classically described by William Blake in two lines:

> ' . . . double the vision my eyes do see,
> And a double vision is always with me,'

even though Blake was actually describing a different dichotomy.

If I may be forgiven for becoming autobiographical, I recall an instance of the poetic process which may throw light on the nature of translation. One idle and restful Sunday during the occupation months in Germany, a sonnet or near-sonnet (tetrameter instead of pentameter)—came into being. Finding what I had written to my liking, I felt the 'double vision' assert itself (since these were English words describing a German scene) in the form of an occasional word or phrase or an entire line sounding in the inner ear in German. Within a few moments an entire German twin poem had come into being. It is interesting in retrospect to see what changes needed to be made in switching from English to German—a switch I was not particularly accustomed to making, not nearly so familiar to me as the other way around.

> This is the way the hours are:
> the morning glare on street and roof,
> the sparrow: lyric and aloof,
> then rain, a book, a slow cigar.

This became (losing completely the line: 'This is the way the hours are' and beginning with the thought-content of the 'morning glare on street and roof'):

> Kommt Morgenglanz auf Weg und Dach,
> singt Vogel: lyrisch und allein;
> Zigarre, Buch.—Am Nachmittag
> prasselt der Regen kühl und fein.

Not only was line 1 lost. The cigar and book moved up to line 3 and the two words: 'then rain' were expanded (or expanded themselves) into the thought-content: 'in the afternoon, the rain patters cool and fine'.

These matters were simple. However, the next line: 'An inward peace no world can mar', simply had to be preserved, but it was altered, by the spirit of the language, as it were, into:

Und Frieden innen, unverkannt.

My German *alter ego* tackled the next three lines:

smooth fabric on whose warp and woof
the spirit's shuttle back and forth
flies silent without jolt or jar

and expressed them with tolerable accuracy and, I hoped, without loss of style, as follows:

der Seele Webstuhl wirkt und flieht
still hin und her und webt und zieht
den Stoff, der schon das Herz bespannt.[1]

Perhaps it is understandable, since the German has so many words to express *spirit*, that the English word *spirit* found itself split into *Seele* and *Herz* and the 'smooth fabric' grew more specific as *der Stoff, der schon das Herz bespannt*.

At any rate, this self-imposed job of transmogrifying myself into German and recostuming my Muse in a sort of diaphanous Rilkean toga, taught me, some years ago, that one must no longer hesitate to switch the position of lines expressing the same thought, to metamorphose an adjective into a noun, if need be, or *vice-versa*, but never to dream of sacrificing the rhyme.

'O qui dira les torts de la rime', cried Verlaine, in his *Art poétique* a good seventy-five years ago, calling rhyme the invention of a deaf child or an insane savage who made this gem sound hollow and false:

O! qui dira les torts de la rime!
Quel enfant sourd ou quel nègre fou
Nous a forgé ce bijou d'un sou
Qui sonne creux et faux sous la lime?

But be it noted that Verlaine spoke thus *in rhyme*, in very effective rhymes which helped get the point of his rhetorical question across.

Let me reverse Verlaine's question by exclaiming: Who can tell the wrongs of *un*rhyme, of rhymelessness in translations, specifically in translating a superb master of the technique of rhyming like Rainer Maria Rilke into rhymeless and therefore unavoidably prosy English? This is the ambiguous service performed by Mrs. Herter-Norton, who offered us in the United States a kind of Rilke pony about two decades ago when Rilke was being discovered in America and was just becoming the rage. She did so with no pose of writing verse, however. Whereas Randall Jarrell did not wince at reciting his adulterated Rilke, his *unreiner Rainer*, in a rhymeless singsong.

But let us compare Rilke's 'Die Erblindende' in two English versions. First, Mrs. Norton, making no pretence at preserving the form, at least not the inner form, nor the outer either:

GOING BLIND[2]

She sat quite like the others there at tea.
It seemed to me at first she grasped her cup
a little differently from the rest.
Once she gave a smile. It almost hurt.

And when people finally stood up and spoke
and slowly and as chance brought it about
moved through many rooms (they talked and laughed),
I saw her. She was moving after the others,

withheld, as one who in a moment
will have to sing and before many people;
upon her bright eyes, that rejoiced,
was light from outside as upon a pool.

She followed slowly, taking a long time,
as though something had not yet been surmounted;
and yet as though, after a crossing over,
she would no longer walk, but fly.

I attempted it in my own way. The difference can be ascribed chiefly to preserving the rhyme:[3]

She sat just like the other ones at tea.
At first it seemed to me she lifted up
not quite the way the others did, her cup.
And once she smiled: a smile it hurt to see.

And when they stood and chatted by their chairs
and slowly, quite as chance might have it, walked
through all those many rooms (they laughed and talked),
I saw her follow as they went in pairs.

She was withdrawn, like one who waits beyond
a turn of time, to sing before a crowd;
upon her clear eyes (happy, almost proud)
light fell as if from outside on a pond.

She followed slowly, and she felt her way,
as though she still must overcome some thing;
and yet, as if, after a certain day,
her steps would lift and lighten and take wing.

17

One American professor, understandably discouraged and bewildered by the profusion of more than forty good, bad and indifferent English translations of *Faust*, has recently added a prose paraphrase to the already glutted market. Another has gone overboard in his over-fidelity to rhyme and given us Goethe's lyrics in a completely unlyrical English style. Choose your favourite wave in this swelling sea of garbled Goethe and rhymeless Rilke. As for me, I am tempted to cry out to the Nortons (and the Jarrells) by slightly misquoting the dying Hamlet:

> If thou didst ever hold me in thy heart,
> Absent thee from facility awhile.

My point is this, then, that the translator, unless he is a mere hack, feels not simply a *cacoethes scribendi* but a real itch to get behind the scenes. As I expressed it in an earlier article: 'The truly devoted translator is impelled almost against his will toward a certain poem, driven by a desire to repeat the original creative act, to re-experience part of the life history of the poem, and thus to come closer to its heart. It is doubtless for this reason that poets "in their own right" not infrequently are the best translators of poetry'.[4]

Be it noted that Rilke himself, in translating poems of Michael-Angelo, Verlaine and Baudelaire, as well as fifteen poems by his contemporary and friend, Paul Valéry, retained the rhyme—nor would he have dreamt of abandoning it in 'Germanizing' a sonnet by Stéphane Mallarmé, not to mention twenty-four sonnets of Louïze Labé and the more than forty *Sonnets from the Portuguese* by Elizabeth Barrett Browning.

One is reminded of what Alexander Fraser Tytler, Lord Woodhouselee, had to say on this point in his *Essay on the Principles of Translation* in 1790;[5] namely: 'To attempt . . . a translation of a lyric poem into prose, is the most absurd of all undertakings'.

I have taken for granted that the prime *donnée* of the translator is an understanding of the two languages and I shall shortly be forced to give some sad examples of this lack. For, as Tytler wrote: 'If the genius and character of all languages were the same, it would be an easy task to translate from one into another; nor would anything more be requisite on the part of the translator, than fidelity and attention'. Tytler does, however, imply fidelity and attention as desiderata, but let us allow Tytler to continue: 'But as the genius and character of languages is confessedly very different, it has hence become a common opinion, that it is the duty of a translator to attend only to the sense and spirit of his original, to make himself perfectly master of his author's ideas, and to communicate them in those expressions which he judges to be best suited to convey them. It has, on the other hand, been maintained that in order to constitute a perfect translation, it is not only requisite that the ideas and sentiments of the original author should be conveyed, but likewise his style and manner of writing'. It is not surprising, therefore, if Alexander Tytler, who, though somewhat gusty, is always robust and alive, concludes some hundred and three pages later, in his chapter devoted specifically to translating lyric poetry, that 'none but a poet can translate a poet'.

18

Rather than reserve my conclusions until later, let me state the obvious now. It is a *sine qua non* that the translator know the language of the original, be it Goethe's or Heine's or Rilke's German, the French of Baudelaire or Valéry, the Spanish of Jiménez or Garcia-Lorca, and that he know it well: not only grammatically but with a feeling for style, with *Sprachgefühl*, indeed with the delicate fingers of a safe-cracker, *i.e.* with *Fingerspitzengefühl*. But he must also (if at all possible) be a poet within the second language into which he is moving his Goethe, Baudelaire or Lorca. To this point Tytler quotes Sir John Denham's 'Preface to the Second Book of Vergil's Aeneid' as follows:

'It is not his [the translator's] business alone to translate language into language, but poesie into poesie; and poesie is of so subtle a spirit that in pouring out of one language into another, it will all evaporate; and if a new spirit is not added in the transfusion, there will remain nothing but a *caput mortuum*'.

Is it not predictable that so delicate and perceptive a sensibility as that of William Butler Yeats was able, in a few lines, to effect a partial re-capture of the spirit of so elusive a poet as Pierre Ronsard?—And here we encounter not a full translation but a partial one; perhaps it is not translation at all but an inspired and loving paraphrase. The outcome, the message—the moral or lesson one might almost say—of the two poems is not the same, but that Yeats was inspired by the first quatrain of Ronsard's sonnet seems inevitable. The spirit and the situational pictures coincide:

> Quand vous serez bien vieille, au soir, à la chandelle,
> Assise auprès du feu, dévidant et filant,
> Direz, chantant mes vers, et vous émerveillant:
> 'Ronsard me célébrait, du temps que j'étais belle!'

> When you are old and grey and full of sleep
> And nodding by the fire, take down this book,
> And slowly read, and dream of the soft look
> Your eyes had once, and of their shadows deep.

From here the poets deviate from one another and the poems with them, till Ronsard ends with the admonition that, lest she regret it, the lady Helen abandon her proud disdain and gather rosebuds while she may:

> Cueillez dès aujourd'hui les roses de la vie

whereas the more modern Yeats is less optimistic and more introspective, and, being the one man who 'loved the pilgrim soul' in his lady,

> And loved the sorrows of your changing face

he knows that she will

> Murmur a little sadly, how love fled
> And paced upon the mountain overhead,
> And hid his face amid a crowd of stars.

3   19

Forgive me if I have shown something off our subject—or is it off the subject to demonstrate the process of *dis*sociation often experienced by the poetic sensibility? For Yeats, this image of the faded beauty by the fireside translated itself quite beautifully, according to its own laws, into something else, something new and for a different age.

That inaccuracy is a serious fault in a translator goes without saying. Obviously, a pretty Flaubertian sort of Catalogue of Human Errors might with patience be compiled. Such a list would include a few great names. Turning from the lyric o the drama, Sir Walter Scott's translation of *Götz von Berlichingen* contained a prize boner. If I recall it correctly, in translating a speech by Brother Martin (whom Goethe apparently intended to suggest the figure of Martin Luther) where the good friar has said that the monastery's garden is its *bee-hive*, Sir Walter rendered *Bienenkorb* as 'basket of beans', obviously influenced by the next sentence which contains an enumeration of other vegetables. The sense, to be sure, suffers only slightly.

The whole matter of the translation of song lyrics, particularly of German *lieder* of the Romantic Period, has occupied and puzzled me for a good while. Here the problem is complicated by a new factor: the melody, and by the necessity—or what *should* be felt as a necessity—of following the composer's lead and of rendering the German into an English which will coincide with the stresses of the music, that is: with whatever emphasis the composer chose to give the line, whether or not the translator agrees with that emphasis. The results are often deplorable—that is, if you place any value whatever on the lyric poem and do not attribute ninety-nine per cent to the music and consider the words an incidental and necessary evil. Admittedly, in some cases the original lyric is trifling. Even such great lieder composers as Schumann and Brahms occasionally selected minor poems by minor poets for what turned out to be major musical achievements, a case in point being Schumann's songs to twelve poems by Justinus Kerner. With perhaps one exception, these poems would not 'make it' into an anthology of the German lyric. Yet they have that indefinable quality known as charm, a melancholy whimsicality which appealed to Robert Schumann. The same is true of his cycle of *Frauen-Liebe und -Leben*, lyrics by the French-born nobleman who became one of the most typically bourgeois German poets of his day, Adalbert von Chamisso. I have rubbed shoulders with this problem when music students, who knew too little German to sing these tender songs in the original language, could not stomach the usual insipid translations and called me in as a sort of poetic troubleshooter. I remember trying, with only limited success, to get the lines straightened out so that Schumann's music should keep its original meaning. In other words, a good lyric translation may not be singable. And, contrariwise, a singable translation may be an otherwise poor one. Unfortunately, many nineteenth and early twentieth century translations of songs are *both* unsingable and otherwise poor. Yet I should not care to have my Chamisso translations, made for students to sing, appear in print. When Chamisso wrote:

> Du Ring an meinem Finger
> mein goldenes Ringelein

Schumann shaped his music so that the longer notes coincided with the syllables Ring—mein—Fing—gold—Ring and lein. To translate this: 'Upon my hand this ring' would throw the stressed notes on such syllables as 'Pon and draw out or spread the word Ring over three notes ('Ri-hi-hing'). So that the song would be ruined. This may not sound exciting when read, but the following *is* singable:

> You ring upon my finger
> my golden ring so fine,
> I press you against my lips with love,
> 'gainst my lips with love, against this heart of mine.

To such expedients is the translator reduced by the composer. But we must not forget that the composer was cramped and curbed by the exigencies of the original verse. Here the original poem was not elevated in tone; Chamisso phrased his thoughts simply and sincerely but not brilliantly, putting them into the mouth of a young girl gazing with rapture on the long-looked-forward-to ring on the third finger.

Yet when we find Brahms's setting of a poem by Daumer ('Wie bist du meine Königin') translated as follows:

> Ah, sweet my love, my gracious queen!
> As now, I've e'er thy subject been:
> Dost thou but smile, then all around sweet spring is smiling
> Thou my queen, thou my queen . . .

we neither feel the poetry of the words, in and of themselves, nor does the music get its due, because one long stress falls, for example, on a minor word like the archaism *e'er* where Brahms placed it on the important noun *Güte* (kindness) and such an expressive word as 'wonnevoll, wonnevoll' (blissfully, blissfully) becomes the rather flat bathos of Thou my queen, thou my queen—a thought which the poet merely touched once, in line one, and then happily dropped. Far worse examples could be adduced, but this is really a *sub-subject* in itself. It may, however, explain the often encountered impression that German lieder are relatively weak concoctions.

A good translation must not be like an umbrella with protruding ribs. Years ago, not exactly flown with insolence but happy over having published my first book-length translation, I sent my English version of some little lyric to the *Washington Post* whose poetry column Kenton Kilmer, son of the poet Joyce Kilmer, was editing. The rejection slip was a collector's item. It read: 'Pardon me, but your translation is showing!'

The author of *Ecclesiasticus* was known as Jesus the Son of Sirach. Writing in the second century before the Christian era and claiming to use the original writings of his own grandfather, he both apologizes for the loss inherent in the translation process by saying that 'the same things uttered in Hebrew and [then] translated into another tongue, have not the same force in them' and also strongly implies

21

that the successful, *i.e.*, the conscientious translator must simultaneously be an interpreter: 'therefore I thought it most necessary for me', he says, 'to bestow some diligence and travail to interpret it'. Horace, in turn, inveighs against what he calls the 'all too faithful translator' who tries to render the original author word for word.[6]

Professor August Closs, in an illuminating treatment[7] of the art of translation, has, as recently as two years ago, cited Grillparzer's objections against bringing a poet too close to us through translation and spoiling the form through slavishly exact rendition, to which Dr. Closs adds the cogent remark that this has been done specifically in the case of Rilke translations, 'die das characteristisch Vage Rilkescher Aussage oft zu sehr verdeutlichen'.

How unbelievably ludicrous the result of this effort can be swam like a new but tarnished planet into my ken a few years ago when I discovered the Pushkin translations of one Ivan Panin. Far from being 'banned in Boston', they were actually published there in 1888: a small collection whose title page is preceded by a charming and disarming Victorian blurb from *The Beacon* to the effect that Panin's book of translations is 'a solitaire and a masterpiece' . . . Mr. Panin's translation, 'thank goodness', quoth the reviewer, 'is literal, even to commas. The volume is beautifully printed and appeals to choice minds'. Whether or not the preservation of commas is a desideratum worth striving for, I should like to leave as a question for another paper—by another critic, preferably. But I am eager to test whether we have any 'choice minds' present who will pay Mr. Ivan Panin his just due of appreciation. For, as Mr. Panin states in his critical preface, 'the highest art is artlessness . . .' a sentiment which he somewhat spoils by adding the word 'unconsciousness', not intended of course to mean unconsciousness of commas. Let me quote three stanzas of his translation of one lyrical ballad of Pushkin. Perhaps a sensitive ear can still somehow tell that this must have been a beautiful poem in the original. The poet's soul glimmers through the translator's murky veil. However, every effort has been made to conceal the merit of the original and we see, at best, as through a glass, darkly:

THE DROWNED[8]

Into the hut the children run,
In haste they called their father:
'Papa, papa, oh, our nets
Out a corpse have dragged.'
'Ye lie, ye lie, ye little devils'
Upon them father grumbled.
'I declare, those wicked brats!
Corpse now too have they must!'

'Down will come the court, "Give answer!"
And for an age no rest from it.
But what to do? Heigh, wife, there,
My coat give me, must get there somehow . . .

Now where's the corpse?'—'Here, papa, here!'
And in truth along the river,
Where is spread the moistened net,
Upon the sand is seen the corpse.

Disfigured terribly the corpse is,
Is blue, and all is swollen.
Is it a hapless sorrower,
Who ruined has his sinful soul,
Or by the waves a fisher taken,
Or some fellow, drunkard,
Or by robbers stripped, perchance,
Trader some, unbusinesslike!

That Pushkin does lend himself to more successful translation into English is, of course, attested to by the performances of Max Eastman, Babette Deutsch (who has also been conspicuously successful with Rilke's *Book of Hours*), Avrahm Yarmolinsky and, more recently, C. M. Bowra and Vladimir Nabokov, to whom we also owe good versions of Michael Lermontov and Fyodor Tyutchev.

Although a while ago I broke a lance for rhyme, and although we have just seen how rhymelessness in translation failed to preserve rationality, still I am haunted by the consciousness that Verlaine's expression of 'the wrongs of rhyme' could in fact sometimes be applied to translated lyric poetry. While many Englishmen, Scotsmen and Americans fared well as translators and managed to be faithful to rhyme (I am thinking of Longfellow, the remarkable James Clarence Mangan, Alexander Macmillan, John Hay, Charles Godfrey Leland and even Elizabeth Barrett Browning, most of whose names are connected with Heinrich Heine's poems in English or with other German Romantics), one little gem behaves like Heine's *Lorelei*—refusing to leave my mind—and makes me exclaim:

Ich weiss nicht, was soll es bedeuten.

It is Margarete Münsterberg's rendition of 'The Hostess's Daughter' by Ludwig Uhland, a long-time favourite in the original. The first three couplets will suffice:

Three fellows were marching over the Rhine,
They stopped where they saw the hostess' sign.

'Dear Hostess, have you good beer and wine?
Where have you your daughter so fair and fine?'

'My beer is good, my wine is clear,
My daughter is lying upon the bier.'

I am afraid we must leave the young lady there, where she has now been lying for many a decade.

23

In translation there is both virtue and hidden danger: not merely to the reputation of the original poet but to the language *into* which one is translating. Some translations become new and original poems in the new language. Few readers would be aware, for example, that Longfellow's 'The Reaper and the Flowers' is actually a skilful adaptation of 'Es ist ein Schnitter und der heisst Tod': an old German folksong found by Longfellow in the Arnim and Brentano collection *Des Knaben Wunderhorn*. Strange phenomena of absorption into the host language occasionally occur, better instanced in the drama than in the lyric, the best example being the virtual naturalization of Shakespeare into German by the Tieck–Schlegel translation in the early nineteenth century. About fifteen years ago Karl Shapiro uttered a warning, however, in his 'Essay on Rime', which is germane to our discussion. Under 'Translations and False Dialects' he speaks of 'the imitation of translation' as follows:[9]

One might have glanced ahead in 1910
And seen the advent of the rime translation
As it is known to us; nor would he then
Have questioned the advantage and the value
Of this revival. Spanish and German rime,
The immediate interchange of foreign genius
Could work no injury upon the English
Or contravene the idiom—which it did
Nevertheless. It may be we can rival
Murray, Cary and Lang in rendering
The foreign poem; I am not qualified
To say. Our present argument, however,
Pertains to the effect of rime translation
Upon the English poem. In the contemporary
Anthology one seems to read at times
A dialect of a dialect, translation
Where no original exists. I mean
The rime of conscious foreign overtones,
Not merely structures like asyndeton
And un-English inversion and the like.
For so suggestible is the modern poem
That out of Spender's Rilke comes a style
The English of which is copied in our verse
As a new idiom. One cannot impugn
The motives of the translator in the least,
But as the fashion of the pony-text
Has increased and become a serious mode,
Our native rhetoric has taken on
An international accent, not unlike
A learned pidgin or a code.

Whether or not translation constitutes a danger of the wrong environmental influence being exerted upon our English heritage, I cannot refrain from a word of tribute to the Spender–Leishman translation of Rilke's *Duino Elegies*. Despite shortcomings inevitable in so extremely difficult a task of rendition and implicit interpretation plus explicit critical notes, the result of their labours is infinitely superior to the translation by Harry Behn, issued in 1957 by the Peter Pauper Press.

Let us hear the conclusion of the whole matter. For it would take a series of separate works to do justice to the task of comparing translations, as, for example, the late Wolfgang Kayser did in publishing, for purposes of a do-it-yourself comparison, German translations of five French symbolists (Baudelaire, Mallarmé, Verlaine, Rimbaud, Valéry) by many hands—fifty translators, to be exact, some ten or a dozen of them poets of stature (Rilke, Stefan George, Richard Dehmel among them).

The conclusion I have already anticipated in part when I said earlier that language mastery, first of all, is essential and, secondly, that we must set a poet to catch a poet. The Swiss–German poet and translator, Max Geilinger, wrote a perceptive essay on translating lyrics in which he cited Mohammed to the effect that God gives unto every people a prophet in their own tongue. But, Geilinger adds, this does not obviate the necessity of translating intellectual and emotional values from one language area into another, especially if we wish to hold to the aim of a common humanity and wish to avoid 'the breaking of bridges' which, according to Chesterton 'is the end of the world'. Max Geilinger asserted that three factors must be considered in this self-appointed task: First: the relationship of one folk-spirit (*Volksgeist*) to the other (and this he elaborates); second: the relationship of one age to another (*von Zeitgeist zu Zeitgeist*) and third: the relationship between the personalities of the poet and the translator, citing Fitzgerald's translation of Omar as supposedly superior to the original, just to prove his point that the comparison is not always to the disfavour of the translator. Could it perhaps at times truthfully be said that the catcher had pitched a beautiful baseball game?

It was André Gide who discovered another aspect of the translator's function when he wrote[10] that 'every creative writer owes it to his country to translate at least one foreign work, to which his talent and his temperament are particularly suited, and thus enrich his own literature'.

There must be a poem on this subject, for only a poem could sum up the relationship between the two sides of this duality: lyric poet and lyric translator. Neither sufficient time exists nor the means to enjoy the fruits of every worthwhile poet who happens to have written in the recondite medium of a foreign language. Without the translator, the poet and his poem remain like the tree in Friedrich Hebbel's lyric *The Tree in the Desert* which we once set over into English:[11]

The Tree in the Desert

In the sanded desert stands a tree,
Alive, alone in a land accurst.
The sun has burnt him cruelly;
No dew or raindrop cools his thirst.

His withered leaves are brightened with
A single fruit. Her spicy skin
Swells tight with sap and all the pith
Of life and force the tree pressed in.

The heavy hour nears when she
Must fall and leave his branches bare.
There comes no wanderer to the tree
And for himself she is not there.

That the thirsting wanderer may find the tree, is this not the mission of the translator of lyric poetry?

DER BAUM IN DER WÜSTE

Es steht ein Baum im Wüstensand,
    Der einzige, der dort gedieh;
Die Sonne hat ihn fast verbrannt,
    Der Regen tränkt den durst'gen nie.

In seiner falben Krone hängt
    Gewürzig eine Frucht voll Saft,
Er hat sein Mark hinein gedrängt,
    Sein Leben, seine höchste Kraft.

Die Stunde, wo sie, überschwer,
    Zu Boden fallen muss, ist nah',
Es zieht kein Wanderer daher,
    Und für ihn selbst ist sie nicht da.

Friedrich Hebbel

DIE ERBLINDENDE

Sie sass so wie die anderen beim Tee.
Mir war zuerst, als ob sie ihre Tasse
ein wenig anders als die andern fasse.
Sie lächelte einmal. Es tat fast weh.

Und als man schliesslich sich erhob und sprach
und langsam und wie es der Zufall brachte
durch viele Zimmer ging (man sprach und lachte),
da sah ich sie. Sie ging den andern nach,

verhalten, so wie eine, welche gleich
wird singen müssen und vor vielen Leuten;
auf ihren hellen Augen, die sich freuten,
war Licht von aussen wie auf einem Teich.

Sie folgte langsam, und sie brauchte lang,
als wäre etwas noch nicht überstiegen;
und doch: als ob, nach einem Übergang,
sie nicht mehr gehen würde, sondern fliegen.

Rainer Maria Rilke

NOTES

1. The English original version, which first appeared in *Poetry* (Chicago), reappears in my first collected poems: *Angel of Our Thirst*, James Decker Press and Grinnell College Press, 1950–51; the German 'self-translation' was published in *The American–German Review*, 1948.

2. *Translations from the Poetry of Rainer Maria Rilke* by Mrs. H. D. Norton; W. W. Norton, New York, 1942; p. 165.

3. Originally published in *Books Abroad*, University of Oklahoma, my translation, together with the German of Rilke, will be found in my *Twentieth-Century German Verse: A Selection*, Princeton University Press, Princeton, New Jersey, 1952; pp. 28 and 29.

4. 'Confessions of a Translator', *Books Abroad*, 1948.

5. In the *Everyman's Library*, publ. by E. P. Dutton.

6. *Ars Poetica*, 131.

7. Übersetzung und Neudichtung: Die Kunst des Übertragens,' in *Unterscheidung und Bewahrung | Festschrift für Hermann Kunisch*, Walter de Gruyter & Co., Berlin, 1961, pp. 79–90. Our passage: p. 86.

8. *Poems by Alexander Pushkin, translated from the Russian with Introduction and Notes by Ivan Panin*; Boston, Cupples and Hurd, 1888.

9. Lines 1272 to 1301.

10. Cf. *Divers*: Paris, Gallimard, 1931 (p. 189).

11. Translation by Herman and Marion C. Salinger in *A Little Treasury of World Poetry*, edited by Hubert Creekmore, Charles Scribner's Sons, New York, 1952.

Discussion

Schoolfield asked why scholars despised translations, although translations were necessary both to students in the early stages of language study and to those studying writings in little-known languages.

Salinger replied that poor writers, who had turned to translating to make a living, had given translation a bad name.

Closs stated that a poet could be at a disadvantage as a translator. He cannot 'jump over his own shadow' in translating, but must keep within the bounds set by his own language.

Salinger agreed and quoted examples of the different associations of so-called equivalent words in different languages. Thus '*Baum*' had not the associations of *cross* or *roof-tree* contained in the word *tree*, while *arbre* was different again.

Mainland referred to the 'discipline of rhyme' and asked whether rhyme was enough, or did the translator also find the equivalent of the light and dark sounds of the original.

Salinger thought the translator could do this if he were translating German and English, because of the similarities between the two languages, or English and French, because of the many words of Norman-French origin in the English language. However, one could not reproduce in English the alternation of masculine and feminine rhymes found in German, because the English language was poor in words suitable for feminine rhymes. English was also 'rhyme-poor'; this meant (1) that English lyric poems *must be short*, and (2) that the English poet had always to be 'on his toes' to find new rhymes. Then there was the difficulty of reproducing in another language the effects created by onomatopoeia.

Körner quoted Karl Kraus's lines:

> 'Er ist das Ufer, wo sie landen,
> Sind zwei Gedanken einverstanden',

and asked what criteria should be used to distinguish between good rhymed verse and mere versification.

Salinger answered by quoting the example of the poet Yeats, who sometimes noted down his rhyme plan before even deciding the subject he wished to write on. Rhythmic patterns could assert themselves in compulsive manner and pre-exist the meaning of the poem.

In reply to the second question the speaker said that rhyme must be functional. One was dealing with mere versification if the rhyme 'showed through' as inorganic ornamentation or like the wallpaper holding an old wall together.

Böckmann asked why it should be necessary to retain the rhyme in translation. It was almost never possible to reproduce a poem completely in another language. Something must always be omitted; why not rhyme? The main function of a translation of a lyric poem was to refer its reader to the original.

Salinger replied that one must decide how important the rhyme was to the original poem. Rhyme was one of several parts of a poem, none of which could be omitted without loss. He thought that a translator who could not cope with the discipline of rhyme usually could not translate the sense of the poem either.

Garland said that translations were of two types. Böckmann had been speaking of the 'ancilliary' translation written for the use of language students, but there was also the 'replacement' translation, written for people who would never read the work translated in its original language.

Stewart spoke of coincidence between an original poem and its translation. Such coincidence was possible but rare. One poet could inspire translations by another poet with similar interests, as had happened with Baudelaire and Stefan George, but the resulting poems did not coincide in form because of the different characteristics of the languages involved. Thus George's translations of Shakespeare's sonnets were superior to his translations of Baudelaire because English was more similar to German than French was.

SECOND SESSION

Chairman: Professor P. BÖCKMANN

Professor G. C. SCHOOLFIELD: Autobiography and biography in the lyric: Rilke's 'Entwürfe aus zwei Winterabenden'.

Chairman: Professor H. M. WAIDSON

Professor BEDA ALLEMANN: Non-representational modern German poetry.

Autobiography and Biography in the Lyric: Rilke's 'Entwürfe aus zwei Winterabenden'

by

G. C. SCHOOLFIELD

Grow old along with me!
The best is yet to be,
The last of life, for which the first was made . . .
(Robert Browning, Rabbi Ben Ezra)

. . . Ihrer zu denken, aus so viel Unruhe, Lärm und
Widerwärtigkeiten, ist fast Sünde . . .
(Lisa Heise, Briefe an Rainer Maria Rilke, p. 53: 24 January 1924)

Ich, die heftige Feindin des Kino, bin in einer Woche gleich dreimal hineingelaufen, es gab eine Expedition eines schwedischen Prinzen nach Afrika . . .man sah die Wilden. Das Kino wurde ein jämmerliches Loch, man fing an zu ersticken, alles war eine Fratze diesen herrlichen Körpern gegenüber, die nie von einer Kleidung verletzt wurden . . . sie tanzten und wirbelten und drehten sich und es war ein herrliches, ein letztes, für uns Zuschauer *erlösendres* Hingeben der Person, denn was wissen die von Erlösung, da nichts in ihnen gefangen gehalten wird.
(Katharina Kippenberg to Rainer Maria Rilke, 27 February 1924)

I

Despite his understandable aversion to reading criticisms of his work, despite his equally understandable refusal to undergo psychoanalysis, Rilke was constantly and desperately concerned with himself, as even the hastiest reader of his letters knows. Similarly, he was not uninterested in the lives of other great men; when he was in his twenties, he planned monographs on Jacobsen and Hammershøj, Zuloaga and Cézanne, and while these books, had they been written, would probably have had more to say about the art than the artist, they could not very well have avoided the artist altogether. Rilke wanted to spend a winter in Copenhagen so that he could use the libraries there (as he put it) for his Jacobsen monograph; this remark of his leads us to believe that, vague as Rilke's notions of library work were, he must have had some idea of consulting manuscripts or letters, the raw materials, in other words, of the biographer. Rilke's plan to write on Hammershøj was abandoned because he could not speak Danish, and Hammershøj was equally unfamiliar with German, as Rilke learned when he visited the painter; from this mutually embarrassing incident we may again deduce that Rilke had laid some sort of directly biographical keel for the proposed monograph on the master of Danish interiors—he could very well look at Hammershøj's pictures in order to be able to write about *them*, but, to find out about Hammershøj himself, he had to communicate with the man.

The biographical fancy returned a few years later, when Rilke decided to write a life of the Venetian admiral, Carlo Zeno; he had begun to think about the great adventurer—so adventurous that he bore the scars of forty wounds on his fourteenth-century body—during his studies for *Malte*. But he was floored almost immediately by the apparatus of the libraries of Venice ('in diesen Büchern und Buchkatalogen bin ich genau so aussichtslos unfindig, wie wenn ich ein Kleeblatt oder Erdbeeren suchen soll', *Briefe 1907–1914*, Leipzig, 1933, p. 101: 5 May 1910); he listened all too intently to the lagoon slapping against the marble foundations of the Palazzo della Zecca, 'als wäre draus mehr zu erfahren als aus den alten Drucken'. Nothing came of the Zeno plan, except the realization that the biographer's lot—or the lot of the poet turned biographer—was not a happy one. He complained to Marie von Thurn und Taxis: 'in allen den Büchern, die ich durchseh, find ich nichts über [Zeno], was ich nicht schon wüsste oder höchstens eben nur immer wieder vergesse' (*Briefwechsel*, Zürich, 1951, I, 124–125: 9 March 1912). After the hard times with Zeno, it would seem, Rilke never again thought seriously of writing a biography; the wish to read biographies swallowed up the wish to compose them. Rilke had long been an avid reader of memoirs, in particular those set down by feminine pens; *Malte* depends heavily on such material: on Bettina's book about her friendship with old Goethe, on Leonora Christina Ulfeldt's *Jammersminde*, on the papers of the Reventlow family as edited by Louis Bobé, on the *Libro de sua vida* of Teresa de Avila, on the *Vision* of Christine de Pisan, on a whole tangle of other, similar sources. The completion of *Malte* scarcely put an end to his love for the autobiographies of others; the *Jammersminde* was still on Rilke's mind in the nineteen-twenties; he made his Swedish friends search the second-hand bookstores for the memoirs of Per Ulrik Kernell; he eagerly read Malla Montgomery–Silfverstolpe's long account of her trip through the Germany of Romanticism; during the war years he praised the 'allegresse' of Tolstoy's *Childhood, Boyhood, and Youth* to Marianne Gilbert; at Schloss Berg he became involved with the memoirs of a Belgian–Austrian, the Prince de Ligne (who may be the Count C.W. of the 'dictated' poem-cycle from Berg); he received Nanny von Escher's account of an old city's old families, *Alt–Zürich*, with enthusiasm; still at Berg, he advised Anton Kippenberg to publish the autobiography of the sixteenth-century Swiss 'pilgrim', Hans Stokar; Jung–Stilling's *Jugend* delighted him in 1922; in 1924 he paid Hans Carossa the compliment of reading *Eine Kindheit* for the second time; in 1925 he told Madame de Sépibus that he was revelling in a double-barrelled autobiography, the book of a 'gentilhomme campagnard d'Armagnac, Joseph de Pesquidoux', who had continued his grandfather's journal with an account of his own life.

But Rilke did not read just what others had to say about themselves; especially in his Swiss years, he indulged in biography as well, and biography of a curiously popular kind. He made his happy way through Constantin Photiades' flamboyant biography of that great and good friend of diplomats and poets, Marie Kalergis, born the Duchess of Nesselrode; at about the same time, late in 1923 and early in

1924, he conducted a campaign among his friends to get them to read André Maurois's *Ariel ou La Vie de Shelley*. 'Eine geradezu wunderbare Monographie' he called it to Marie von Thurn und Taxis (II, 787: 23 February 1924), trading biographical treasures with his Austrian friend, who had just recommended Lytton Strachey's *Queen Victoria* to him. The Duchess Gallarati Scotti got the same message, somewhat extended, in French; Rilke told her of 'ce délicieux "Ariel" ... que j'ai lu en automne avec un véritable enchantement' (*Lettres milanaises*, Paris, 1956: 29 March 1924).

Rilke's lady-friends, succumbing to his persuasions, were apparently not surprised that he liked *Ariel* so much; some of the rest of us, however, may be a little taken aback at his enthusiasm, especially if we remember the strictures he placed upon his own would-be biographers and other students of his work. Maurois's book is popular, and charming, to the point of frivolity: it oversimplifies larger developments in order to achieve dramatic effect, and shows a journalistic predilection for the colourful incident, the intimate detail. Of course, such faults may in fact be virtues; but a fault past redemption lies at the heart of the 'delicious book'—if we did not know beforehand that Shelley was a great poet, or a poet at all, we should have trouble deducing the fact from what Maurois tells us. That Rilke admired *Ariel* so much should give pause to the authors of 'inner biographies' of Rilke, to those who deprecate the use of 'external facts' in retelling the poet's life. Yet the 'inner biographers' could retort that Rilke, when it was a question of himself and not some mere English poet, would have been dismayed, or worse, if he had been given the *Ariel* treatment. The replies distributed to the inquisitive correspondents, Alfred Schaer, Hermann Pongs, and Arthur Fischer-Colbrie in 1924 and 1925 (when an army of students was preparing to pounce on Rilke's oeuvre, and when the army's reconnaissances made the poet reflect seriously upon the figure he would cut in posterity's eyes), show a man willing to offer help, but not quite help enough —not enough, at least, for any dogged biographer. Schaer got considerable information about early influences, although Rilke was careful to deny that the influences were such, in the letter of 26 February 1924 (*Briefe aus Muzot*, Leipzig, 1940, pp. 252–257); a subsequent letter of 3 March (pp. 257–259) gently shut the door in Schaer's face: Rilke told Schaer that he did not wish to read anything written about him, even from Schaer's no doubt intelligent hand, and thus effectively (and without saying so, a technique also employed by the present controllers of the Rilke-archives) refused Schaer further biographical succour. Pongs, who was a professor where Schaer was only a *Privatdozent*, found a longer red carpet run out for him: besides, Pongs, no mean student of human nature, had disclaimed any desire for mere autobiographical 'Zubehör', and so got the very thing he did not ask for. Yet even Pongs was told a great deal only by indirection, as in the long postscript on Leonora Christina Ulfeldt in the letter of 21 October 1924 (pp. 335–337), where Rilke in fact gives an account of the way he conducted, and regarded, his own life. Or was the gift of the postscript intended to console Pongs, whom Rilke apparently liked so much, for all the direct information the poet had withheld? It would seem that Rilke's Austrian compatriot, Fischer-Colbrie, got an answer which betrayed how little sympathy Rilke had for the biographer's cause, at least when the biographer was on Rilke's trail. Since he resided in Linz, Fischer-Colbrie wanted to know something about Rilke's months at the commercial school in the Upper Austrian metropolis; we are frequently blunter with fellow nationals than with foreigners, and the postscript the Linz author received was an abrupt one: 'In Linz könnte freilich niemand über mich "Auskünfte" geben; die unglücklichen, dort verbrachten Monate fassen eine Zeit zusammen, da ich mir selber ganz unkenntlich war: wie sehr muss ichs erst den Anderen gewesen sein' (p. 389: 18 December, 1925). We may sympathize with Rilke's desire to shield an unfortunate episode in his life from prying eyes; yet Rilke, who so gladly captured the pity of outsiders by his tales from the military school, could not very well expect a biographer *in spe* to turn his aroused interest off, once that biographer got to the Linz episode. Rilke read the record of Shelley's youthful amours with an almost lascivious delight; he would surely have been disappointed, if Shelley, living a century beyond his fated span, had forbidden Maurois to investigate, say, his early London days, on the grounds that Shelley was not Shelley then. Yet such compliance is what Rilke demanded of his own would-be biographers, at least by implication.

Or, perhaps, Rilke wanted to have his cake and eat it too. He was possessed by a strong drive to autobiography, he wanted to talk about himself, and not always in an entirely friendly way; but, as a member of that pan-European generation of neo-romantics who, too much in love with themselves for direct and painful autobiographical revelation, had hidden inside their various literary *alter egos* (Louys' Bilitis, Housman's Shropshire Lad, George's Algabal, Karlfeldt's Fridolin),[1] he made a clear trail, then carefully covered it. We are all familiar with the running starts at autobiography disguised which Rilke took; with *Die Turnstunde*, *Pierre Dumont*, and *Ewald Tragy*; with the autobiographical elements in *Die weisse Fürstin*;[2] with the monk of the first version of *Das Stundenbuch*; with the many childhood poems from 'Aus der Kinderzeit' in *Larenopfer* to 'Kindheit' and 'Das Kind' in *Neue Gedichte*; with the long-cherished plan of a 'Militärroman'; with the often repeated *curriculum vitae*, distorted in many of its details, which got its classic form in the early letters to Ellen Key (and which was fed, with larger or smaller emendations, to other soft-hearted correspondents); with the protracted tales of illness past and present—these too a kind of autobiography—of which Lou Andreas-Salomé was the chief but by no means the only recipient. We are, of course, all familiar with *Malte Laurids Brigge*, which appeared in 1910 and was the last of Rilke's masked autobiographies for a while. Once *Malte* was off Rilke's chest, the autobiographical impulse was forced into another channel by the events of the so-called 'Wendung' crisis. Now the talk is less of the wretched Rilke who *was* than of the wretched Rilke who *is*; and now, too, the distinction between a 'lyric of present experience', where the poet states his reaction to events which have just befallen him, and a true 'autobiographical lyric', where a recent misfortune (or, less commonly, a piece of good fortune) prompts the poet to give an *apologia* for his entire existence, becomes especially plain: the crisis, as in the case of that fit of 'spleen' which befell Esaias Tegnér, causes both types of lyric to flower.[3] In the former category there are such poems as 'Winterliche Stanzen', 'Die grosse Nacht', 'Du im Voraus verlorene Geliebte', 'Ausgesetzt auf den Bergen des Herzens'; the poet's situation, as it stands at the present moment, is explained, illuminated, lamented.

Into the latter category, however, there falls the climactic poem of the crisis-period, 'Wendung', which looks backward, lists and interprets past events which have led to present misery, and then proposes a new programme for life:

> Denn des Anschauens, siehe, ist eine Grenze.
> Und die geschautere Welt
> will in der Liebe gedeihn.

> Werk des Gesichts ist getan,
> tue nun Herzwerk.[4]

The excitement and the anxieties of the First World War, the temporary quality of the Munich years, made Rilke less self-indulgent—autobiographically speaking —than he had been before. War keeps autobiographic expression fragmentary; witness the anniversary-sonnets of the Baroque, in which the poet rejoices (or laments) his survival of another perilous year, and the burgeoning of diary-literature (which deals with the present self and can be broken off anywhere) during World War Two. The author needs some guarantee of permanence before he can settle down to an examination of his past; Rilke's Austrian draft-board—and the atmosphere of the time—saw to it that he was kept on pins and needles. And, apart from the 'provisory air' of Munich, a new factor entered the game. Rilke suspected that, erotically, he was becoming a new man; the 'Fluss-Gott des Blutes', about whom Rilke had entertained some strong reservations when he wrote the Third Elegy in 1912 and 1913, was turning out to be a friend, even a saviour. We still do not know exactly what brought the change about, and perhaps we never shall; but it seems more than likely that the affair with Lou Albert-Lasard, which inspired not only the poems addressed directly to her but the 'Ode an Bellman' and the skeleton in the closet of pious Rilke-scholarship, the 'Sieben Gedichte', had much to do with the passage from brotherly lover to Don Juan. Of course, Rilke had to practise being his new self for some time before he could write of the transformation autobiographically, before he could fit it into his life's whole pattern. As a matter of fact, the first longer work he wrote after arriving in the comfortable 'pre-war' world of Switzerland in 1919 made it seem that he had retreated to the carefully masked autobiography of *Malte* and before; the words of the 'Nachlass des Grafen C.W.' were recited to Rilke, he claimed, by a ghost clad in a costume from the Biedermeier—Rilke had done no more than take them down. At first glance, Rilke would seem (if we do not give credence to his tale of a phantom) to be writing biography, not autobiography, since the spooky visitor to Castle Berg tells what amounts to the story of his life. But the tale's elements are taken from Rilke's own and fairly recent career: his new doctrine of sexual fulfillment, in which the woman is an authentic partner, not a being superior by reason of her skill at unrequited love ('Kurve der Liebe, lass uns sie zeichnen. Ihr Steigen / soll uns unendlich rühmlich sein'); his dawning conviction that the new manhood has grown out of childhood experiences, and that childhood, after all, had not been unbearably wretched ('Ach, ich war die Muschel, Aphrodite, / die dich trug, und in mir war das Meer'); and finally, a cause for unhappiness to replace those just abandoned: his growing awareness of age ('Wunderliches Wort: die Zeit vertreiben!/Sie zu *halten* wäre das Problem'). The new Rilke, at once reborn and ageing, is only dimly perceptible under disguises, amidst returns to older thoughts ('Da Geliebt-Sein noch nicht band und mühte'); but he is there, nonetheless.

The years immediately after the ghost's trip to Berg are occupied, of course, with the completion of an older task, the *Elegies*, and the sudden production of the *Sonnets to Orpheus*, whose all-encompassing affirmation might have one of its roots, perhaps its chief one, in the special erotic affirmation we have just noted. Once these tasks are finished, once the poet realizes that his major work is done, then he begins to look backward at his life, to review it, even as he attempts, *rerum novarum cupidus* like the old Thomas Mann, a new and not altogether serious career in another tongue. (Rilke's French poetry could be taken as an acting-out of the wish for rejuvenation, the new beginning in the new medium.) The 'Entwürfe aus zwei Winterabenden', from the middle weeks of February 1924, are the expression of this mood of review; they are autobiographical lyrics, they take the place of a much longer prose work, which would look back to the past and connect it with the present.

The events which provide the direct occasion for the composition of the 'Entwürfe' are worth reviewing in some detail, if only for the contrast which then may be made with other events (perhaps still more important ones), whose connexion with the cycle is not immediately apparent. Anton Kippenberg was to celebrate his fiftieth birthday on 22 May 1924; in recognition of the event, a *Festschrift* was planned, *Navigare necesse est*. Rilke's 'Fest-Beitrag', the poem 'Der Reisende', was sent off to Katharina Kippenberg on 17 July 1923; its 'occasional verses' were inspired, as Rilke told Frau Kippenberg, by a sight, scarcely an unusual one, he had seen from a train window: a young man and a young woman stood together by the right-of-way. The poem's suitability as a birthday gift (at least this must have been Rilke's not altogether cheerful line of reasoning) seems to lie in its numerous thoughts about the evanescence of human relationships; and Kippenberg, if he read the poem carefully, must have detected his identity with the attractive little trackside figures for whom Rilke had felt such a sudden and Olympian liking. Human beings are essentially lonely, the poem implies, and should be thankful for every spark of friendship they may feel toward other members of their kind, however one-sided or fleeting the contact may be. The poem does contain one tiny trumpet call, a summons *en mineur* to the affirmation of the *Sonnets to Orpheus*; for we are told, in a subsidiary reflection, about the dependency of the adult on the emotional richness of his childhood, something that will be expanded into a major theme of the 'Entwürfe':

> ... wir jagen
> dieses köstliche Herz, das wir nur in der Kindheit ertragen,
> das *uns* seither trug.

(SW, II, 142)

Otherwise, though, the poem has none of the glad spirits we associate with birthday verse; Rilke, who had impressed the visiting Kippenbergs just a year before by his glowing health,[5] was not at his physical best, and his woes quickly found their way into the spirit if not the letter of his verse. A month after 'Der Reisende'[6] had been sent to the organizer of *Navigare necesse est*, Rilke repaired to Sanatorium Schöneck on the Vierwaldstättersee, a lake which, stretched out 'like four handkerchiefs, waving in different directions,' did not appeal to him, for all its literary connexions. After a less than satisfactory month in the hands of Schöneck's physicians, Rilke departed, to visit Guido von Salis at Malans in the Grisons; in September, 1920, a stay at Malans, and a stroll through the Salis family's Schloss Bothmar, with its 'entzückender verzauberter Schlossgarten,' had preceded, and perhaps inspired the stage settings of, the dictations of the Count C.W.[7] Back at Muzot for the remainder of the autumn, the poet sent the Kippenbergs, as thanks for birthday greetings they had sent him (he turned forty-eight on 5 December 1923), a poem which expresses, too determinedly, his joy at existence:

> Alles ist Überfluss. Denn genug
> war es schon damals, als uns die Kindheit bestürzte
> mit unendlichem Dasein. . . . Damals schon
> war es zuviel. Wie sollten wir jemals Verkürzte
> oder Betrogene sein: wir, mit jeglichem Lohn
> schon Überlohnten . . .

(SW, II, 250)[8]

It was the well-known tune of affirmation, and of a rich childhood as the basis for a happy adult life; but the tune was whistled in the dark. Three days after Christmas, Rilke took himself to Sanatorium Val-Mont, the place, where just three years and one day later, he would die amidst 'ich weiss nicht wie viel Höllen'. Released from the sanatorium on 20 January 1924, Rilke continued his whistling for the Kippenbergs: he read the Seventh Elegy, the elegy of 'Hiersein ist herrlich', to Katharina Kippenberg when she and her husband visited Muzot on their way home from Italy late in April ('Ich wusste schon, dass Sie diesen Wunsch hatten,' he said to her);[9] he sent Frau Kippenberg, early in May, the brave little poem 'Frühling' ('Blätterschatten lindert unsern Schrecken');[10] finally, he sent Anton Kippenberg a congratulatory letter for the publisher's fiftieth birthday, enclosing the 'Entwürfe', which were intended as a personal birthday gift, quite apart from 'Der Reisende', formally presented in the *Festschrift*. Actually, the letter and the poems were dispatched from Muzot a week before the great day, addressed to Katharina, so that she might present them to her husband at the proper time; the envelope was made still more crowded by an explanatory letter to Katharina and *another* poem of affirmation, 'Schon bricht das Glück, verhalten viel zu lang, / Höher hervor' (RMR–KK, *Briefwechsel*, p. 534; 15 May 1924; and *SW*, II, 163). Having let down his guard to the Kippenbergs with 'Der Reisende', and with some pathetic letters from Val-Mont, Rilke was now determined to convince his friends in Leipzig that all was right, or almost right, with his world.

The letter to Kippenberg which accompanies the 'Entwürfe' is an odd document, having an intention, or several intentions, quite different from its apparent aim of congratulation. It begins with a set of four elaborate paragraphs, expressing a variety of birthday wishes and reminding us, in their exquisite obliqueness, of Rilke's Austrian heritage. In the fifth paragraph, the congratulator gets around to mentioning the 'Entwürfe'; they are 'keine Zueignung, nichts durch die "Gelegenheit" Hervorgerufenes oder Bestimmtes' (RMR, *Briefe an seinen Verleger*, Wiesbaden, 1949, II, 455). The statement is true enough: the poems do not contain a reference to Kippenberg's birthday, although they are still, in their backward glance into time (a glance not infrequently prompted by birthdays), birthday poems just the same, as we shall see. Having made this disavowal, Rilke reminds his publisher that the latter is familiar with his practice of returning now and then to an earlier style; probably Rilke has the poems of the Count C.W. in mind, for he had sent Kippenberg the first series of the 'Nachlass' in February 1921.[11] He continues: 'solche Rückfälle führen das, was wir zwischen uns im Vertrauen das Werk nennen mögen, kaum weiter, und sie bereiten dem, dem sie widerfahren, eine gewisse Befremdung und Verlegenheit'. (The words 'Rückfälle' and 'Verlegenheit' are worth remembering in connexion with the medical background of the cycle, to which we shall come presently.) He was on the point of destroying the poems, Rilke says, when it occurred to him that, if to anyone, then they might appeal to Kippenberg, the friend who had so often demonstrated his sympathetic interest 'über einem menschlich oder bürgerlich dringenden Anlass', and who now was to be given, in these poems, 'ein Spielplatz, eine Erholungsstunde seiner Teilnahme'. The poems may indeed be just a playground, an hour of relaxation for Kippenberg's well-trained sympathy, but they demand his sympathy nevertheless; anyone who has studied the weather-signs in Rilke's letters will know that a request of some sort is in the offing. The signs do not fail; the request comes in the letter's last paragraph. The paragraph very properly makes a final reference to Kippenberg's birthday; the plea is mingled with it, like medicine with the sugar candy in a pill. 'Und zum Schluss noch dies: mein lieber Kippenberg, der Sie so geübt sind, mir beiständig zu sein, verwenden Sie nun auch *dies* mir zum Beistande, dass Sie mir ein Jahr voraus sind, und geben Sie mir ein Beispiel, wie man diese Wendung über das fünfzigste hinaus, in einem zusammenfassenden und fortschreitenden Sinne, sich zu eigen mache. Lassen Sie mich in diesem Begriffe, eh ichs dann selber versuche, Ihr Schüler sein.'

The psychiatrists tell us that the fiftieth birthday is an even more frightening milepost of mortality than the thirtieth or the fortieth; for a man of Rilke's peculiar makeup it must have been a prospect particularly upsetting to contemplate. Rilke would have said that Rabbi Ben Ezra talked nonsense; he did not want to grow old gracefully, he did not want to grow old at all (perhaps, like Peter Pan, he did not even want very much to grow up), and his appearance gave him every encouragement in his wish. Marie von Thurn und Taxis reports that Rilke looked 'unwahrscheinlich jung' when she visited Muzot in 1923; one would have taken him for a man in his thirties.[12] There is a wealth of corroborative evidence for her observation; seeing Rilke for the first time in 1916, Max Mell noticed the odd youthfulness of his movements, which, in turn, emphasized his 'knabenhafte Schmalheit'; almost everyone who met him heard the boyishness in his laughter, which Kassner called 'das treuherzigste'; according, once again, to Marie von Thurn und Taxis, children loved him for his special skill in choosing toys, although he was oddly uncomfortable (did he sense rivals?) in the presence of the little ones.[13] The 'entzückendes Kind' (who became an 'armes Kind' to Hofmannsthal when he was drafted) liked to draw profit from his childlikeness; he played the child for all his older women friends, from Ellen Key on. Not having grown up, he got favours all the more easily; and his conviction that he was a child served him as a kind of ever-ready excuse to himself (he frequently had to salve his conscience after he had done things he wanted to do) for his peccadilloes. Shortly before his death, he exculpated Verlaine (and himself) by saying that he was 'rein wie ein Kind' in what he did.[14] It is only fair to add that an inner child in Rilke bolstered the useful external one; the pose, if it deserves to be called that, had truth beneath it. We shall never be able to determine, of course, what respective roles calculation and instinct played in the transmission of the inner child to the world without; but Kassner was probably correct in his often quoted dictum about Rilke's poetic kingdom, where the man was the intruder, and only children, women and the old were at home.[15] Dieter Basserman was right, too, when he argued in *Der andere Rilke* that the poet, young as he seemed on the outside, stayed spiritually younger still; thus there frequently arose, as in the case of Rilke's marriage, painful incongruities between Rilke's situation and his emotional development.[15a] At any event, the nourishment of an inner child was fairly easy for the man in his twenties: becoming a father himself, he simply left the scene of his mistake. The inner child's maintenance was not impossible for the artist in his thirties, who had escaped by the skin of his teeth from domesticity, or even, after some strain, for the victim of crisis in his early forties; but a man who approached fifty and still wanted to be a child was in a bad way, and Rilke knew it. And then, to make matters worse, he was caught in a landslide of reminders of his age.

Rilke had become a grandfather on 2 November 1923; little Ruth, lately wed to Carl Sieber, had given birth to little Christine; and Rilke, not always with the readiest will, announced the blessed event to selected friends. To Frau Gudi Nölke he wrote on 3 December: 'Ich habe ja auch inzwischen Zeit gehabt, Grossvater zu werden ... So treibt es die Zeit mit uns' (RMR, *Die Briefe an Frau Gudi Nölke*, Wiesbaden, 1953, p. 125). On 22 December Nanni von Escher got the same message with variations: 'nebenbei erwähnt, darf ich selbst mich, seit November, in die Generation der Grossväter rechnen, bürgerlich gesprochen, also zu den "Alten"' (*Briefe aus Muzot*, p. 230). To a recent grandmother, Gertrud Ouckama Knoop, he observed that she had not mentioned any ill effects: 'Sie schreiben ja nichts davon, dass Grossmutterschaft an und für sich die Anwendungen einschränke, die man sich zutrauen mag—so will ich auch mon art d'être grand père ... einfach für einen Zuwachs halten' (*Briefe aus Muzot*, p. 238: 13 February 1924). The talk about the art of being a grandfather persists well into the spring of 1924; when Clara Rilke arrives at Muzot for a visit that will turn out much better than expected, Rilke informs Marie von Thurn und Taxis that he is receiving 'eine Art Elementarunterricht in der Kunst "Grossvater zu sein"' (*Briefwechsel*, II, 806: 24 May 1924); he repeats the story of his education to Anton Kippenberg: 'wir haben uns in den einfachsten und elementarsten Übungen der Grosselterlichkeit gegenseitig nach Kräften unterstützt und gefördert' (*Briefe an seinen Verleger*, II, 462: 28 May 1924). Plainly, since he has no plans whatsoever to see his new grandchild, resident in distant Germany, his concern is not with the care and feeding of infants, but with himself, with the fact that he now, 'bürgerlich gesprochen', is an old man. And yet he still works at being a child: announcing Christine's birth to Kippenberg on 21 November 1923 (II, 440), he requests, in a single breath, not just a larger stipend for Clara and Ruth but more 'Taschengeld' for himself. There were painful incongruities in the situation: the new grandfather, not very enthusiastic about his new state yet 'respectable' enough to announce it properly, must request more money for his semi-dependents, a larger allowance for himself. The incongruities existed; Rilke was aware of them and perhaps even felt them keenly—but he would do nothing to remove them. They were a part of the payment for staying young.

In the letters about the new granddaughter we come across other familiar references. Having congratulated Clara on the new addition to the clan (*Briefe aus Muzot*, p. 218: 17 November 1923), he brings up his ageing mother, who has moved to Franzensbad from the hateful capital of the new Czechoslovakian Republic; as a prelude to informing Kippenberg of the baby's christening, he recalls his late father's name-day, 19 March, and the way it was celebrated in Old Austria. Joseph Rilke's little son had not wanted to wear an old coat over the new suit he had received to mark the great day; instead the boy insisted on going out 'im blossen Anzug, "blank", wie man damals in Oesterreich sagte—und das wollte dann natürlich bezahlt sein' (*Briefe an seinen Verleger*, II, 446–447: 19 March 1924). The family event, coupled with childish vanity, made the boy Rilke catch cold; family events also brought illness down on the head of the fledgling grandfather—and illness at forty-eight is not a product of youthful pride but a sign of coming age. Rilke's reasoning on this point—that illness or death in his family weakened *him*—is a little difficult to grasp; but however obscure it may be in itself, it bobs up repeatedly in the letters from this period. He frequently meditates on death; lengthy reflections of this sort are prompted by the serious illness of a relative of Dory von der Mühll, by the death of the grandmother of Duke Gallarati-Scotti, by the passing of Countess Sizzo's aunt.[16] These people, whom Rilke did not know, had no direct emotional claim on him; but their familial ties to his *correspondantes* made him think long, long thoughts—had the ladies (or, in the Gallarati–Scotti case, the lady's spouse) been somehow damaged by the fates that befell their kin?

Recently, Rilke had lost two close relatives of his own, Oswald von Kutschera and Paula Rilke, while his grandmother, Caroline Entz, had come so close to dying that Rilke, in a letter to Kippenberg (II, 449: 12 May 1924), made it sound as if she were already dead; in actual fact, she outlived Rilke, hanging on until 1927. (Recently, the Kippenbergs had been treated to the saga of Rilke's family straight from the mouth of its principal member; during the Muzot visit of April, 1924, when Rilke, visibly failing, told Kippenberg he had finished his literary career, he entertained his guests from Germany with long stories about his relatives.)[17] An outburst, a rash, of deaths in a single family is, to be sure, not an extremely unusual event; the superstitious among us might recall the old saying about deaths coming in threes. However, Rilke had discovered what he thought was a scientific explanation of his illness as a part of the family's cycle of misery and death. In a letter to Clara Rilke (*Briefe aus Muzot*, pp. 247–252: 26 February 1924), he first suggests that 'das Alter' is to blame for his troubles, but hastily shoves this unpleasant notion aside; instead, he decides, 'irgendein kritischer Moment des Blutes' must be overcome before he will regain his health. Twenty years ago, he writes, he had experienced similar illnesses; but in the meantime he had become aware of an understanding between himself and his 'blood'; presently, he feels left in the lurch. But his trusted 'blood' could not help going back on the tacit agreement; the two deaths in his family had signalled to his blood that the whole Rilke tribe was in a phase of decline, and so his blood, obedient to the command, had to misbehave. Rilke had read the works of Wilhelm Fliess[18] (whose name and theories are mentioned in this letter to Clara), and so was not at all surprised by what had taken place; nor, if we are aware of Rilke's egocentricity, are we surprised to see him transform a quasi-clinical inquiry into an excuse for somewhat grisly recriminations. By dying, Ossi and Paula (his relatives had never been very considerate of his feelings) had done him a bad turn; 'so sind ja schon genug Ursachen genannt, die, zusammenwirkend, Veränderungen des Blutdrucks hätten herbeiführen können'.

Age, if not debilitation and death, was brought home to him in another intimate connexion, too; he did a good turn for 'Merline', Baladine Klossowska, and lived to regret it. He arranged for Pierre Klossowski, Merline's elder son, to stay in Paris under the tutelage of André Gide; Pierre had hopes of becoming Gide's private secretary, and Rilke informed Frau Nölke, who had also had a part in Pierre's upbringing, that everything, after all, was possible—had he not become Rodin's secretary with a knowledge of French orthography still faultier than Pierre's (*Briefe an Gudi Nölke*, p. 124; 3 December 1923)? The letters about Pierre's case to Gide and to Merline contain strong hints of identification and envy: he had been in Paris as a young man—would that he had enjoyed Pierre's advantages! (Rilke forgets that, like his admired Shelley, he was already married and a father when he first came to Paris, while Pierre is a seventeen-year-old boy.) When lucky Pierre is installed in rooms overlooking the Luxembourg Garden, Rilke confesses his envy to Gide: 'J'espère qu'il profitera de toutes ces circonstances' (RMR–André Gide, *Correspondance*, Paris, 1952, p. 233: 19 December 1923); earlier, he had told Gide the reason for his envy: 'Si autrefois, dans ma jeunesse, une telle main s'était tendue vers mois, combien de retours et de recommencements cela m'eût épargné' (p. 226: 23 November 1923). To Merline,[18a] who has not taken the edge off Rilke's envy, we should guess, by telling him about Pierre's Parisian love affairs, Rilke is considerably more circumspect, providing resumés, without comment, of the accounts Gide gives him. But in a letter from the very days of the production of the 'Entwürfe' (15 February 1924), where Pierre is *not* mentioned, we can perceive the boy's healthy and handsome form between the lines; telling Merline about a new book of Henri de Montherlant, Rilke rather surprisingly becomes an advocate of intelligent physical training, and decides that modern youth is especially fortunate in this respect. Such was not the case in Rilke's day, 'surtout en Autriche' (RMR–Merline, *Correspondance*, Zürich, 1954, p. 502). The envy of the ill and ageing man, probably mindful of the nightmarish 'Turnstunden' at Sankt Pölten and Mährisch–Weisskirchen, is switched from Pierre to all the world's vigorous young men.

Minor literary events made Rilke feel his age, even as Pierre's trip to Paris did. He agreed, upon request, to the printing of a poem he had dedicated to Christian Morgenstern in 1896; he reminisced to Duchess Gallarati-Scotti about the halcyon days he had spent at Viareggio between 1897 and 1905; he read the latest edition of the letters and papers of his old flame, Paula Modersohn-Becker, dead seventeen years past; he read the correspondence of the late Richard Dehmel, where he could find, if he wanted to, a terrifying example of a poet unable to outgrow noisy adolescence. The most serious blow came, however, from Vienna, the city in which, once upon a time, his bold flight from the 'Linzer Handelsakademie' had ended; he learned that Hugo von Hofmannsthal, the youthful poet *par excellence* of Rilke's generation, had turned fifty, and, moved by the information, sent his Viennese colleague the poem 'Das Füllhorn'. Meanwhile, Katherina Kippenberg unwittingly underlined Rilke's realization that Hofmannsthal (and Rilke) were middle-aged by quoting to her prize poet a sentence from Hofmannsthal's contribution to *Navigare necesse est*: '"Es ist, als hätte dieser Morgen im Voraus den Abend verzehrt"' (RMR–KK, *Briefwechsel*, p. 521: 27 February 1924).[19] Simultaneously, the literary world of the present began to treat Rilke as if he were a grand old man; and Rilke did his best to escape the classification. The young Carl Viëtor wanted Rilke's permission to anthologize some of his sonnets; he got it, together with a long recommendation of Wolf Kalckreuth, one of those 'Frühvollendeten' whose early passing (Rilke seems almost envious of them, too) prevented them from winning an assured position in literature (*Briefe aus Muzot*, p. 260: 24 March 1924). If Rilke is a spokesman for young poets of the past in the Viëtor letter, then, in a letter to Werner Milch, he begs to be allowed to stay in youth's ranks. He thanks Milch for permitting him to examine a volume of the novice's poetry, and tells the youth—Milch was only twenty-one at the time—that he most definitely is 'open' to the new generation: 'Oh, das bin ich mit ganzem Herzen und denke übrigens nicht daran, mich zu den "Alten" zu zählen; was wäre unser métier, wenn es das Herz nicht über die Kleinlichkeit der Zeitzählung hinaushöbe' (*Briefe aus Muzot*, p. 243). The letter to Milch was written on 14 February 1924; thus, like the letter on sports to Merline, it is exactly contemporaneous to the 'Entwürfe'. Proust, whom Rilke read in these Swiss years with the warmest enthusiasm, had made at least a literary recapture of his youth by remembering it;[20] Carossa, if less impressively, had done the same thing with *Eine Kindheit*, which Rilke was re-reading just at this time. By remembering, in the 'Entwürfe', Rilke intended to get at least a part of his youth back, to raise himself, in the phrase he used to Milch, above the pettiness of chronology.

Finally, some other young writers (apart from Maurois and his *Ariel*) also attracted Rilke's attention in the autumn and winter months of 1923–24: Robert de Traz, with a long essay on Sweden which brought Rilke's Scandinavian days back to him; Henri de Montherlant, whose war novel, *Le Songe* (like Carossa's *Rumänisches Tagebuch*) found Rilke's approval; and, especially, Jacques Sindral (a pseudonym of Albert Fabre-Luce),[21] whose *Attirance de la Mort*, bearing a motto,

'The amorous deep', from Shelley, aroused a flurry of excitement in Rilke's letters. As Rilke pointed out, the author was such an extremely young man, only twenty-five (at this age, Rilke had accomplished a great deal more than Sindral, but these accomplishments were meaningless to the man suddenly growing old); furthermore, the book dealt with a subject very close to Rilke's anxious heart. The hero, 'averti par la maladie et s'effrayant de la mort', takes refuge from death first by flight to a cloister, then by falling in love, and at the end, as if to anticipate 'toute cruauté finale', by casting himself into the arms of death itself; the summary is the one Rilke sent to Merline (*Correspondance*, pp. 498–499). Sindral's thoughts are completely comprehensible to him, Rilke says, in these weeks of his illness; the letter on Sindral's novel bears the date of 11 February 1924. Unlike Sindral's hero, Rilke did not try to make up with death; we have the reports of Dr. Haemmerli on Rilke's blank refusal to accept the imminence of his passing. He took another of the solutions of Sindral's hero—love, its description, its substitutes.

It would require much more space than we have here even to outline the history of Rilke's illnesses, a history culminating in the flight to Val-Mont at Christmas, 1923. In summary, however, the following may be said: when Katharine Kippenberg told Rilke (on 5 January 1924) that she had never heard him speak of physical illness before, she revealed herself as a relative late-comer, and something of an outsider, in the circle of Rilke's epistolary friends. The letters from the early and middle periods of Rilke's life are full to overflowing with laments about, and descriptions of, physical ill-being. Lou Andreas-Salomé hits the nail on the head with her recollection that one of Rilke's earliest remarks to her was: '"Ich werde ohnhin bald zu liegen kommen—sei's Herz oder Lunge"'.[22] She concludes that Rilke was 'unsicher seinem eigenen Körper gegenüber', a judgement which, if we recall the countless minor ailments and frequent trips to the dry-dock of the sanatorium he catalogues in his letters, can scarcely be called unfair. Of course, Lou, with her semi-medical interests, got to bear the brunt of his complaints, although she was by no means the only recipient of them; it is to her that Rilke addresses the long case-history of the 'Wendung' crisis and its aftermath, where he says 'Mein Körper ist wie eine Falle geworden' (RMR–LAS, *Briefwechsel*, Zürich–Wiesbaden, 1951, p. 352: 26 June 1914). During the next years the complaints become less frequent, without ceasing altogether; the brief military experience caused an equally brief ascent of the line on the fever-chart. By the time Rilke had finished the *Elegies* and the *Sonnets*, he was convinced that his body, his mind, and his soul, as he put it, lived together in perfect harmony; indeed, he is able to give an exact date for this harmony's inception. Writing to Lisa Heise on 27 January 1924, just after his return from the first stay at Val-Mont, he says: 'Seit dreiundzwanzig Jahren [thus since 1901, the year Ruth was born] . . . bin ich immer allein mit allen Störungen des Körpers fertig geworden . . . Ich habe nie genaue Grenzen gezogen zwischen Leib und Geist und Seele: eines hat ins andere gedient und gewirkt, und jedes ist mir wunderbar und köstlich gewesen' (RMR, *Briefe an eine junge Frau*, Leipzig, 1930, pp. 52–53).[23] This tale of harmony is, obviously, a very different story from that told by countless letters from the very twenty-three years Rilke has staked out as his golden age. A few months after the letter to Lisa Heise, Rilke moves the *terminus a quo* back further still; to Frau Amann-Volkart he writes that his recent illness is 'ein Zustand, den ich, seit meiner kränklichen Kindheit, nicht gekannt habe' (*Briefe aus Muzot*, p. 264: 7 April 1924). The novelty of the experience of illness, then, is given by Rilke as the cause for the special shock he received when he was forced to seek medical aid at Schöneck and Val-Mont. But we have seen that neither illness nor the consultation of a sanatorium physician was a new experience for Rilke; that the harmony he boasted of was of relatively recent origin. Other reasons must have existed, then, for the violence of Rilke's emotional reaction to his illness, an illness never very clearly defined by him, despite all the lengthy accounts he gives of it.

There is no denying that Rilke had enjoyed general well-being from about 1915 until 1923. In these years, too, he had been involved in a series of what may be called successful love affairs, with Lou Albert-Lasard, with Claire Studer, with Merline, with others. As we have noted above, a new attitude toward the erotic life became apparent, or rather, the trickle of 'flachem klaren Wasser', discernible to the careful eye from the very beginnings of his oeuvre, became 'der Männer Ströme': the phrases just quoted are from 'Hetären-Gräber' in *Neue Gedichte*, a poem from 1904 which is a harbinger of the change. We have likewise mentioned that it was probably the liaison with Lou Albert-Lasard which broke the dam; the poems written for her at Irschenhausen in September, 1914, will provide at least a sketch, if not a whole picture, of what happened. Rilke fights hard ('Lass mich nicht in deine Arme sinken, / denn mich fassen Arme nicht'), but finally succumbs to normalcy ('Doch mein Aufblick wird Dich immer wieder / sammeln in den lieben: Deinen Körper'); it should be observed here that Lou Albert-Lasard had not just her fascinating red hair but the potent memory of another Lou on her side: it was at another Alpine village near Munich, at Wolfratshausen in 1897, that Rilke had sunk into the arms of Lou Andreas-Salomé. Of course, red hair and memories did not do the job by themselves; in the previous year, Rilke—still busy with a 'geschwisterliche Geliebte', Magda von Hattingberg, who reacted in a surprisingly human way when, later on, she saw her replacement[24]—had informed Lou Andreas-Salomé of his plan for a set of 'phallische Hymnen'.[25] These poems were finally put on paper in 1915; and Rilke's editors have given them the innocent name of 'Sieben Gedichte'. The 'Sieben Gedichte' are one of the two programmatic documents of Rilke's phallic worship; the other is the 'Brief des jungen Arbeiters', composed at Muzot in the same remarkable month as the last *Elegies* and the *Sonnets*. In the 'Brief' the young worker is made to say that he has found a new faith: 'mein Geschlecht ist nicht nur den Nachkommen zugekehrt, es ist das Geheimnis meines eigenen Lebens' (*Ausgewählte Werke*, Leipzig, 1938, II, 306). However, Rilke was profoundly shy about announcing his discovery to the world; neither the phallic hymns nor the 'Brief' were released for publication during his lifetime; while the sentiments of the letter, put into the mouth of the young worker, are addressed to a mysterious 'Herr V.'—the late Emile Verhaeren who, resting in his grave, could not very well agree or disagree. Rilke probably felt relieved upon learning that someone else had broadcast the message of phallic salvation in his stead; after reading D. H. Lawrence's essay on religion, Rilke wrote to Kippenberg:

'[der Aufsatz] enthält Sätze, die ich, beinahe wörtlich gleich, in meinen Anmerkungen weiss' (*Briefe an seinen Verleger*, II, 473: 5 December 1924).

Rilke's hesitancy to spread his new gospel abroad would suggest that his faith in the flesh was not entirely firm; in his own case, the body in which he placed his trust betrayed him, and not merely by growing feeble. Lou Andreas-Salomé described the Rilke body as follows: it was 'fast ein Körper ohne Altern, als sei die Reifung der Jahre ersetzt durch kränkliches Zögern und Nichtmitkönnen mit dem wahrhaften Geschehen der Zeit'.[26] The Rilke who now celebrated the *man* had wanted to remain a *child* in every other respect except the sexual; the child is even granted a share, a main one, in manhood's special realm, for the sexual experience is called, in 'Der Brief des jungen Arbeiters', the one instance in adult life where the naiveté, the wholeness, of childhood is retained: 'Um die eigentliche Lage unserer Sinnlichkeit zu bezeichnen, müsste man also sagen dürfen: Einmal waren wir überall Kind, jetzt sind wirs nur noch an einer Stelle' (*AW*, II, 306). Now, Lou Andreas-Salomé knew that, as a child, Rilke had been of an unusually erethic nature; and she knew that such a child had only one outlet for its precocity, an outlet about which Rilke's father had been much concerned (*In der Schule bei Freud*, p. 209). She also knew that Rilke, the eternal would-be child, had not been able to rid himself of the childish vice for which Josef Rilke had been on the lookout; finally, she knew that the vice beset Rilke in particular at times of crisis. In 1904, preparing himself for the final break with domesticity's world, Rilke had comforted Kappus, and himself, about the appearance of the vice in adults;[27] Malte was not free of the vice, and equated it with illness ('Und jetzt auch noch diese Krankheit, die mich immer schon so eigentümlich berührt hat'[28]; in 1912, during the 'Wendung' crisis, Rilke talked of it in oblique terms to Dr. Gebsattel, who almost became his psychiatrist ('was einfach nur eine schlechte Angewohnheit war ... bekommt Resistenz und kann nächstens eine Wand geworden sein', *Briefe 1907–1914*, Leipzig, 1933, p. 170: 14 January 1912); Lou Andreas-Salomé got the same story in slightly clearer terms: 'ich schäme mich einzugestehn, wie sehr mich oft wochenlang dieser geheimnisvolle Cirkel umtanzt, in dem ein Elend dem andern jeden Gefallen thut' (RMR–LAS, *Briefwechsel*, p. 261: 20 January 1912). The vice accompanies the symptoms of disease which drive Rilke to Schöneck and its 'fremden Beistand' in 1923, and then to Val-Mont. Embarrassment keeps him from discussing the matter frankly; he talks to Katharina Kippenberg of the 'obedience' (Joseph Rilke's precautions come to mind) with which he follows the directions of the Schöneck physicians (RMR–KK, *Briefwechsel*, p. 511: 21 November 1923); he mentions 'diesen fatalen Intermezzo' to Anton Kippenberg (*Briefe an seinen Verleger*, II, 445: 13 January 1924); but he makes a clean breast only to Lou.[29] Evidently he tells her his story in the letter of 22 April 1924 (RMR–LAS, *Briefwechsel*, p. 490), but the letter's printed version has had several sections removed; we must take recourse to the somewhat less badly mutilated letter of 31 October 1925, to find out what has happened. The vocabulary of 1912 is repeated: 'ja ich lebe seit zwei Jahren mehr und mehr in der Mitte eines Schreckens ... Es ist ein entsetzlicher Cirkel, ein Kreis böser Magie ... ich sehe nicht, wie ich so weiterleben soll ... in meinem Thurm ... in dieser völligen Abgeschiedenheit, [würden] diese mesquinen

Teufel erst recht ihr Spiel mit mir übertreiben...' (RMR–LAS, *Briefwechsel*, p. 500). It is an absurd situation for a great poet of almost fifty: 'Es lag wohl in einer Einfalt meiner Natur, dass [meine Niederlage] in so absurden Gegebenheiten sich abspielen sollte'. The situation, then, of 1923 and 1924, has been the following: the convert to an affirmation of life, the recent discoverer of a phallic cult (or, put less melodramatically, of garden-variety heterosexual love), has found himself betrayed by a remnant of the childhood he did not want to abandon. The man's work, the deed which transforms the male, however briefly, into an erotic god, has been changed into 'das hilflose Laster', and the 'Laster' is the accompanying sign of what Rilke, ageing and terrified of death, thinks may be a mortal disease. The situation is at once ridiculous and desperate; it is a situation which demands autobiography, since it involves the whole of life, childhood, manhood, and age. The situation is so painful that it requires the immediate release of the poem instead of the long gestation of the prose autobiography; the situation is so painful (in another sense), that the poem, affording the disguise of symbolic language, thrusts itself upon the poet as the only possible medium for autobiography.

II

On 15 September 1923, Rilke was at Schöneck. There, at the request of a chief forest ranger named Burri, he wrote a poem, 'Imaginärer Lebenslauf', for the *Festschrift* of Lucerne's 'Freie Vereinigung Gleichgesinnter.' Having nothing else on hand, he told Burri, he had jotted down 'ein paar Verszeilen' for the club's book (*Briefe aus Muzot*, p. 217). The poem is a trial balloon, an effort at confessional autobiography to be published in an out-of-the-way place and for an audience of which not a single member, save Burri, knows the poet personally; such a corner-confession, we suppose, is designed to give at least limited relief to the sufferer. The title itself, 'Imaginärer Lebenslauf', and some of the poem's details, are likewise designed to lead the well-informed reader, who might detect autobiography in the poem, off the track—but not so far off that he cannot find his way back again. Rilke is like the criminal who wants to get caught, concealing some clues but leaving others in plain view.[30]

'Childhood', in the poem's first two lines, begins happily, in contrast to the pictures of nursery 'Ängste' Rilke had painted in the past with such a generous hand, and in keeping with the newer programme of total affirmation:[31]

> Erst eine Kindheit, grenzenlos und ohne
> Verzicht und Zeit. O unbewusste Lust.

Then we meet that obligatory hell, the military school ('Auf einmal Schrecken'), a hell which has stayed the same except for an added dash of frankness about conditions there, conditions which may have been rather as Robert Musil, a cadet at Mährisch-Weisskirchen a few years after Rilke, described them in *Die Verwirrungen des Zöglings Törless*. The famous anecdote of the curse which René Rilke hurled at his tormentors is recounted, or seems to be;[32] it gets a whole strophe:

> Trotz. Der Gebogene wird selber Bieger
> und rächt an anderen, dass er erlag,
> Geliebt, gefürchtet, Retter, Ringer, Sieger
> und Überwinder, Schlag auf Schlag.

Nevertheless, the claims of the last two lines are almost too boastful for the military school's reality: Rilke never became an Austrian Frank Merriwell, captain of the team and champion of bullied younger boys. On the other hand, the lines can be taken to mean a somewhat older Rilke struggling for literary recognition, but in this case they describe a poet considerably more embattled than Rilke ever was: he never had *that* much trouble with his critics, except in his theatrical fiascoes. (We are reminded of the self-flattering overemphasis Richard Strauss gave his opponents in the 'Critics' section of *Ein Heldenleben*; the bigger Goliath is, the braver David seems.) Perhaps the double meaning of the strophe, simultaneously indicating 'military school' and 'trials of the young artist', is purposeful, a bow in the direction of the 'imaginariness' of the title. The third strophe achieves 'imaginariness' not by ambiguity but by radical contraction; the poet on the heights of his ability, the isolated master of the *Neue Gedichte* and *Malte*, of the *Elegies* and the *Sonnets*, is passed by in a single line:

> Und dann allein im Weiten, Leichten, Kalten ...

But Rilke's haste cannot be ascribed to a desire for concealment alone; he is anxious to get on to the erotic renaissance which has become the major fact of his existence, the basis of his affirmation of 'Hiersein'. He goes straight—it is a revelatory detail—to what he thinks is the spark of the renaissance, the vital connexion between childhood's 'unbegrenzte Lust' and the 'single point' of the young worker:

> Doch tief in der errichteten Gestalt
> Ein Atemholen nach dem Ersten, Alten ...

Then the poem ends abruptly, with a line certainly mysterious and perhaps sinister:

> Da stürzte Gott aus seinem Hinterhalt.

What god? In a recent essay on Rilke's 'phallic motif',[33] Klaus Kanzog has taken the line as a statement of the old vice's sudden reoccurrence; we might expand his interpretation to include the concomitant and frightening *illness* (not just the renewed attack of the vice) of what Lou Andreas-Salomé liked to call the 'Rückschlag', the revenge life took for the productivity of February, 1922. Indeed, Rilke had studied Wilhelm Fliess's theory of the danger implicit in 'schöpferische Tage'; querulous as he was, he would not have been slow to apply Fliess's gloomy thought to himself, and it likewise lay within his nature to clothe the event in ominously sublime language. The very sublimity of the poem's last line admits, of course, other interpretations: in his paper, Professor Prawer has suggested a parallel with the passage in Exodus iii, where God calls to Moses from the burning bush. However, God speaks to Moses at the beginning of his 'Lebenslauf', while Rilke's hero is ambushed only after he has, it seems, his career behind him; the God who talks to Moses may be terrifying (He pops up suddenly from a burning bush) but not threatening, for He merely speaks to Moses, while Rilke's god plunges out of an ambuscade, and his intention is plainly an assault upon the hero. A Christian (or a Greek) interpretation of the Rilke line would be that God, or the gods, had decided to take vengeance for a long arrogance, or a long hybris; but Rilke does not concern himself elsewhere with the problems of pride—he thought of himself as an exceedingly humble man. In trying to interpret the line, it should be remembered that Rilke's God in his last years was the affirmative song-god of the *Sonnets* or the erotic god of the well-known poem from February, 1924: 'Masken! Masken! Dass man Eros blende'—he had stopped trying to find any other deity than those directly a part of 'Hiersein'. Could there be an obfuscation on Rilke's part here, half intentional, the last of his stabs at 'imaginariness', and half the product of his own bafflement at his situation? The god who plunges forth so menacingly from his ambuscade could indeed be the vice, as Kanzog claims; but the vice is an aspect of the whole god of affirmation whom Rilke worships. The crux lies here: will the aspect get command of the whole? Will the saviour-god turn altogether into a 'mesquiner Teufel'? Rilke did not know the answer; the sudden breaking-off of the 'Imaginary Career' (to which Rilke could only imagine the end) leaves the autobiographer without relief, his question unanswered.

Six months later, after getting back from Val-Mont, Rilke wrote the 'Entwürfe aus zwei Winterabenden', which would try, as *Malte* once had, to 'accomplish childhood once again', but this time the accomplishment would be carried out in accordance with the new party-line of affirmation, not with the old story of 'Ängste' Rilke had peddled so often in the past. The 'Entwürfe' would, perhaps, set biographers (biography was so much on Rilke's mind now) on what he conceived to be the right track about himself; they would see him once and for all as the poet of 'Rühmen', not of terrors. More intimately, more importantly, and more pathetically, the 'Entwürfe' might transform the erotic god, gone bad, into a saviour again; they might prove that Rilke's 'body, mind, and soul' were still friends, still that unity of which he had so often boasted. Like the rest of us, Rilke wanted to put his best foot forward for posterity; like the rest of us, Rilke did not want to grow old and die.

In *Malte*, autobiographical intentions were disclaimed by the fiction of the Danish nobleman, in the poems of Count C.W. by the ghost's visit, in 'Imaginärer Lebenslauf' by the very title; in the 'Entwürfe' the disclaimer is reduced to a device, one taken from the nineteenth-century German novella, for establishing a certain distance between the narrator and his story. Rilke's shyness makes him use the 'Rahmen' of time but no heavier disguise; the autobiographical criminal is determined to be caught at last. The 'Prélude' leads us into a framed well and into a framed picture, [34] downward and backward into the past:

> Warum, auf einmal, seh ich die gerahmte
> Park-Quelle unterm Ulmen-Dach?
> Das Wasser in dem alten Rande ahmte
> dem Hintergrund in Bildnissen nach.[35]

We step into the image world of the water and, simultaneously, into the 'Bildnis' of the past (that the picture is a portrait indicates its specifically personal nature); the fact that the water is a spring, in movement, should not disturb us, for water in movement can still reflect images, lending them movement from its own flow—and there will be some important movements, of time and development, in the figures who will inhabit the portrait. The spring, and the picture, are 'unterm Ulmen-Dach' and 'in dem alten Rande'; the phrases make us recall the wish which Rilke expressed upon seeing the park of Schloss Bothmar a second time, in September, 1923: 'unter den alten Bäumen lichte Kleider zu sehen, die Frauen und Mädchen von einst'. Going into the castle itself (he described the experience to Countess Sizzo, in a letter from the following December, just before he fell seriously ill), he was entranced by the 'stattlichsten Frauenporträts des siebzehnten und achtzehnten Jahrhunderts'; several of the ladies, Rilke observed, held lemons in their hands—he cannot explain, and neither can his host, von Salis, why they should do so; he adds, however, that he always keeps lemons in his workroom in winter, as, we assume, aids to inspiration and memory (*Briefe an Gräfin Sizzo*, Wiesbaden, 1950, pp. 52–55: 16 December 1923). In the second strophe of the 'Prélude' the lemon is not mentioned, but its shape is. And to the oval is subjoined another magical object, the shawl, which is also mentioned in the letter to Countess Sizzo; Rilke had been enchanted by the collection of shawls he had come upon in Berne's National Museum:[36]

> War es die Hoffnung eines Kaschmirshawls,
> die ich ans Blätterspiegelbild verlor?

Both the oval's gentle shape (in sexual symbolism, the complementary opposite of Rilke's often-employed 'Turm'[37]) and the shawl tell us what Rilke is going to remember: his discovery of womankind, a more graceful version of Henri Brulard's first memory, or of that dreadful incident when André Gide, just a toddler, bit his cousin's bare shoulder. But Rilke seems to grow irresolute for a moment at the beginning of the third strophe; it is the first of several hesitations which he will use for rhetorical contrast, to make the cycle's affirmations appear all the more powerful:

> Wer weiss es jetzt, da Jugend nicht mehr täuscht?

Now that youth is gone (and for Rilke so reluctantly gone), how can we be sure of the validity of the youthful experience to be described? This hesitation has helped to produce the cycle, of course; the doubt must be overcome, and it is, but not yet permanently, in the 'Prélude's' last three lines:

51

> Wie viele Griffe in das Leere
> hat reines Wasser wunderbar verkeuscht
> und glänzt noch jetzt herauf, dass es den Traum vermehre.

How often has reflection, the look into memory's water, helped us to put the major experiences of life into order, cleansed ('verkeuscht') of the meaningless events which surrounded them? We think of the 'Wendung' crisis, when the glance into Narcissus' pool and into the 'Waldteich' taught Rilke that he must abandon 'eye-work' for 'heart-work'. The glance into the 'reines Wasser' of the 'Entwürfe' will perform the same functions of purifying and arranging life's blind stabs ('Griffe in das Leere'), the necessary preliminaries to the explanation of life which autobiography should offer. (Perhaps there is a hint here too of the autobiographer's claim of telling the 'whole truth': 'ich werde dir reines Wasser einschenken'.) The first half of the concluding line ('und glänzt noch jetzt herauf') continues the claims for the validity and importance of the autobiography; the experience *is* still alive; but the last words of the poem, with their reference to the 'Traum', make us pause again. Does the 'Traum' imply still another reservation about the reality of the experience (it was 'only a dream')? Or is the 'Traum' part of an extremely ancient literary and subliterary tradition, that of the 'Liebestraum', which has flourished in particular in romantic songs: the supreme experience of life is like a dream because it is so wonderful. The cycle contains enough elements of the romantically banal later on, particularly in the fifth poem of the first part ('Dass ich die Früchte beschrieb'), to make us suspect that the latter possibility is the correct one.

The first part of the cycle proper is composed of seven poems which alternate, in their material, according to an easily discernible pattern, a simplicity which is quite in keeping with the *soi-disant* 'childlikeness' of the whole cycle: one poem presents a scene, the next presents a reflection connected with the scene, and so on, until the seventh poem combines scene and reflection. In the first poem we are made to attend one of those dramas which, in life as in letters, can leave lasting scars on the beardless hero; a boy, not up to the situation in size or in social graces, is humiliated at a dance—we can think of companion examples in literature from Booth Tarkington's *Penrod* to Thomas Mann's *Tonio Kröger*. But the coals to be heaped on the boy's head are cooled before the tale begins: 'Nichts blieb so schön'. It was the fairest experience of life, even though the narrator, like the youngest child in another Mann story, *Unordnung und frühes Leid*, was too small for the party: 'Ich war damals zu klein'. The background is a country house,[38] or a house with a large garden, perhaps the country house in Friuli which, during the Duino days, Rilke had revisited in the company of Marie von Thurn und Taxis; here, he told her, he had, as a child, fallen in love with 'die kleine Amélie'.[39] The children decide to roll up the carpets for an impromptu dance, and Rilke is given the chance to get a splendid triple effect out of the last line of the strophe:

> Sie wollten plötzlich tanzen
> und rollten rasch den alten Teppich ein.
> (Was für ein Schimmer liegt noch auf dem Ganzen.)

In our mind's eye we are made to see, all at once, the shine of the unworn varnish on the floor just revealed, the shimmer of water in the pool, and the patina which lies on the memories of what happened   Rilke fools us: the girl, suddenly appearing, dances, and we guess that the boy can see only her in the crowd, because she is so lovely; still, the press of dancers can sometimes conceal even her beauty. This is what we think until we read the next lines:

> weil ihr Geruch die Welt geworden war,
> in der man unterging.

Then we learn that the experience was more elemental; the watcher is so intoxicated by the odour she emanates (we remember the lemons of Malans) that he can see no longer, cannot follow her with his eyes. Then the lament is repeated: 'Ich war zu klein', but with a new sense; he was too small then, and he will forever be too small to become the master of such an aroma. Plenty of evidence, epistolary and anecdotal, attests to Rilke's dislike of the pronouncedly masculine man—Kassner says somewhere that he could not stand to be in the same room with persons of this sort. He wants neither to become the 'Herr aller Schöpfung', the man who uses the excitement woman provides for what might be called his own selfish ends, nor does he want to become the master of the odour in a directly opposite sense, the ascetic who can eliminate woman from his life. 'Mastery' of either sort would make him fall out of the special and miraculous order of things into which he has been placed, of which he grew aware as a boy and again, belatedly, as a man:

> Um aus dem unbeschreiblichen Bezug
> herauszufallen wie ein Stein.

The last strophe of the poem merely repeats what has gone before, as if to nail fast this most important of happenings in the reader's mind: 'Nein, dies blieb schön! ...Ihr blumiger Geruch...Nie kam ein Widerspruch...Unendlicher Ertrag'. His discovery has given him infinite profit.

   The second poem of the cycle's first part offers a reflection, as has been promised, on the events just past; it would seem at first glance to be another hedging, like the 'Wer weiss es jetzt' of the 'Prélude'. The 'Unendlicher Ertrag' is cut down to a 'Möglichkeit des Glücks', which winged its way past, an echo of the old Rilkean doctrine that unrequited, unrealized love is the best love; then the profit is reduced still further into '*Un*-Möglichkeit sogar', into a mere suspicion:

> dass dieser Sommer, dieser Gartensaal—
> dass die Musik hinklingender Minuten
> unschuldig war, da sie uns rein betrog.

In other and coarser words: the experience deceived us, it had no validity in our case, the best we can say for it is that it misled us unintentionally, without malice. But the doubt has been anticipated here, as in the previous poem, by the opening words: 'Dies ist Besitz'—the *possibility* of possession is admitted, even though the possession turns out temporarily to have the negative form postulated in Abelone's song in *Malte*: 'weil ich niemals dich anhielt, halt ich dich fest'. And the hesitation the strophe expresses is vitiated by a second detail, the hyphen and the italics in '*Un*-Möglichkeit' (which make the word imply not that happiness is literally impossible, but rather unbelievable, miraculous); it is weakened again by the 'innocence' of the music played for the dance and the 'purity' of our betrayal. Hesitation, in this curious strophe, hovers constantly on the brink of acceptance. Rilke was in a tight spot, as far as his doctrines were concerned; having preached non-possessive love so long and so loudly, he could not abandon it straight out; and his new phallic cult had to include the act of possession, however brief.[40] Skilful as he was at arguing for two opposed sides simultaneously, not even Rilke could be comfortable on a fence.

In the next strophe, Rilke climbs down on the side of his new doctrine, as we suspected he would. In the course of the dance, the girl has had the effect of a mature woman upon the boy; she has also matured in the poet's memory. Meanwhile, the poet himself enjoys a double age. He is the boy of his memory, he is at the same time his present self; and the two beings, boy and man, are joined by the god-like condition which came upon the child then, in the 'Gartensaal', and which befalls the poet now, as he remembers.[41] The recognition of the link between child and man does not inspire sadness at time's flight, as in Hofmannsthal's 'Terzinen über Vergänglichkeit', but joy; the urge toward the other sex is something time has *not* been able to change. The poem ends as it has begun, with hesitation, but of the mildest and most hopeful kind. If the hours of the god's descent are indeed immortal (and their reoccurrence in the man, remembering their first appearance, indicates at least their longevity in the individual), then what promises might life hold, both for the boy at the dance and the man who recalls passion's birth! The 'Gebäude' erected are doubtless Rilke's 'Türme', but their erection is not caused by a bestial lusting; the towers are built of (or aroused by) those evanescent and mighty materials, 'Geruch und Schein', or, returning to the somewhat more concrete language of the 'Prélude', oval and shawl.

The third poem is again a scene; following the customary affirmative introduction ('Alles ist mir lieb' corresponds, in position and tone, to 'Nichts blieb so schön' and 'Dies ist Besitz'), the feminine partner reappears, again double-aged:

> Alles ist mir lieb, die Sommersprossen
> und die Spange, die den Ärmel schloss.

The painting is done with a minimum of strokes, by the listing of the freckles of childhood and the grown-up brooch closing the sleeve of a woman's dress; she is a child, but she will play the woman's role in what is to follow. After two more lines ('oh wie unerhört und unverflossen / blieb die Süssigkeit, drin nichts verdross') which, in the miniature dimensions of the lyric, would take the place, as it were, of the long crescendo in *Tristan's* love duet, we see the boy himself, standing to one side, stunned. The child's heart overflows (there is a verbal link, as well as a possible indication of physiological events, between the 'unverflossen' of the first strophe and the 'Überfluss' of the second); the convolvulus blossom, held half-chewed in the boy's little fist, tells us, if we do not already know, what has happened. Like the 'sanftester Oval', the calix of the convolvulus, the morning-glory, has a suggestive shape; on at least two other occasions in these years, in the first poem of the 'Sieben Gedichte' and in the paralipomena to the *Briefwechsel in Gedichten mit Erika Mitterer*,[42] Rilke used similar imagery of the 'weiblichen Kelch' and, correspondingly, the 'männlichen Blume'. Here the feminine calix of the morning-glory is almost devoured by the boy as he experiences something he has never experienced before. For his gentler, or less perceptive, readers, Rilke (perhaps a little embarrassed at his boldness himself) provides a kind of blanket prophecy of future joys for the child, somewhat less specific than the promise of 'Gebäude' at the end of the previous poem:

> Oh wie will das Leben übersteigern
> was es damals, schon erblüht, beging,

but a second key to the actual event is provided in 'schon erblüht', the chain-phrase (above, 'Überfluss' has the same connexion with 'verflossen') between the concluding strophe and the 'Blüte' of the strophe before it. Continuing the flower imagery to the end, Rilke describes the condition of the hapless and yet so happy onlooker after the event; passive before,

> als es von dem eigenen Verweigern
> wie von Gartenmauern niederhing,

the flower of the boy (or 'das Leben' itself, as Rilke says) now realizes what strength it has.

After the narration of the rather shocking events of the third poem, Rilke turns once again to a reflection, this time (another example of the fine sense for contrast so often demonstrated in the cycle) of a superbly ideal nature. Rilke has just spoken of the convolvulus, the morning-glory, and the morning hour of desire; now, by expansion, the whole morning of life is celebrated. In *Arbeitsstunden bei Rilke* (pp. 13-14), Marga Wertheimer tells how much Rilke admired Albrecht von Haller's 'An die Morgenstunde'; she no doubt means 'Morgengedanken', the initial poem of the *Versuch schweizerischer Gedichte*, of which Haller, anticipating Rilke's remarks on his own 'Entwürfe', said that he thought 'this fruit of a single hour' so imperfect that he hesitated to include it in his published work:

> Durchs rote Morgenthor der heitern Sternenbühne
> Naht das verklärte Licht der Welt;
> Die falben Wolken glühn von blitzendem Rubine,
> Und brennend Gold bedeckt das Feld.

Rilke's poem, which in its language is closer to the late Goethe than to Haller, likewise opens with a praise of the morning light:

> Nein, ich vergesse dich nicht,
>   was ich auch werde,
> liebliches, zeitiges Licht,
>   Erstling der Erde.

The pious Haller once rejoiced, and Rilke rejoices, at the coming of the morning light; but in Rilke's poem, which is of course part of an autobiography, the poet looks back to his first awareness of the light's first coming. Thus an avenue is opened to the second strophe, where a direct connexion is made with the little boy's initial erotic experience:

> Alles, was du versprachst,
>   hat sie gehalten,
> seit du das Herz mir erbrachst
>   ohne Gewalten.

The 'sie' of the second line is 'die Erde'; we think of 'Erde, du liebe, ich will' of the Ninth Elegy and of the praise of the earth which is the ground-bass of the *Sonnets to Orpheus*. However, if we remember the preceding poems in the cycle, the 'sie' will conjure up the girl-woman of the 'Gartensaal' for us. The morning light and the 'Geruch und Schein' of the feminine being play the same role; the heart, of whose 'Überfluss' we have just heard, is broken open gently, 'ohne Gewalten', in an experience which, while it may be stunning ('Taumelnd stand ich'), has nothing brutal about it. In either case—whether the boy is awakened to the whole of life by the sun, or to desire by the sight and smell of the girl—he has become alive. The third strophe of the hymn to the morning light returns to the general statement, a praise of the light itself:

> Flüchtigste frühste Figur,
>   die ich gewahrte,[43]

but the special instance of the erotic awakening crops up again in the conclusion:

> nur weil ich Stärke erfuhr,
>   rühm ich das Zarte.

Only since he has known the strength of the morning light, and of desire's beginning, has he been able to praise the tender concomitants of these experiences, all the delicate beings and things ('Ihr Zärtlichen') apostrophized in the fourth *Sonnet to Orpheus*, and the 'sanftesten Oval' of the 'Entwürfe'.

The autobiographical lyricist can take advantage, in his poetic *apologia*, of his special weapon, the lyric outcry; 'Nein, ich vergesse dich nicht' is a happy example of such a usage—too happy, indeed, since by its ability to stand alone, out of context, ready for inclusion in some treasury of German verse, it indicates an inherent flaw in the autobiographical lyric. The autobiographical lyric may be at its most interesting when it informs on the poet, as in the opening strophes of Tegnér's 'Mjältsjukan', yet it would seem to reach its aesthetic peak when it leaves autobiography; in assaying the poetic gold of Tegnér's poem, we should probably give the highest value to lines not specifically descriptive of the poet's personal misery, lines that speak for all mankind:

> Säg mig, du väktare, vad natten lider!
> Tar det då aldrig något slut därpå?
> Halvätne månen skrider jämt och skrider,
> gråtögda stjärnor gå alltjämt och gå.

On the other hand, we cannot understand Rilke's hymn (or Tegnér's dirge) completely unless we realize it is part of an autobiographical statement; in fact, can we claim fully to comprehend any of Rilke's late lyrics, including those *Duino Elegies* written in 1922 and the *Sonnets to Orpheus*, unless we know what prompted the composition of 'Nein, ich vergesse dich nicht'? And such knowledge can be won only by an investigation of all the 'Entwürfe'.

The fifth poem is again a scene; now we are no longer in the 'Gartensaal' and the actors are no longer children but, at the least, adolescents. Although the opening provides a continuation of the morning lyric (the poet begins immediately to praise 'das Zarte' in some of its manifestations) it becomes apparent that this poem's statement will be made in less exalted terms:

> Dass ich die Früchte beschrieb,
> kams vielleicht durch dein Bücken
> zum Erdbeerbeet [?]

The girl has gone outside, and the boy, suddenly changed from a nonplussed child into a stormy youth, has followed her; his passions burn even brighter, once he has caught sight of her as she bends down to the strawberry bed: when writing erotic poetry, Rilke was not infrequently played false by his taste.[44] The trite follows on the vaguely vulgar; after a re-introduction of the flower theme:

> und wenn keine Blume in mir vergeht,
> ist es vielleicht, weil Freude dich trieb,
> eine zu pflücken?,

we are presented with an episode which reminds us that Walter Killy has given Rilke a place in his anthology of *Deutscher Kitsch*. The girl runs away—not too fast, of course; the boy pursues her; out of breath, she turns toward him, waiting ('Ich weiss, wie du liefst, / und plötzlich, du Atemlose, / warst du mir wartend zugewandt'). We can only guess at what happens next; one of those grand pauses ensues which may contain the same events as the famous skipped love-scenes in Theodor Fontane, where the reader's imagination must supply the missing embraces between Ebbe Rosenberg and Holk, between Effi and Crampas. Then the girls falls asleep; her left hand lies 'like a rose'.

In the fragments connected with the 'Entwürfe', a grown woman appears, who instructs the boy in love after he has evidently had an unsuccessful experience with a girl nearer his own age:

> Einmal kam die Frau, die reiche, reife
> die zerstreut den Jüngling unterwies,
> wenn er störend, noch mit Knabensteife,
> an die blumige Geliebte stiess.
>
> (*SW*, II, 484)

The poem, which Rilke rejected, is at once too obscure and too clear: too obscure because of the conjunction 'wenn' (we expect 'als') with its implication of repeated action, too clear because it draws a demarcation line between the grown woman and the young beloved, between the instructress and the cause of passion. Disputable and indisputable evidence points to such a separation in Rilke's actual erotic training; the legendary typing-teacher at Linz may have taught him other skills, too, and there is no question that Lou Andreas Salomé's lessons went beyond Russian. Yet the unity of the young girl at the dance with all the women to follow (like the unity of the perplexed boy with the man who is 'almost like a god') remains the essence of the erotic autobiography, the truth of it, even though the 'identity' of girl and woman has no support in the facts of the matter as we know them. Rilke had learned the device of giving the beloved simultaneous and separate ages from Herman Bang; long ago, poring over *Haabløse Slaegter*, he had discovered the figure of Kamilla Falk, Høg's seductress, girl *and* woman, and added her to his own bag of literary tricks: he employed her as a template for Abelone in *Malte Laurids Brigge*. Lacking her double age, Abelone would be a great deal less fascinating than she is; and what adds lure to Malte's aunt becomes a necessity in the 'Entwürfe'. The connexion of child and adult in the realm of love is a life-nerve of the cycle; 'Einmal kam die Frau' would have cut that nerve, or damaged it badly, while 'Dass ich die Früchte beschrieb' leaves it unharmed, or even strengthens it. And the fragment is less felicitous than the story of the strawberry patch in another way; it states the initiation of the boy into the 'increased realm' of sexual love too explicitly, and so, admitted to the 'Entwürfe', would have jarred against the purposeful vagueness (which, as we know, permits the indication of 'worse' improprieties) in the other poems:

> Dann erschienen reizende Gestalten,
> traten ins gesteigerte Bereich
> wo sich Menschen aneinanderhalten
> zum vergöttlichten Vergleich.

58

We have had cruel things to say about 'Dass ich die Früchte beschrieb', about its sly hint of shapes revealed ('durch dein Bücken'), about the puffing and panting of its chase and capture; but the sexual union itself is indicated only by the silence, the girl's satisfied slumber, and the impudently elegant symbolism of her left hand, lying 'wie eine Rose'. In fact, the last detail's meaning would escape us, if we did not remember the flowers of the earlier 'Entwürfe', and the overture to the phallic hymns:

> Auf einmal fasst die Rosenpflückerin
> die volle Knospe seines Lebensgliedes . . .
>
> (*SW*, II, 435)

The close of 'Dass ich die Früchte beschrieb', then, is both subtler and bolder than 'Einmal kam die Frau', with its proposal of gymnastics. Bearing in mind that Rilke's theme is an extremely delicate one, and that he frequently lost his sense of proportion when dealing with it, we must give him credit for having chosen, between the two accounts of early embraces, the better part.

Again, in the next of the 'Entwürfe', reflection follows narration; again, a certain uneasiness (like that in 'Dies ist Besitz') is apparent. Was the woman not the ruler from the start? Was she not forever superior to the male lover? Would he ever be her equal? The questions are part of an old story in Rilke; but the very asking of them would cancel them out. The songs about 'die im Voraus verlorene Geliebte' have ended; however much of a head start the woman may have, she is not *lost* in advance; we know from the preceding poem that she has been won. And however superior an unrequited lover she may have been, the male lover ('beinah wie ein Gott', after all) can imagine his eventual equality with her on his own terms of possession, terms that would have been anathema to Rilke in *Malte*'s day. It is as if Rilke were still apologizing to his former tenets for giving them up; but his apologies contain the kernel of defiance, and the next strophe wipes out his timidity altogether, since he returns to 'Dass ich die Früchte beschrieb' and the girl's surrender:

> Du warst so recht, dass nicht einmal die Mode
> an deinem Kleide mich beirrt.
> Wie mir dein Flüchten gehört . . .,

lines to which we could give, from the standpoint of the male lover, a salaciously exultant interpretation. No technical barriers kept the youth from his victory amongst the strawberries.

But the recollection of the game in the garden is suddenly broken off; the poet feels the stab of his illness, the intimations of death, and wonders what will happen to his urge to exist, of which the drive to love is the most concentrated expression, when he dies. Can something so vital vanish?

> Wie mir dein Flüchten gehört . . . Wird
> es hinschwinden in meinem Tode?

The death-thought likewise appears in a second fragment which Rilke did not include in the 'Entwürfe'. Here the beloved, instead of fleeing into surrender, disappears altogether, leaving the youth desolate. However, the suggestion that the erotic muse may have vanished for good and all at the very beginning of the boy's 'manhood' cannot be made to agree with the main argument of the 'Entwürfe', which is (although Rilke would have blanched at the comparison) not so very far from Tosca's in her aria, 'Vissi d'arte, vissi d'amore', save that Rilke claims his 'arte', and everything else, grew out of his 'amore'. The fragment would destroy the 'Entwürfe', and so he rejects it; indeed, he torpedoes it from within, saying in its second strophe that he could not exist in a loveless world (cf. *SW*, II, 485).

It is a catalogue of increasing bleakness: life would have no direction; those unfortunate to partake of life would withdraw within themselves, there to find only confusion, not wisdom; the partings of which life is composed would be meaningless, since no attraction preceded them. Leaving the fragment, Rilke returns to love's world, where he *is*; he attempts to calm his fears about his individual destruction by asking another question, less desperately interrogatory, more rhetorical than 'Wird es hinschwinden in meinem Tode?' It is intended to console, even as 'Stirb und werde' and the last lines of the Tenth Elegy are:

> Oder werf ich in die Natur,
> als meines Untergangs Widerlegung
> deinen Einfluss zurück? die lange Erregung
> auf deiner Spur?

The individual will perish, but his urge to procreation is so strong that it will guarantee him a kind of immortality. The passage thus contains the single instance, in this suite of poems about desire's role in life, where reproduction is hinted at. Fatherhood becomes the last straw clutched by the poet drowning in fears of oblivion; like Rita scolding Alfred Allmers after little Eyolf's drowning, we should chide Rilke for his huge egocentricity, if we did not see the same all too human fault within ourselves.

The main body of the 'Entwürfe' has been made up of six poems, with scene and reflection alternating; we expect the seventh poem to close the ring. It does, as far as the locations of the poems are concerned, since it returns to the 'Gartensaal', and to the world of childhood. The poet is a small boy again, unaware of what excitement the dance may bring. Now he can still refuse to surrender to the aroma which would capture him; he can stand to one side, contemptuous—like his fellows —of the dancers:

> Auch dies ist möglich: zu sagen: Nein.
> Und stolz bei den Knaben zu bleiben;
> statt eines Mädchens Widerschein
> in sich zu übertreiben.

The tableau is familiar and comic; it smacks again, for American readers, of Tarkington. But then a question is put which shatters our vision of a bashful little Rilke in an Indiana dancing school; growing up, will the 'youths' be comparable to the girl's gentle power?

> Sind die Jünglinge später vergleichbar
> einer so sanften Gewalt? . . .

We are brought up short here by what is apparently the introduction of the theme of homosexual love, a subject which Rilke, otherwise so intensely interested in the emotional life, always treated with the greatest circumspection. Nothing is known of any such involvement on Rilke's part, although the very circumstances of his later boyhood would have encouraged it; the sudden and almost inexplicable fascination he developed, in 1919, for Hans Blüher's *Die Rolle der Erotik in der männlichen Gesellschaft*,[45] throws a flickering light into this murky corner, as does the odd pair of lines about school life in 'Imaginärer Lebenslauf':

> Auf einmal Schrecken, Schranke, Schule, Frohne
> und Absturz in Versuchung und Verlust.

What prompted Rilke to bring homosexuality up near the end of a cycle celebrating heterosexual eroticism? Can he have done it for the sake of contrast, his favourite rhetorical device in the 'Entwürfe'? Or did he decide, moved by the autobiographer's compulsion to frankness, that the 'Entwürfe' would not be complete unless they recorded how he had considered, once upon a time, the possibility of remaining 'stolz bei den Knaben'? He had rejected the possibility, or been saved from it; for otherwise, to quote from the first scene in the 'Gartensaal', he would have fallen 'aus dem unbeschreiblichen Bezug' like a stone, quite as rapidly as the 'masterful man' or the ascetic would. There may be some association, too, with the vice which recently had made a fresh attack upon Rilke, a vice which he was forced to regard as still another cause for expulsion from the 'indescribable relationship' of man and woman. It is worth noting that: '*auch* der Freund bleibt im Hinterhalt', a line which not only calls the conclusion of the 'Lebenslauf' to mind ('Da stürzte Gott aus seinem Hinterhalt') but supports Kanzog's contention that the abrupt return of the solitary vice is meant. Both vice and friend are minatory figures, waiting in ambush, dangerous aspects of the god of love: the one plunges forward with destructive force, the other remains outside the order of things, unattainable, destructive by the lure of its inaccessibility. Homosexual love is not condemned straight out, not, in a way, condemned at all; instead it belongs to another and incomprehensible world. Strangely, it is given a place in the world of love not unlike that assigned to God the Creator in the *Elegies*; it lies so far away that men, whose task it is to praise the here-and-now, cannot bother with it.

The poem's final strophe, and the conclusion of the main body of the 'Entwürfe', is a joyful homecoming to the heterosexual world, and a recommendation to the boy of the past that he ready himself for the life of a lover. He will be rewarded. The conclusion offers an almost ribald series of *doubles ententes*; after practice as a lover ('am Zarten und Harten', with its not very mellifluous inner rhyme, reduces the exercise to a formula), the lover will be blessed, with pleasure, by the women

LIBRARY

he loves, and they, in turn, will bless him for the pleasure he gives them. Much the same kind of verbal trickery is to be found in the last line of the fragment, 'Einmal kam die Frau', where the 'Seligen, die er erfuhr' (*SW*, II, 484), at once bestow and receive sensual bliss. The lover and the beloved have become equals at last, answering the old question, 'Wann werden wir gleich?' Or, perhaps, the lover even has got the upper hand, for he is one, while the ladies he favours are many.

The 'Entwürfe' end with a coda of two poems, in which the affirmation of the love experience, and so of all life, is repeated. How was the discovery made? Love succeeded, when in school nothing succeeded at all as yet—an echo, it may be, of the sideswipe at homosexuality in the conclusion of Part One, or a suggestion, not a surprising one to come from Rilke, that eroticism is the foundation even of intellectual life:

> Wie geschah es? Es gelang zu lieben,
> da noch in der Schule nichts gelang!

Then we are confronted with an observation less readily understood:

> Das Unendliche bleibt unbeschrieben
> zwischen Auf- und Niedergang.

The lines do not surrender their mystery until we remember the boy's hasty rise and fall of passion in the 'Gartensaal', and the infinite implications, 'unbeschrieben', of the experience for the boy—'undescribed' because he could not describe them or even comprehend them. The experience was 'unbeschrieben' until the 'Entwürfe' were written; it was also 'heimlich', unknown to others, since, as Rilke says with a pun, the boy's mouth was not mature enough to describe it:

> Heimlich hat es sich in *dem* vollzogen
> dessen Mund nicht mündig war . . .[46]

Yet the boy's heart unconsciously embraced and preserved the experience, which would give form and content to his whole future life:

> doch das Herz beging den grossen Bogen
> um das namenlose Liebesjahr.

(Rilke's vocabulary is reminiscent of the title he gave, in a letter written at this time to Alfred Schaer, to another formative influence, J. P. Jacobsen, whom he called the 'Jahres-Regent meines Himmel–Erdenjahrs'.[47]) For the boy, the experience of passion was 'undescribed', 'secret', 'nameless', but nothing else had a comparable importance:

> Was war Mahlzeit, Schule, Ballspiel, Strafe,
> was war Wachen, was war Schlaf?
> Da in jäh geordneter Oktave
> aller Zukunft Klang zusammentraf.

The rest of childhood was forgotten, once all the future's notes had been played in the single erotic octave. In one of the French poems to Eros, composed simultaneously with the 'Entwürfe', Rilke says the same thing, and in the same image:

> Il faut que les Orgues grondent,
> pour que la musique abonde
> de toutes les notes de l'amour.

(SW, II, 529)

The first coming of Eros may have been as jarring as all the octave's notes, struck together, or as the rumble of the organ's pedal tones; but these sounds are the stuff of music, just as the initial erotic experience contained all the stuff of love.

The coda's second poem opens a little tiredly: 'Oh so war es damals schon genossen'. Even then the heart got the upper hand ('und das Herz nahm überhand'), giving a course to the drifting life of the child:

> während noch das Leben unentschlossen
> um die Knabenspiele stand.

Everything had been decided in the 'Gartensaal'; as a child, the poet received the profit which he could measure all his life through—what really mattered was the reception of that profit:

> Damals war ihm Übermass gegeben,
> damals schon entschied sich sein Gewinn;
> ihn zu messen, später, war das Leben,—
> ihn zu fassen, reichte hin.

Following these repetitions of the cycle's main theme, handsomely phrased but a little boring, the master poet summons up all his strength for a grand finale. The god—beheld one last time in his triumphant and beneficent aspect—took the shape of the boy on that day, unknown to the girl who had inspired his coming:

> Denn der Gott, der Partnerin verschwiegen,
> fühlte sich in diesem Kinde ganz,
> da er in des Knaben Unterliegen
> gründete das Überstehn des Manns.

Again Rilke uses a pun, a heroic one; for the child not only survived the fiasco of long ago ('das Unterliegen'), but on his fiasco was founded 'das Überstehn'—not merely the man's survival ('Wer spricht von Siegen? Überstehn ist alles'), but his victory.[48] He stands like a tower, he rises above himself, he becomes a god. In German poetry, we must look to the Baroque for a comparable boast of sexual prowess, to the sonnet of Georg Rudolf Weckherlin:

> Das prächtigste Kriegsschiff, dem ie das Meer war kund,
>   Hat keinen Mast so hoch, als hoch ist mein begehren.

The 'Entwürfe' are a boast, however, from a man in mortal trouble, a man who would like to convince his putative biographers that his later message, of affirmation, had been built on the solid ground of personal experience; equally, he would like to convince himself. Rilke used the autobiographical lyric to make his *apologia*; had he lived in Wordsworth's age, when the long narrative poem was a popular poetic genre, he might have used *The Prelude's* form to tell his story. Yet, even if the book-size poem still had been in fashion, it is unlikely that Rilke would have taken recourse to it; he was too frantic, too rushed. His statement must be made at once, before it was too late; it must be sent to Kippenberg, for in the publisher's careful hands, Rilke knew, it was safe—it would reach the world, as its author wanted it to, but not before he had died. On 5 April 1924, Rilke sent his wife some reflections on the fate of Rodin. How different Rodin's life would have been, Rilke says, had the sculptor not been deprived of approval for years, and if the approval, when it came, had not oppressed and burdened the artist 'in falscher Weise'. Such situations are hard to change; but 'noch schwerer ist es, zu erreichen, dass der, der alle diese Dinge gewahre und "rette", selber auch gerettet sei' (*Briefe aus Muzot*, p. 261). One may 'save' the works of a great colleague in art by correct appreciation and interpretation, one may see to it that one's own works are 'saved'—but one cannot save one's self. Does the artist not throw his works overboard like a sailor on a sinking ship, 'wie ein Schiffbrüchiger', in hopes that they will reach the shore, 'während er selbst im Untergang treibt, gehalten immer wieder eine kleine Weile durch das, was seine Liebe, seine Einsicht rettet?' With the 'Entwürfe' Rilke thought he had given posterity (or Kippenberg, his messenger to posterity) substantial hints about the 'right' interpretation of his life and works; but he had not saved himself. He was a castaway, like William Cowper in his last poem, itself an autobiographical lyric:

> No voice divine the storm allay'd,
>   No light propitious shone;
> When, snatch'd from all effectual aid,
>   We perish'd, each alone.

NOTES

1. These mouthpieces must have proved particularly satisfactory to their respective creators, since they were used not just in single poems or short cycles, but as the central figures of whole books of poetry. It is not hard to see why the poets of the *fin-de-siècle* loved them; beyond allowing the relief of a hidden confession (which could also be obtained in the autobiographical novel, such as Huysmans' *À Rebours*, or fictional memoir, such as Gissing's *Henry Ryecroft*), they afforded the poet the chance to confess repeatedly in his special medium, the lyric poem.
2. Erna Zoller, 'Autobiographisches in R. M. Rilkes "Weisser Fürstin",' *Schweizerische Rundschau*, LV (1955–56), 168–174.

3. Between 1820 and 1825, the great Swedish poet underwent a radical inner change, from what might be called humanistic idealism to cynical pessimism. He gave an account of the transformation in 'Mjältsjukan' ('Spleen') from 1825, a masterpiece of the Swedish lyric and a fine example of the use of the lyric for autobiographical purposes. In it, Tegnér tells not only what is presently happening to him, but what *has* happened; the standpoint of 1820:

> Jag stod på höjden av min levnads branter,

and the catastrophe:

> Då steg en mjältsjuk svartalf upp, och plötsligt
> Bet sig den svarte vid mitt hjärta fast . . .

are put in the past tense. The experience is not sung about directly, but instead is seen at a distance, from the autobiographer's vantage point. Once the statement of previous events is made, to be sure, the poet changes to the present tense; but the autobiographer, working at his lengthy book in prose, would do the same: he would use the present tense as he made his *apologia*, his explanation, for the past, and as he tried to connect the past to his present self:

> Du himlabarn, hos dig det enda sanna
> är kainsmärket, inbränt på din panna.

In 1825, Tegnér wrote another poem, 'Fågelleken', which also has an honoured, if somewhat scandalous, place in the Swedish *florilegium*. Five years before, the Lund professor had fallen in love with Martina von Schwerin; their affair was interrupted by Tegnér's election as Bishop of Växjö in Småland. On one of his last visits to the lovely Martina before his departure for the dark Småland forests, the bishop-elect wrote 'Fågelleken' about the tragedy of parting:

> Allt hvad ömmast längtan säger,
> allt hvad gladast hoppet äger,
> suckar och jubelskri
> blandas däri . . .

'Mjältsjukan' and 'Fågelleken' are from the same poet, the same time, the same crisis; but the former is an autobiographical lyric, it attempts to describe and explain, albeit in foreshortened form, the poet's adult life, while the latter gives the poet's reaction to a single and immediate experience, and can be called 'autobiographical' only to this limited extent.

4. Rainer Maria Rilke, *Sämtliche Werke* (Wiesbaden, 1955 ff.), II, 83; hereafter *SW*. For an account of the 'Wendung' crisis, see the present writer's 'Rilke and Narcissus' in *On Romanticism and the Art of Translation: Studies in Honor of Edwin Hermann Zeydel* (Princeton, 1956), pp. 197–232.

5. Katharine Kippenberg, *Rainer Maria Rilke: ein Beitrag* (Wiesbaden, 1948), p. 334: 'Rilke sprach viel und lebhaft, er war etwas stärker geworden in Gesicht und Figur, hatte eine gesunde gebräunte Hautfarbe und raschere Bewegungen als sonst'.

6. 'Der Reisende' had in fact been written on 20 June 1923, a month before Rilke dispatched it to Frau Kippenberg.

7. That Rilke expected some poetic profit from his second visit to Malans may be seen from a letter to Mme. Sépibus (in Maurice Zermatten, *Der Ruf der Stille*, Zürich, 1954, p. 95: 13 September 1923): 'Je me déciderai probablement a faire encore une espèce de "Nachkur" au château de Malans, auprès de mon ami de Salis. Je connais là le vieux jardin, un peu abandonné du "Bothmer" [sic] et depuis longtemps je me sens attiré vers la tapisserie royalement mélancolique qu'il forme en automne.'

8. In the letter which accompanies the poem, Rilke calls their recognition of his birthday the 'schönster Teil meiner unwillkürlichen Feier' (RMR–KK, *Briefwechsel*, p. 513); 'unwillkürlich' is a hint that he would have preferred not to be reminded of the anniversary.

65

9. It was a great moment for Frau Kippenberg; 'das beglückendste Ausruhen lag in [Ihrer] Lesung der siebenten Elegie, ein mystisches,' she wrote to Rilke (*Briefwechsel*, p. 530 and note, p. 690).

10. See *SW*, II, 162; Rilke had enclosed the poem for Frau Kippenberg in a letter to her husband.

11. 'Da kommt auch schon das Heftchen mit dem wunderlich gefundenen Nachlass des Grafen C.W.' (*Briefe an seinen Verleger*, II, 379: February, 1921).

12. Maria von Thurn und Taxis, *Erinnerungen an Rainer Maria Rilke* (Munich–Berlin–Zürich, 1932), p. 95.

13. Max Mell, 'Begegnung mit Rainer Maria Rilke', *Corona*, VI (1936), 696 and 703; Rudolf Kassner, *Buch der Erinnerung* (Leipzig, 1938), p. 304; Carl J. Burckhardt, 'Ein Vormittag beim Buchhändler' in *Reden und Aufsätze* (Zürich, 1952), p. 74; Maurice Zermatten, *op. cit.* p. 87; Marie von Thurn und Taxis, *op. cit.*, p. 22.

14. Marga Wertheimer, *Arbeitsstunden bei Rilke* (Zürich and New York, 1940), p. 40.

15. Rudolf Kassner, *op. cit.*, p. 295.

15a. Dieter Bassermann, *Der andere Rilke* (Bad Homburg v.d.H., 1961), p. 81 ff.

16. *Briefe aus Muzot*, pp. 278–279: 16 May 1924; *Lettres milanaises*, p. 42: 4 January 1924; *Die Briefe an Gräfin Sizzo* (Wiesbaden, 1950), pp. 61–62: 23 January 1924.

17. Anton Kippenberg, 'Rainer Maria Rilke' in *Reden und Schriften* (Wiesbaden, 1952), p. 108: 'als der Verleger die Frage stellte, was bei neuen Auflagen mit dem Zuwachs geschehen solle, meinte Rilke, er würde nicht wesentlich mehr sein . . . was ihm zu sagen aufgetragen sei, habe er gesagt'; also Katharine Kippenberg, *op. cit.*, pp. 345–348.

18. See Rilke's letter to Fliess, *Briefe aus Muzot*, pp. 65–67; for a brief introduction to Fliess's teachings on the 'periodicity' of births and deaths within a single family, see Wilhlem Fliess, *Zur Periodenlehre* (Jena, 1925), pp. 70–78, 83–93, and 110–118.

18a. On his forty-eighth birthday, Rilke got a letter from Merline, in which she said: 'Je me sens très Vénus en écoutant quelque aventure amoureuse de son fils' (*Correspondance*, Zürich, 1954, 1954, p. 473: 4 December 1923).

19. The full text can be found in Hugo von Hofmannsthal, *Prosa IV* (Frankfurt, 1955), p. 205.

20. For Rilke's remarks on *À la recherche du temps perdu*, see RMR–Marie von Thurn und Taxis, *Briefwechsel*, I, 348: 21 January 1914, and *passim*.

21. Among the other items Rilke read at this time were Roger Martin du Gard's *Les Thibault*, Maurois' *Les Discours du Docteur O'Grady*, Montherlant's *Le Paradis à l'Ombre des Épées*, Valery Larbaud's *Amants, Heureux Amants*, and a *Vie de Balzac*, author not specified.

22. Lou Andreas-Salomé, *Rainer Maria Rilke* (Leipzig, 1929), pp. 9- 10. See also Lou Andreas-Salomé, *In der Schule bei Freud* (Zürich, 1958), pp. 149 ff. for further observations on the health of Rilke, this 'typischer Hysterischer, sich an seine körperlichen Zustände verlierend'.

23. Rilke also attempted to put the story over on Marie von Thurn und Taxis (*Briefwechsel*, II, 786: 23 February 1924: 'die meisten Menschen leben ja in einer Art Feindsäligkeit mit ihrem Körper . . . der meine . . . hatte, sozusagen, die Prokura für die ganze Firma'), but she had received plenty of epistolary evidence to the contrary in the past fifteen years of their friendship.

24. In 1916, Magda met Rilke and Lou Albert-Lasard on the street in Vienna: 'an seinem Arm hing eine Frau mit fahlem, verblühtem Gesicht, das von Schminke entstellt war. Sie hinkte und stützte sich schwer auf ihn'. (Magda von Hattingberg, *Rilke und Benvenuta*, Vienna, 1943, p. 291).

25. Lou Andreas-Salomé, *In der Schule bei Freud*, p. 208: diary entry of 10–16 October 1913.

26. Lou Andreas-Salomé, *ibid.*, p. 171.

27. RMR, *Briefe an einen jungen Dichter* (Wiesbaden, 1954), p. 49: 12 August 1904.

28. RMR, *Die Aufzeichnungen des Malte Laurids Brigge* (Zürich, 1948), p. 69.

29. J. R. von Salis, *Rainer Maria Rilkes Schweizerjahre* (Frauenfeld, 1952), p. 249, reports that Rilke also made an epistolary 'confession sans retenue', contents not further specified, to Nanny Wunderly-Volkart after the first stay at Val-Mont.

30. Salis, who has had access to more first-hand information about the Swiss years than any other scholar, takes the poem to be an autobiography ('in dem er rückschauend seine eigene Biographie auf die knappste Formel brachte', *op. cit.*, p. 167), and there is no good reason to think that it deals with a fictional subject.

31. The 'uncompleted elegy', 'Lass dir, dass Kindheit war' (*SW*, II, 457–460), from November, 1920, appears to mark an important stage in Rilke's re-appraisal of *his own* childhood; childhood in general had already been tested, and not found wanting, in the Fourth Elegy, from November, 1915.

32. E. M. Butler has listed the various forms and sources of the legend in her *Rainer Maria Rilke* (Cambridge, 1941), pp. 14–18.

33. 'Wortbildwahl und phallisches Motiv bei R. M. Rilke: Beitrag zu einem zukünftigen Rilke-Wörterbuch', *Zeitschrift für deutsche Philologie*, LXXVI (1957), 226, note 35.

34. Rilke apparently considered the possibility of enclosing the well in a bench of stone, then abandoned stone for wood because of the latter's implication of a picture frame. The 'Entwürfe' were begun both in German and French; the extant fragment of the French version runs:

> Soudain il me souvient d'une place
> auprès d'une source prise de manière
> qu'un banc en pierre qui s'enlace
> vous invitait à vous taire.
>
> (*SW*, II, 704)

35. The germ-cell of the cycle may have been present in Rilke for some time; compare the opening of the poem, 'Liebesanfang', from the spring or summer of 1915:

> O Lächeln, erstes Lächeln, unser Lächeln.
> Wie war das Eines: Duft der Linden atmen,
> Parkstille hören—, plötzlich in einander
> aufschauen und staunen bis heran ans Lächeln.
>
> (*SW*, II, 99–100)

36. See the fragmentary poems on shawls which Rilke wrote in October, 1923 (*SW*, II, 476–477) and the later shawl poem, 'Wie Seligkeit in diesem sich verbirgt' from July, 1924 (*SW*, II, 488); also the first poem in the cycle called 'Éros' from 15–20 February 1924:

> Tout ceci serait pour le mieux;
> mais tu es, *en nous* (c'est pire)
> comme le noir milieu
> d'un châle brodé de cachemire.
>
> (*SW*, II, 525)

37. In rococo poetry, the lemon had a directly sexual connotation; compare the girl in C. M. Bellman (*Fredmans epistlar*, No. 63) who has made a good thing of the loss of her virtue:

> Korgen med citroner
> tynger inte mera hennes arm;
> Nu ibland baroner
> Dansar hon sig varm.

On the other hand, the lemon implies death, too; it was frequently placed in coffins, or given to funeral guests. Gryphius combines both aspects of the fruit's meaning in the second act of *Das verliebte Gespenst*, where Sulpice, pretending to be mortally ill, revives upon the appearance of his beloved Chloris:

> O Chloris, schönste Blum, auff meine Todten-Baar!
> . Ruff allen, doch gib mir von den verdachten Früchten
> Die grosse Citronat.

38. Fascinated as she was by the *ambiance* of nobility, Phia Rilke frequently took her son during summer-vacations to the country houses of the great, or at least to the village that served the manor. For example, he told Marie von Thurn und Taxis that he had visited the Bohemian seat of the Thurn und Taxis family as a boy—in the company of a sick rabbit (Marie von Thurn und Taxis, *op. cit.*, p. 14). Could this experience, by the way, be the source of 'Liebes-anfang', mentioned in note 35 above? Its second strophe begins:

> In diesem Lächeln war Erinnerung
> an einen Hasen, der da eben drüben
> im Rasen spielte.

39. Marie von Thurn und Taxis, *op. cit.*, pp. 47–48.

40. The poem, 'Eros', from 20 February 1924, contains the lines:
> Oh verloren, plötzlich, oh verloren!
> Göttliche umarmen schnell . . .

41. How easily aroused Rilke was by memory or anticipation can be seen from the evidence of note 42 below.

42.
> (Da ich dir schrieb, sprang Saft
> auf in der männlichen Blume,
> die meinem Menschentume
> reich ist und rätselhaft.
> Fühlst du, da du mich liest,
> ferne Zärtliche, welche
> Süsse im weibliche Kelche
> willig zusammenfliesst?)

> > (*SW*, II, 492)

43. Beda Allemann, *Zeit und Figur beim späten Rilke* (Pfullingen, 1961), pp. 75–76, quotes these lines in connexion with the late Rilke's urge to the abstract. Scholarship has otherwise been chary of comment on the 'Entwürfe': Else Buddeberg (in *Rilke: eine Biographie*, Stuttgart, 1954, p. 479), takes Rilke's deprecatory remarks in the accompanying letter to Kippenberg at face value and dismisses the poems as unimportant. O. F. Bollnow (*Rilke*, Stuttgart, 1951, p. 350), notes a 'ganz neues Vertrauen des Menschen zu seiner eigenen Leistungsfähigkeit' in them, but does not grow any more precise. Salis (*op. cit.*, p. 168) implies an unfavourable comparison with 'Der Magier', which latter poem is called 'bedeutungstief'. Actually, only Hans Egon Holthusen, in *Der unbehauste Mensch* (Munich, 1952) has taken a somewhat closer look at them. There he says (p. 62): 'Es stellt sich heraus, dass "die im voraus verlorene Geliebte" . . . in Wahrheit dennoch gefunden ist . . . Der Dichter hat den verlorenen Prozess seiner Kindheit sozusagen in der Berufungsinstanz gewonnen'.

44. The 'Ode to Bellman" offers particularly painful examples of what is meant: 'schon fühlt sie her, schon fühl ich hin' and 'da nimmt ihn erst das Leben ans Geschlecht / und schläft mit ihm' (*SW*, II, 100–101).

45. Hans Blüher, *Werke und Tage* (Munich, 1953), pp. 347–350; see also RMR–Lou Andreas-Salomé, *Briefwechsel*, p. 412: 21 February 1919.

46. A study of the word 'Mund' in Rilke would be profitable: it might range from Rilke's sensitivity about his own large and ugly mouth (he grew his moustache to hide it) to the sublime mouths of the *Sonnets to Orpheus*: 'sind wir die Hörenden jetzt und ein Mund der Natur' and 'O Brunnen-Mund, du gebender, du Mund'. Probably the study would provide still more evidence for the major influence which Rilke's physical being had upon his poetic thought.

47. *Briefe aus Muzot*, p. 253: 26 February 1924.

48. The third of the 'Fünf Gesänge', the hymns to the war-god of August, 1914, contains a directly parallel usage of 'überstehn':

> Und nun aufstand er: steht: höher
> als stehende Türme, höher
> als die geatmete Luft unseres sonstigen Tags.
> Steht. Übersteht.

Discussion

Böckmann commented on how interesting it was to see how the poems interpreted in the lecture had touched on several themes from Rilke's life. He mentioned how this cycle of poems reflected ideas found in other poems by Rilke, especially in the 'Neue Gedichte' and the 'Duino Elegies'.

Closs asked whether one could speak of a genre of autobiographical lyric in Germany.

Schoolfield replied that every lyric poem was autobiographical in a way, but that a sub-genre of autobiographical lyric poetry also existed. Here the poet was intentionally using lyric poetry as a substitute for prose autobiography. He did well to use his own instrument when writing of himself, for a poet's prose autobiography was often poor. A poet could be more direct in poetry and could hide and reveal himself at the same time. He found it hard to cite examples of German autobiographical poetry, though there were many Scandinavian examples.

Closs asked what kind of biography Rilke would have liked written about himself.

Schoolfield thought he would have liked the kind of biography that he had in fact received, the biography concentrating on the inner life.

Rowley asked if there was a difference between the autobiographical lyric and verse autobiography.

Schoolfield replied that the autobiographical lyric was only one part of verse autobiography. A single lyric poem was usually too short for autobiography. He quoted 'Prelude' as an example of verse autobiography, and referred to Lermontov's poem 'In the Spring', in which an occurrence similar to that in Rilke's cycle was recorded.

Salinger thought that the title of the Symposium 'Reality and Creative Vision' had been beautifully illustrated by the lyric autobiography in the poems which the lecturer had interpreted. He explained that he was interpreting 'reality' to mean 'biography, facts', and 'creative vision' to mean 'the poet's vision, non-facts'.

Allemann brought up the problem of 'Verwandlung' and related the poems under discussion to the Narcissus poems.

Non-representational modern German poetry

by

BEDA ALLEMANN

My present theme is non-representational poetry.

Is there in fact any sense in transferring the conception of non-representational art from its original place in the sphere of plastic art to modern poetry? Are similar processes to be found there as in the history of painting in the twentieth century? Do we find here a certain tendency to de-objectify, so that as a result we may speak of a non-representational form of poetry? And as we do so, is the meaning of the term 'non-representational' still the same as in connexion with formative art? We will attempt to examine these questions with the aid of some examples chosen from different periods of modern German poetry. I need not mention that these examples can give only a kind of cross section through the problem. They do not pretend to suggest a continual development, which would be rather difficult to recognize in German poetry of the last fifty years.

Since the idea of abstraction has its origin in the sphere of plastic art, we may well assume that a certain historical connexion exists between the abrupt change towards abstraction in the world of painting about the year 1910, and a comparable development in poetry. It is a fact that an equally violent revolution took place at the same period in the sphere of lyric verse, at any rate in Germany: this year marks the birth of Expressionism. It may well prove impossible to produce a clearly de-fined common denominator for literary Expressionism, but it is at least possible to characterize it in a negative sense (as is the case with all revolutions) by observing what it rejected and what it attempted to overcome: that is, the literary Impression-ism of the fin-de-siècle and the Naturalism of the same period. These were, as we know, movements which can be interpreted each in its own way, as the closing phases of a conception of art, in which the main principles were imitation and representation of a non-artistic reality—whether this was in fact the social reality of the under-privileged classes as in Naturalism, or of the over-civilized groups of society as in Impressionism. As Expressionism relegated these programmes to the past, it is clear that the potentiality of poetic abstraction was directly forced upon it. We shall see in what way we can discern the traces of the revolutionary develop-ment from Impressionism to Abstraction in the works of expressionist poets. Here lies a parallel with the development of the most consistent of all abstract painters, Piet Mondrian, who began as an impressionist.

However, the literary movement which has gone down in history under the name of Dadaism, completed the change to abstraction at the time of the First World War in a still much more obvious manner than Expressionism. We may, in this case, well conceive of a direct influence from the sphere of abstract painting. As Kandinsky formulated it at a very early date, the principle of this painting was the subordination of presentation itself to the means of presentation, which were thus judged absolute. When the artist represents the back of a fish by one line, the line itself is the essential artistic element, and not the fish. That is to say, one can abstract the fish and make the line as such the aim of the presentation. Today, more than fifty years later, this idea has long since become a truism, but at the time it was revolutionary. Were not the painter-poets of Dada—Tristan Tzara, Hans Arp and others—compelled to attempt the transposition to poetry? For them, Dada was in any way identical with abstract art, as Richard Huelsenbeck pointed out rather reproachfully in 1920.

What then is the result in the sphere of lyric poetry, when the hitherto existing form of presentation is superseded by absolute means? The answer of the Dadaists can be found in their poetic production. In the foreground stands the repudiation of the conventional meaning of words and the logical sequence of the sentence. The pure material of language—that is, the complexity of sounds, metres and melody —is made independent. Hugo Ball's well-known Caravan poem of 1917 does not *describe* a caravan by impressionist or other means, it composes a string of word-like sounds:

> jolifanto bambla o falli bambla . . .

Echoes of familiar words play a part up to a point, and a certain degree of sound-painting is apparent, as if the sounds of the march through the desert were imitated, but the primary element of such verses is to be found in neither the one nor the other method, but in the free association of pseudo-verbal sounds. Ball called such forms 'Lautgedichte' (sound-poems) and wished to differentiate in this way between them and the usual type of word-poems. What we may term the acoustic material of language comes here into its own right, independent of the meanings, which are repudiated and suppressed. Such attempts base their justification on the fact that poetry has always made use of acoustic-musical phenomena from the very beginning; that they have been used in sound-painting quite successfully from the earliest times, even if not to the exclusive extent as in this particular case.

The potentialities of pure material in the sphere of language are not yet exhausted at this point. The acoustic means form only one side of language-substance. The other side—at least in modern literature, that is to say, writing-language—is formed by the optic-*graphic* substratum, of which linguistic expression makes use. This purely graphic side of a poetic text played a certain part in earlier centuries. The age of mannerism was familiar with the verse form consisting of artistically formed silhouettes (carmina figurata). But we find here the same condition as in the case of the figures of rhetoric: these things, which were in mannerism still ornamentation and addition, became in the twentieth century an aim in themselves, charged with the essence of the poem. Symbolism had led the way: in the case of Mallarmé we can fix the point where the poetic text breaks apart under the pressure of the symbolical content, and the abstract-geometrical buds of the calligram begin to open. Apollinaire accentuated the significance of the dilettant element of this reversion to the graphic potentialities of the written poem and the free grouping of letters.

His friends, the Cubists, incorporated calligram-like forms into their painting. In this respect Apollinaire also forms the bridge to Dada. The technique of the calligram has never disappeared from modern lyric poetry since then. The surrealists took possession of it. Among the young German lyricists Franz Mon particularly makes use of it, but we find traces of it also in the works of Paul Celan: in his poem 'Eng-führung' the graphic form is an apparently natural means of marking the joints in the structure of the poem.

In general, we may say that recourse to the graphic picture of the poem-text introduces a new sensuous dimension and partly removes the poem from the sphere of acoustics, so that it becomes a poem designed specifically for reading, a poem which—in extreme cases—cannot be absorbed quite adequately by the ear. However, this solution appears to be happier than reducing the poem to a pure sound-phenomenon, as Ball tried to do, the result being, instead of an absolute sound-poem, in most cases a more or less virtuous form of sound-painting. The attempt to attain abstraction comes down to a perhaps amusing, but very simple form of imitation of sound and at the most of movements. As long as this imitation remains one means among means, in order to confer particularly sensuous qualities to poetic language, it would appear legitimate. But when it is made absolute, the suggestive force which radiates from the sound-painting degenerates into an unconvincing dilettantism, which very quickly bores us. So we come to the critical question, namely, whether there is in fact any point in trying to transfer the reduction to the material, as we can observe it in abstract painting, also to the art of literature. One cannot overlook the fact that the 'material' plays quite a different part in plastic art and of course in music from that in a work of literature. A simple sequence of sounds, grouped in a suitable manner, is comprehended at once by the hearer as a form, as a melody, with its unmistakable inner line and wide span of rich subject-matter. A simple display of colour-splashes can strike the eye in the same way, as a form, as a highly intensive material interwoven with immanent conceptions. The same thing applies to lines, surfaces and tints. The possibility of nonrepresentational art is based on these facts.

The situation with regard to literary material is quite different. As long as only the sensuous, that is to say the optic and acoustic substrata of literature and literary expression are taken into consideration, the material remains relatively poor. A certain magic charm radiates from a string of vocal sounds, but it is still far removed from attaining the plastic suggestivity of a musical sequence or a chord. What we may call a language-melody remains amorphous from the purely acoustic point of view and no less than childish in comparison with melody in a musical sense or with the twelve-tone scale. A test can be made by listening to a poem in an unfamiliar language: we are able indeed to catch one or the other of the acoustic effects, if we know at least something about the theme, but taken by and large the acoustic impression is strangely monotonous and in a certain sense even unaesthetic. The text, taken simply as sound, is literally meaningless, and that not even primarily because we do not understand the contents of the poem and its various parts. We must take care to make a distinction at this point. Frequently we do not understand the contents of a poem in a familiar language at the first reading. And we have great difficulty even with poems we think we know well, in producing a resumé of the contents in our own words, and we are convinced, and quite rightly so, that such a summary, if we succeeded in producing it, would never reach the artistic heart of the poem. Poems make no statement of fact, in the strict sense of the word, they impart no knowledge, at least not in the sense of the modern theory of communication, which is bound up with the conception of information. We are no better informed after reading a poem, whatever its subject may be. In the poetic context the words lose the character of mere tokens and makeshifts, which they so often have in colloquial speech, where they appear to be merely a cipher to render a presumed reality easily intelligible. If we often speak of 'ciphers' (Chiffre) in the theory of modern poetry, if the poetic word itself is often defined as a cipher, we do not mean by this a mere symbol of reference to a non-literary reality. The cipher in the poetic sense is a secret formula, the meaning of which must be acquired from within itself. Gottfried Benn said in his famous poem *Ein Wort*:

> Ein Wort, ein Satz—: Aus Chiffren steigen
> erkanntes Leben, jäher Sinn ...

In these verses, the accent falls on the 'jähe Sinn' (sharp sense) rising from the word-ciphers, which is one of the most mysterious phenomena known to us. The 'sense' in lyrical poetry has little to do with the logical communication of a declaratory statement. At the same time it is much more than the mere sound-magic which has its origin in the sensuous substratum of language. The poetical sense of words and sentences cannot be brought down to either the sensuous-material substratum or to the logical structure of the grammatic standard sentence. The science of phonetics, even in its most fundamental form of phonology, cannot produce any causal connexion between sound and sense: the same sound can have a variety of 'meanings'. On the other hand, the theory of meaning (Bedeutungslehre) provides no space for the decisive 'sense' of words and sentences as mentioned by Gottfried Benn, because it concentrates on the meaning of the words within a closed system of symbols, and not on that 'significance' of the poetic cipher, which is so much more difficult to formulate. Syntax finally, the theory of sentence-formation, always anticipates already the sense of the sentence it analyses. An example may illustrate this. Paul Celan's *Todesfuge*, which is perhaps the most famous poem of German post-war poetry, begins with the words:

> Schwarze Milch der Frühe wir trinken sie abends ...
> (Black milk of the early hours we drink it in the evening ...)

From the point of view of syntax, the expression 'Schwarze Milch der Frühe' is a preposed apposition to the accusative object 'sie' in the main sentence 'wir trinken sie abends'. However, this does not reveal very much as far as the artistically relevant elements within the verse are concerned, and requires further interpretation, which can only be gained from the special context and not from the general rules of syntax. We may understand the 'sense' of a sentence as a function of the sentence-construction, but in order to track down the artistic sense of a poem in this way, we need a new conception of 'sentence-construction'. This conception would have to encompass the actual sense-giving elements of the sentence, which go far beyond the merely logical relations between the parts of the grammatically 'complete' standard sentence. Gottfried Benn, in one of his most important programme-poems, makes a demand in this direction:

> Was aber neu ist, ist die Frage nach dem Satzbau
> und die ist dringend . . .

As things stand in the sphere of modern lyric poetry, there can be no doubt that the question of abstraction can only be dealt with adequately in close connexion with this question of sentence-construction as a whole.

Helmut Heissenbüttel, one of the particularly consistent representatives of specifically abstract lyricism, and one whom we must take seriously, places an assertion of René Wellek in the forefront of his latest publication, namely:

'A work of literature is, first of all, an organised, purposeful sequence of words'.

This is a principle almost generally accepted by modern literary criticism. We have to realize that the 'sequence of words' mentioned here means considerably more than just a mere grouping of words. This corresponds with the fact that in the sphere of music the melody is very much more than just a sequence of notes. A certain element is added to that sequence, which Christian von Ehrenfels has denoted as 'form-quality' (Gestaltqualität) and which rises from the simple fact that the whole is more than the total of parts. It is not mere coincidence that Helmut Heissenbüttel places a quotation from Husserl next to that of Wellek, which recalls in phenomenological terms the insight of Ehrenfels.

The word-sequence as produced by aesthetic sentence-construction is more than the amount of the single words. Its particular form-quality is what we commonly call 'sense', this sharp sense which, according to Gottfried Benn, radiates from the ciphers. If we could succeed in formulating precisely this process of radiation, without all distracting elements of 'content', we should have certainly described a form of poetic abstraction worthy of the name.

In fact we do find already in early expressionist poetry certain tendencies to develop new possibilities out of the phenomenon of word-sequence. This is displayed with special clearness in August Stramm's lyric poetry, which in addition to this shows the historical change from impressionism to abstraction in the sphere of poetry. If we look at it from this point of view, Stramm's poetic technique is of particular importance in the development of the modern lyric. Up to now the critics, while respecting the final results, have not been able to make much of Stramm's method, which appears strange and violent. This man, who was a high official in the imperial postal service and a captain in the Army Reserve, and who was destined to die during an attack in 1915 at the head of his battalion—this man carried out experiments in sentence-construction in his spare time which are in reality very much more than the hectic expression of a soul bubbling over with expressionistic enthusiasm. Indeed, they were attempts to blaze a way to a new form of syntax. The most striking feature of this technique is the way in which it tries to overcome the conventional types of word-categories by changing nouns into verbs and vice versa, transitive verbs into intransitives; depriving adjectives of their typical inflexions and thus making them absolute. An example of this is the following poem:

KRIEGGRAB

Stäbe flehen kreuze Arme
Schrift zagt blasses Unbekannt
Blumen frechen Staube schüchtern
Flimmer
tränet
glast
Vergessen

The word 'kreuze' at the beginning is not a noun, it is a newly-formed adjective applying to 'Arme', instead of 'gekreuzt'. Vice versa, in the second line the adjective 'unbekannt' is made into a noun, without the introduction of a case-ending which would denote the noun. On the other hand, the intransitive verbs 'flehen' and 'zagen' are used in a transitive sense. In the following line two new verbs are created out of adjectives: 'frechen' and 'schüchtern', intransitives and without prefix, where conventional language recognizes at the most the forms 'erfrechen' and 'einschüchtern'. Such examples are to be found ad libitum in the works of August Stramm. It is as if mutations take place by leaps and bounds within the customary word-forms under the pressure of expression. The rutted tracks along which colloquial speech has formed logical-grammatical combinations, appear to be broken up and the formal possibilities of word-formation are newly utilized in an almost fantastic and arbitrary manner, whereby the 'sense' of the poem radiates only the more strikingly. We find his technique not only in Stramm's war poems, in which the subject-matter might justify the violence at least superficially, but we find it also in that group of his poems which we should have to classify as 'love-lyrics', if we were still able to divide poetry into the conventional categories. In the *Untreu* we find the line:

im Atem wittert Laubwelk!

The unusual use of the verb 'wittern' fits into the general scheme of Stramm's poetic technique as we have described it. Then he creates the new noun 'Laubwelk'. In the rough copy of this line—twenty-one drafts preceded the final poem—we read:

Im Atem flittert Falschheit, Vergessen, Verachtung, Unrast. Im Atem wittert

Wandel, Moder, Abscheu, Ekel, totes Laub, welke Blätter. Im Atem wittert Sterben, Todluft, Grüfte. Im Atem schwelet Asche. Im Atem wittert meine Leiche.
(Handschriften-Archiv der Universität Münster in Westfalen. Zitiert nach Paul Pörtner, August Stramm, in: Neue Zürcher Zeitung, 19.6.1960.)

(In breath glitters guile, oblivion, scorn, turmoil. In breath breathes change, decay, abhorrence, disgust, dead foliage, withered leaves. In breath breathes mortality, the odour of death, vaults. In breath ashes smoulder. In breath my corpse smells.)

All these variations may be interpreted as typically impressionist paraphrases of a common fin-de-siècle theme, namely, the faithless lover. But in the final version, the abstract abridgement to the new creation 'wittert Laubwelk' replaces the abundance of impressionist images. Up to the end August Stramm considered whether he would not rather say 'im Atem wittert welkes Laub'. In a letter to Herwarth Walden he justified his decision in favour of 'Laubwelk' with subtle arguments. He gives up a more easily understandable form in favour of the demands of the style, to attain complete congruity between the artistic intention and the expression.

It is easy to see that such a technique of abstraction reaches deeper into the structure of language than the simple retreat into sound-magic or into the calligram as practised by Dada. The actual 'material' of poetic language is not the sensuous substratum but those immaterial elements of tension between the words which are so difficult to define and which Stramm emphasizes in their complete nakedness by his austere technique. The impressionist lucidity of metaphor is sacrified to this process. But something more essential is revealed—the pure form-quality of the word-sequence.

We cannot however overlook a certain danger within Stramm's poetic technique and this is closely bound up with the problem of word-sequence. Stramm has the tendency to lay the emphasis of the poetic contents on isolated single words. It is symptomatic that very many of his lines are composed of single words. The example we have given of his technique showed us how he attempts to reduce the essence of a whole poem in its drafted form into a single new word as 'Laubwelk', pregnant with a wealth of meaning. For this reason the poem threatens to break up into single words. A further development in this direction seems hardly possible. The writers of the post-expressionist generation had to approach the problem of word-sequence from a new aspect—in as far as they did not remain at the stage of Dadaism, which was the case with most of the lyric poets who are today still regarded as being particularly avant-garde.

In this situation, a certain influence came from French surrealism, which had in turn developed out of Dada. One of the younger German descendants of surrealism, Franz Mon, puts the conception of an 'Artikulationsspur' (trace of articulation) into the very centre of his poetic theory. This is a specific definition for the 'sequence of words' in a poem. It follows its own rules and according to Franz Mon belongs to a more general 'process' in which each single poem participates.

To be sure, we must admit that Franz Mon stands under the influence of certain surrealist dogmas about the hallucinatory character of poetry and this renders an analysis more difficult. In the case of Helmut Heissenbüttel, who is not to be classified as a surrealist, the sequence of words in their abstract form is more clearly visible. In Heissenbüttel's texts we find repeatedly sentences of the type:

'Was ist Wirklichkeit? Wirklichkeit ist etwas das'.

'Reality is something which' we must judge to be merely a broken-up and incomplete sentence, looked at from the point of view of grammar. However, from the point of view of word-sequence, we find that the critical element is brought to light and accentuated through this same abrupt break: that is, the self-mobility of speech mentioned by Franz Mon, even if it is only in the plane sequence of two words: 'etwas das'—'something which'. Because the combination begun with a pronoun is not completed, its function as syntactic link is emphasized all the more. From here equally abstract variations can be developed:

Wirklichkeit ist etwas das. Etwas Erfahrbares. Etwas worüber man reden kann. Etwas worüber man nicht reden kann. Etwas das etwas wovon etwas worüber.

These are relatively simple specimens of the terseness and rhythmic buoyancy which are bestowed on the movement of language in Heissenbüttel's work, in his technique of varied sentence-construction. He creates in this way step by step a new language, which is—as it is stated in his text 'Grammatikalische Reduktion'—no longer foreign to his speech, by which he means the actual language-movement. The speech in this particular sense again becomes supple and frees itself from the stiffness of its conventional grammatical form. A technique of word-combination is developed here, which is not forced to give up the meaning of words in order to be abstract in the best sense of the word. Indeed, the meaning of the words becomes an intrinsic element in the variations of the sentence-construction. One text of Heissenbüttel bears the title 'Gruppentheorie'. We can compare it directly with the prose of Franz Mon entitled 'gruppe und reihe'. These titles remind us of advanced mathematics, and this analogy is equally legitimate here as in the sphere of music, where the mathematical foundation of the intervals is particularly clear, or in non-representational art, which developed its own particular form of mathematics. This is not to say that the word-sequence of a poem can be reduced subsequently to an arithmetical formula which would 'explain' it. But we find in principle the pure word-sequences so precise and full of meaning that we can only compare them, if to anything at all, to mathematical phenomena.

The references and examples already given should have proved the fact sufficiently. We have been forced to leave out a number of intermediate stages which might be assigned to a place between early expressionism and the non-representational lyric of the present day. But we have done enough, if we have succeeded in showing that the technique of abstraction in literary art cannot be mastered by over-hasty analogies to abstraction in the sphere of plastic arts, even if the historical impulse originating in abstract art may be considered important enough. The main difficulty lies in the fact that language does not have at its disposal a 'material' in the same sense as music or the plastic arts have it, but that its material is something quite different from its sensuous substratum. This is in itself a highly complex phenomenon, which we have tried here to define with the conception of the 'sharp sense' deriving from the cipher, of word-sequence and of the 'Artikulationsspur'. With the insight in this fundamental relationship it is no longer difficult to admit the full potentialities of non-representational poetry and to acknowledge that the so-called 'Bildlichkeit', the figurative character of poetic speech—this dogma which has passed by unexamined for so long—really concerns a secondary phenomenon.

A final and quite justified objection to the conception of non-representational lyric poetry may well be made. It is the same objection which Kandinsky and Mondrian made fifty years ago against the label 'abstract painting': what we call 'abstract' from the usual point of view of descriptive representation is in fact fundamentally the concrete form, if we look at the work of art within the bounds of its own legality. We may say with reference to the lyric that it is its apparently so abstract development of the word-sequence which in actual fact causes the language to shine in its full richness of variety and terseness, as it is thus freed from its supposed function of being a system of symbols for non-literary elements. The renunciation of plastic presentation in the usual sense does not mean loss of breadth and wealth. On the contrary, a deeper-laid stratum of reality is uncovered by such concrete abstraction, an 'intermediate world' (Zwischenreich) as Paul Klee called it. In Paul Celan's poem 'Engführung', which forms a later pendant to the *Todesfuge*, we see the characteristic transition to this intermediate world specifically completed:

> Verbracht ins
> Gelände
> mit der untrüglichen Spur:
>
> Gras, auseinandergeschrieben. Die Steine, weiss,
> mit den Schatten der Halme:
> Lies nicht mehr—schau!
> Schau nicht mehr—geh!

The 'trace of articulation' does not demand primarily that we look at poetic pictures, but that we wander through the landscape of language. Here is 'Gras, auseinandergeschrieben'. Observed reality and linguistic description do not fall apart here as object and subject: the grass itself *is* only as written grass—a highly abstract form, we may well say, but it is, considered as a poetic form, infinitely more concrete than it could ever be as 'real grass', beyond the limits of language.

Discussion

Prawer mentioned the lecturer's approval of Gottfried Benn's assertion that the question of syntax was new and urgent. Prawer claimed that it was *not* new; it had been brought up by Klopstock and the Storm and Stress writers.

Allemann agreed, but stated that Benn had understood something different from what had occupied Klopstock's attention. This great difference was perhaps illustrated more clearly by the example of Stramm, a modern poet more extreme than Benn. Moreover, it was only since the modern writers had been paring down language to produce an 'abstrakte Kunst' that readers had begun to see something similar in Klopstock's work, something which Klopstock's contemporaries failed to notice.

Mainland suggested that Benn's statement should be interpreted as meaning 'new' in the sense of 'actual', not in the sense of 'never before occurring'.

Allemann added that Benn had considered that traditional themes in traditional modes had been exhausted, that newness must now be sought in language.

Mainland asked if this 'Gestaltungsproblem' could be regarded as 'democratization'. He quoted Dutch examples from the early days of Expressionism to show the correspondence of poems with advertising lay-out, so that the reader both hears and sees at the same time.

Keith-Smith, taking up the theme of 'Reduction', quoted Barlach, who had said that he could not do in words what he could do in sculpture (where the longer he worked the fewer the cuts he made in the wood). He added that Barlach had taken refuge in irony because words were intractable.

Allemann thought that Barlach, the poet, was still imprisoned in Naturalism, despite a few superficially Expressionist features. For Barlach, irony meant escape. He was a representative of the dilemma which leads to a new style.

Prawer did not consider that awareness of these problems meant that one must take refuge in irony. He quoted the example of Paul Celan, a poet who made emotive and personal statements about such problems and who did not turn to irony.

Allemann thought Celan went to the extreme limits of possibility in his use of language and metaphor and spoke of Celan's frequent use of certain concrete words (e.g. Auge, Stein) which had special significance for him.

Böckmann asked where the connexion could be found between this modern verse and traditional lyric poetry, in which the poet goes back into himself, and maintained that, to him, lyric poetry meant 'Selbstzeugnis'.

Allemann stated that Heissenbüttel was an example of a modern poet who did not use the traditional word, 'Gedichte', for his poems, but called them instead 'Texte', and his volumes of poems 'Textbücher'.

Closs quoted Eugen Gomringer's 'Das schwarze Geheimnis' as an extreme example of abstract word-structure with its two diagonals meeting in a nihilisitic vacuum.

Allemann thought this was an experiment in the fashion of Dadaism, but considered that since Enzensberger there had been a revolt against experimentation in lyric poetry.

Peacock brought up the question of emotionality. 'Abstract' poems seemed to be 'abstracted' from emotionality too, at least from emotionality as understood in the nineteenth century. He asked if they had an emotional content in their own terms.

Allemann felt that in this context words like 'emotionality' lost their meaning. He stressed the importance of studying the poem rather than the poet who wrote it. He thought we were too involved in changes to be able to evaluate them.

Bednall asked to comment on the modern poets' tendency to dwell on this problem of syntax. Was this because the poets—having abandoned language as a public medium—needed to instruct their readers in their private language? Or did the poets themselves feel the need of new creation? With this interpretation, they would be experiencing disintegration as a stimulus to integration.

Allemann agreed and considered that behind the provocative façade of the modern writers there was an attempt at a constructive approach.

THIRD SESSION

Chairman: Professor K. BROOKE

Professor W. D. WILLIAMS: Nietzsche and lyric poetry.

Chairman: Professor G. C. SCHOOLFIELD

Professor W. C. MAINLAND: Brockes and the limitations of imitation.

Nietzsche and lyric poetry

by

W. D. WILLIAMS

In his long and careful history of the German lyric, Professor Johannes Klein devotes some interesting pages to Nietzsche and commits himself to what may seem to be a somewhat controversial position when he says 'Erst in seiner Lyrik ist Nietzsche wirklich ein Umstürzer eigensten Gepräges'.[1] If we wished to argue this question fully it would take us very far afield indeed. We would have to consider the whole nature of Nietzsche's thinking, and perhaps attempt to subsume much of his prose writing under the general category of lyric production. Certainly we would have to consider the notion, first, I think, propounded by Professor Barker Fairley many years ago, that in *Zarathustra* something went wrong with Nietzsche's expression in the sense that much of his writing here, while essentially lyric in its substance, emerges in the guise of philosophical reflection, has been, as Fairley puts it, consigned to the 'wrong box', and thus makes a blurred impression causing uncertainty in the reader and failing to speak with that unified voice which is the mark of artistic coherence. I do not wish today to pursue this topic, fascinating though it is. I would simply start by saying that I think it wrong to regard *Zarathustra* as 'prose poetry' and to apply to it the sort of criteria one applies to lyric poetry. With that side of the question I am not now concerned. Rather I would like to consider the far from inconsiderable body of properly lyrical writing in Nietzsche's works, since one of my contentions will be that one has no need to apologize for him as a lyric poet, nor to explicate his poems solely in terms of his philosophical ideas, as is so often done. I believe that he knew very well what he was doing when he wrote most of his work in prose and that when he wrote verses he was expressing himself in a properly lyric spirit. From the earliest days, with the poem *Dem unbekannten Gott*, to the end of his intellectual life, he pours forth a stream of purely lyrical verses, which he frequently incorporates into or appends to his prose works, but not by any means always. One of the few criticisms one can make of the new three-volume edition of Nietzsche by Paul Schlechta is that it does not print the poems separately, indeed, it does not include all of them. And one of Schlechta's great services, on the other hand, is to have made clear the error of regarding the *Dionysos-Dithyramben* as a sort of extension of *Zarathustra*. We shall be much concerned with these poems, which constitute Nietzsche's most sustained lyric production, so I will only indicate now that I feel it wrong to interpret them as philosophical poetry, and certainly wrong to regard them as the songs of Zarathustra. They are very much the songs of Nietzsche.

But before we start considering Nietzsche's achievement as a lyric poet, let us remember an oft-quoted remark of his on this subject. In *Götzendämmerung* he says:

Den höchsten Begriff vom Lyriker hat mir Heinrich Heine gegeben. Ich suche umsonst in allen Reichen der Jahrtausende nach einer gleich süßen und leiden- schaftlichen Musik. Er besaß jene göttliche Bosheit, ohne die ich mir das Voll- kommene nicht zu denken vermag—ich schätze den Wert von Menschen, von Rassen darnach ab, wie notwendig sie den Gott nicht abgetrennt vom Satyr zu verstehen wissen.

This is worth more consideration than it is usually given. It is not difficult to see general affinities between Nietzsche and Heine and to understand Nietzsche's admiration for the 'gay science' of Heine, the refusal to be committed, the sovereign play, the Voltairean freedom of the spirit, and of course the continual unmasking of humbug and pretence. Satire is an important activity for both of them, and irony the main weapon. But none of these things is essentially lyrical, and it is significant not only that Nietzsche hails Heine as the highest lyrical talent he knows, but also that he characterizes his quality on the one hand as sweet and passionate music (and this is a not surprising judgement) and on the other as a combination of divinity and spite, the union of the god and the satyr. Plainly Nietzsche has in mind here a fundamental doubleness and ambivalence of response which he sees in Heine and which for him constitutes the highest art. We must see how this is apparent in his own lyrical poetry.

We may start by noting that throughout his life Nietzsche writes poetry of three fairly distinct types. First the short lyric, impressionistic, often fragmentary, highly concentrated. The best-known of these pieces, *Venedig*, is in all the anthologies, and we shall have something more to say about this sort of poetry later on. Second, the longer ode or hymn, or dramatic scene, highly charged with mystical and religious symbolism, elegiac or tragic rather than purely lyrical. These are to my mind the most interesting of his poems, the *Dionysos-Dithyramben* being the most elaborate effort in this manner, and we shall have a great deal to say about them. The third type, the witty epigram or aphorism in verse, frequently just an outburst of temper, sometimes profound, often using parody or puns as its main device, is well exempli- fied by the famous lines, parodying the concluding chorus of Goethe's *Faust*. I do not propose to consider this third type of writing today, not because I regard it as out- side my subject (and indeed what we said just now about Heine indicates how close this is to the central nerve of Nietzsche's self-expression), but simply because of the shortness of time.

Consider these lines:

> Nun, da der Tag
> des Tags müde ward, und aller Sehnsucht Bäche
> von neuem Trost plätschern,
> auch alle Himmel, aufgehängt in Gold-Spinnetzen
> zu jedem Müden sprechen: "ruhe nun!"—
> was ruhst du nicht, du dunkles Herz,
> was stachelt dich zu fußwunder Flucht . . .
> weß harrest du?

The highly compressed syntax, the telescoped imagery, the ramming of impressions into one another—these are qualities we find elsewhere in Nietzsche, and they give an effect here reminiscent of Mörike perhaps. But a fundamental difference remains. These are not visual impressions, nor even auditory, but purely cerebral. Nietzsche is often credited with being the real founder of impressionism in Germany lyric poetry, but if it is so, it is impressionism of a very special kind. There is no sensuous sound-painting here, no colours, simply the purely abstract pattern of ideas and mental images. I regard this as a limitation in this particular poem, but it was one which can be overcome, and in *Venedig* we have the overcoming of it. *Venedig*, as you know, occurs in *Ecce Homo*, from the year 1888, the last of Nietzsche's intellectual life. I make no apology for quoting it once again:

> An der Brücke stand
> jüngst ich in brauner Nacht.
> Fernher kam Gesang:
> goldener Tropfen quoll's
> über die zitternde Fläche weg.
> Gondeln, Lichter, Musik—
> trunken schwamm's in die Dämm'rung hinaus . . .
> Meine Seele, ein Saitenspiel,
> sang sich, unsichtbar berührt,
> heimlich ein Gondellied dazu,
> zitternd vor bunter Seligkeit.
> —Hörte jemand ihr zu? . . .

Again a string of statements, of impressions, each hard and clear, each leading to the next and deriving increasing precision from it, little imagery in the real sense of the word, and what there is simple and arresting. The drops of song which flow, the harp of the poet's soul—these are the only two true images. For the rest, simple, ejaculatory sensations, physical and nervous. Though the subject, a distant gondolier's song, is by its nature and traditional associations romantic and dreamy and vague, the poem is a perfectly precise and exact depiction of an experience which is in a sense mystical, and certainly not complete without the tragic question at the end. The final question in both these poems, in fact, is very typical indeed of Nietzsche; and produces the same effect as in many of Heine's poems. We shall see it again in the longer odes. It is an indication of that ambivalence we mentioned earlier, which is always present even in Nietzsche's most lyrical moments. Here the colour—and this poem is full of colour—is laid on with a technique similar to that of pointilliste painting—each speck is perhaps incongruous, but the total effect, each one modifying all the others, is of an immensely rich and complex inter-weaving and harmony. A close analysis of the various devices of alliteration and assonance would reveal just how this effect of shimmering brilliance is achieved. Shimmering brilliance—yet the poem, despite its imagery of colour and light, does not produce a visual effect at all, it is the shimmering of the soul which is conveyed. Once again, as always in Nietzsche, the subject is the lonely individual conscious-ness, trying in its isolation to comprehend the universe by, so to speak, vibrating to it. The essential thing here is the crystallization of the moment when, for an instant, the two are one, the distinction between the self and that which it perceives is obliterated. But only for an instant. The intuition of ecstasy is cut across by the essential isolation. The last line poses an unanswerable query, an insuperable obstacle.

Perhaps this is the moment to mention Nietzsche's frequent use and elaboration of the symbol of the 'großer Mittag' to which O. F. Bollnow devoted an interesting chapter some years ago in his book *Das Wesen der Stimmungen*. A moment of intense bliss, and often intoxication, often linked to the hot Mediterranean midday, of time-lessness and perfection, the hour so to speak of the Eternal Recurrence—this is a theme we cannot escape in Nietzsche. We have it again and again in *Zarathustra*—it is as though eternity breaks through into time, we inhabit for an instant a different world, life is at its highest intensity yet totally hushed and still. Nietzsche uses many symbols for this, of which the circle is perhaps the most frequent. The well-known description of Pan sleeping in *Der Wanderer und sein Schatten*, gives the essential points:

Wem ein tätiger und stürmreicher Morgen des Lebens beschieden war, dessen Seele überfällt um den Mittag des Lebens eine seltsame Ruhesucht, die Monden und Jahre lang dauern kann. Es wird still um ihn, die Stimmen klingen fern und ferner; die Sonne scheint steil auf ihn herab. Auf einer verborgenen Waldwiese sieht er den großen Pan schlafend; alle Dinge der Natur sind mit ihm eingeschlafen, einen Ausdruck von Ewigkeit im Gesichte—so dünkt es ihm. Er will nichts, er sorgt sich um Nichts, sein Herz steht still, nur sein Auge lebt—es ist ein Tod mit wachen Augen. Vieles sieht da der Mensch, was er nie sah, und soweit er sieht, ist Alles in ein Lichtnetz eingesponnen und gleichsam darin begraben. Er fühlt sich glücklich dabei, aber es ist ein schweres, schweres Glück.—Da endlich erhebt sich der Wind in den Bäumen, Mittag ist vorbei, das *Leben* reißt ihn wieder an sich, das Leben mit blinden Augen, hinter dem sein Gefolge herstürmt: Wunsch, Trug, Vergessen, Genießen, Vernichten, Vergänglichkeit. Und so kommt der Abend herauf, stürmereicher und tatenvoller, als selbst der Morgen war.—Den eigentlich tätigen Menschen erscheinen die länger währenden Zustände des Erkennens fast unheimlich und krankhaft; aber nicht unangenehm.

(Sect 308.)

One can parallel this mood time and again in Nietzsche—it is frequently conveyed in *Zarathustra* for instance—and it is plain that for him it is linked to many of his dearest conceptions. It can lead directly for instance to the conviction of eternal recurrence, though this particular passage was written long before Nietzsche underwent the curious experience which led him to this belief. But more important than any philosophical or metaphysical belief or series of beliefs which are here crystallized, is to my mind the mere fact of the mood felt and conveyed, which Bollnow easily shows is by no means confined to Nietzsche. Indeed throughout our Western poetic tradition this is a not uncommon theme for poets, and Nietzsche is by no means original in using it.

But the long passage we quoted is not a poem. When Nietzsche uses this or similar material for direct expression lyrically, as in the poem *Venedig* for instance we have seen that immediately an ambivalent situation occurs. It is this which we indicated earlier when comparing him to Heine. Nietzsche, in fact, cannot make his lyrical expression anything but ambivalent, just as Heine could not, and for fundamentally the same reasons. Though for Nietzsche, standing two generations later than Heine, this quality comes out far more tragically and is far more agonizing, he is less able than Heine was to mask his pain (and I am speaking of artistic pain, not personal unhappiness) in a joke or a piece of persiflage. For Nietzsche lyric expression, where language is freed from the obligation to portray anything at all and becomes entirely its own master, where the writer is truly a maker and not an imitator—lyric expression is the noblest calling he can conceive, and yet is essentially, so his innermost experience tells him, circular and self-destroying.

Professor Gombrich, in his recent book *Art and Illusion*, has tellingly argued that our perception of the visible world is not ever a passive recording, but involves a continual feed-back process in which our expectations are matched and corrected by outside reality and we finally arrive at what for us is 'the truth'. The pictorial artist, then, is not trying to render some one true and real thing which is outside reality, he is proposing schemata, ways of looking at things, which can be made to yield significance. The same general line of argument can be applied, can it not, to literature, and to lyric poetry in particular. It has often been said, and it will bear saying again and again, that poetry is made, not of ideas or sensations, or emotions or feelings, but of words. The poet does not seek to 'render' anything, his own feelings or the effect of moonlight on the lake or what have you. He may do these things by the way, but his poetry does not consist in this and is not measured by his success or failure in doing this. What he is concerned with is setting up schemata of language, making language behave in ways in which it does not normally behave. Lyric poetry is essentially making, not recording. And what is made is a linguistic construct which may or may not be representational. This is all, I hope, elementary, but we should keep it in mind when considering Nietzsche's poetry, since it is one of his main claims to attention that he consistently followed this idea and his work derives its intense pathos from the fact that he was unable ultimately to persuade himself of the sovereignity of language which it entails. 'Die Dichter lügen zuviel'.

Let us now look at the *Dionysos-Dithyramben*, the most sustained cycle of poems of Nietzsche's that we have, arranged in a definite order by him, and plainly to be read as a whole, the development of a consistent theme. I propose not to go into the question of their *Entstehung* and the relation between the cycle and those parts of it which occur in *Zarathustra* itself. I treat these poems as a work in their own right, not an offshoot from *Zarathustra*. And secondly I propose to take as read the whole philosophical and religious 'meaning' which is plainly indicated in them. This has been exhaustively analysed by H. Rehder[2] and others, and we must have it all in mind, but I submit not in the front of our minds, when considering these poems. I would like to regard them as poems, 'pure' poems if you like, that is poems whose real subject, whatever is ostensibly being related, is poetry itself, like many of Hölderlin's odes, say, or much of Rilke's work.

The first of the nine aptly illustrates some of the points we made earlier. A short introduction conjures up an evening situation, with the comfort of the dew, and recalls how the poet's heart had thirsted for comfort and been repulsed by the cruel rays of the sun. And at the end we are in an evening-situation again, this time with moonlight, with the poet's heart sinking out of his 'Wahrheits-Wahnsinne', thirsting still but able only to say 'Daß ich verbannt sei / von aller Wahrheit'. There has been no movement, no progress or solution. But in between these short passages put in the poet's mouth, the main body of the poem is the long ecstatic characterization by the sunlight of the poet's being and function, and it is this which carries the main burden of the poem. It starts uncompromisingly:

'Der Wahrheit Freier—du? so höhnten sie—
nein! nur ein Dichter!
ein Tier, ein listiges, raubendes, schleichendes,
das lügen muß,
das wissentlich, willentlich lügen muß,
nach Beute lüstern,
bunt verlarvt,
sich selbst zur Larve,
sich selbst zur Beute,
das—der Wahrheit Freier? . . .
Nur Narr! Nur Dichter!
Nur Buntes redend,
aus Narrenlarven bunt herausredend,
herumsteigend auf lügnerischen Wortbrücken,
auf Lügen-Regenbogen
zwischen falschen Himmeln
herumschweifend, herumschleichend—
nur Narr! *nur* Dichter! . . .

This is a fair sample of Nietzsche's style in these poems—staccato, disconnected, broken up into spurts of expression, leaping from one image to another. Here the fundamental image of the poet as beast of prey, seen in this first version as entirely negative, springs over into the image of masks and then this is associated with word-bridges and finally rainbows of lies between false heavens. And in the next stanza an explicit distinction is drawn. The poet is *not* a calm serene smooth temple-figure, a monument to the divine, he is the enemy of all such, he is at home in the wilderness not in the temple, he is

. . . voll Katzen-Mutwillens
durch jedes Fenster springend
husch! in jeden Zufall,
jedem Urwalde zuschnüffelnd . . .

The image is of an alley-cat—still a beast of prey, but with no nobility or pride, 'mit lüsternen Lefzen'.

And then suddenly, a new note is struck:

> Oder dem Adler gleich, der lange
> lange starr in Abgründe blickt,
> in *seine* Abgründe . . .

The beast of prey, skulking in his dark corner, has become an eagle, freely hovering over the chasm. The feeling is akin to that of Goethe at the opening of *Harzreise im Winter* (Dem Geier gleich, / Der auf schweren Morgenwolken / Mit sanftem Fittich ruhend / Nach Beute schaut, / Schwebe mein Lied.). And the succeeding lines build up this picture of power and independence, the sovereignty of the poet as he swoops upon his prey from above. All of it following that innocuous 'Oder'. The eagler swoops upon the lambs, and the lambs are all that we normally call virtue.

> Also
> adlerhaft, pantherhaft
> sind des Dichters Sehnsüchte,
> sind *deine* Sehnsüchte unter tausend Larven,
> du Narr! du Dichter! . . .
>
> Der du den Menschen schautest
> so *Gott* als *Schaf*—
> Den Gott *zerreißen* im Menschen
> wie das Schaf im Menschen
> und zerreißend *lachen*—
>
> *Das, das ist deine Seligkeit,*
> eines Panthers und Adlers Seligkeit,
> eines Dichters und Narren Seligkeit!'

This ends the message of the sunbeams, which is very reminiscent indeed, is it not, of Heine's similar invocation in the Nordsee poem *Der Gesang der Okeaniden*, where the sea-nymphs puncture the pretensions of the poet to the enjoyment of his love. Only here in Nietzsche the sunbeams have, almost despite themselves, drifted from a negative to a positive evaluation of the poet's role, and the coda, where the poet resigns himself to the fact that he is excluded from all truth, does not and cannot unsay the eagle-feeling that has been expressed.

Something of this general landscape of wild beasts, savagery, ruthlessness and the freedom which scorns civilization, 'virtue' and the generally-accepted values, is retained throughout all the nine poems. The second, 'Unter Töchtern der Wüste', with its mock oriental style, its theatricality, its on the whole not very good jokes, and its general opposition of Europeans and desert-girls, pursues a similar general direction. There is incoherence here, and a certain laboured quality in the elaboration of a rueful conceit. This is often judged one of Nietzsche's failures, and perhaps it is, but I would like you to notice the force of the build-up of Nietzsche's imagery.

We open with a lion, rather a stagey lion, it is true, as befits the throw-away tone of absurdity of the whole. He is linked to the desert girls and the palm-trees. The desert and the oasis—so far this is stage-setting. Then with the notion of the desert swallowing the poet we have pure fancy and soon Jonah and his whale are presented. The poet is next a date, yearning to be sucked by juicy girls' lips and chewed by their teeth. But he is still sitting in the oasis, watching the palm-trees which seem to be dancing, as a girl dances, but apparently with one leg only. And soon he is hunting for the leg, which may have been eaten by a lion. In mock-grief, he weeps and strength comes from what he calls the bellows of virtue. With a quotation of Luther's famous words, he is back at the beginning and closes the poem with these lines:

> Die Wüste wächst: weh dem, der Wüsten birgt!
> Stein knirscht an Stein, die Wüste schlingt und würgt.
> Der ungeheure Tod blickt glühend braun
> und *kaut*—, sein Leben ist sein Kaun . . .
> Vergiß nicht, Mensch, den Wollust ausgeloht:
> du—bist der Stein, die Wüste, bist der Tod.

I am suggesting here that though all this is a joke, it is not a joke without a point. And the impression which has been built up is not a medley of incongruous elements, but a carefully-calculated picture of wild revelry, dance and song, with an undertone of sexual abandon, soft and flowing and liquid, but with cruelty and brutality bound up with it, and set against the forbidding rock-hard dryness of stone and desert. And this confrontation of hardness, ossification, deadness, against joyful savagery and movement is a central theme in Nietzsche's poetic experience.

This was a long very loosely-constructed poem. By contrast the third, 'Letzter Wille', consisting of only seventeen lines, operates with an extremely taut economy, celebrating, in incantatory exultation, the hero-figure who hovers in the implication of the whole cycle. The opening is one of Nietzsche's most precise and vivid pictures, linking, in a few words, death and victory, lightning and youth, the divine and the human, dance and battle:

> So sterben,
> wie ich ihn einst sterben sah—,
> den Freund, der Blitze und Blicke
> göttlich in meine dunkle Jugend warf.
> Mutwillig und tief,
> in der Schlacht ein Tänzer—,

And the close, in its dying fall, echoes the opening:

> So sterben,
> wie ich ihn einst sterben sah:
> siegend, *vernichtend* . . .

92

It is apparent already that the cycle is no mere random collection of Dionysian poems, surging and welling up in waves of ecstasy or abandonment, but is a unity, a carefully-graded and musically-composed series of dithyrambs, each celebrating one aspect of the total committal and involvement which is Nietzsche's poetic burden, and each carefully placed so as to form with its neighbours, by similarity or contrast, by echo and discord, a progression with a poetic logic which is much clearer than a first reading might suggest. The first brought into question the validity of poetry in relation to the quest for truth, the second was concerned with an aspect of the Dionysian quality of life, the third with the hero in his isolation and his example, his victory-in-death, and now in the fourth we return, completing, so to speak, the first circle, to the figure of the poet. He is also a prophet, and here he is named—Zarathustra. 'Zwischen Raubvögeln' is appropriately his place, since this poem is dominated by the commanding image of the bird of prey, which we have seen before. And tied to a particular landscape, as Nietzsche so consistently does. Earlier we had the landscape of the desert, against which the dancers appeared in the hallucinatory haze. Now the landscape of ravine and crag, of roots and rocks, of streams and precipices and avalanches, is the fit home for the symbol of iron-hard determination and ruthlessness which are here expressed.

The central part of the poem here addresses Zarathustra and, operating with a string of reflexives, indicates the curiously inward-turning nature of the prophet's consciousness, which is twisted back on to itself in continual self-consuming.

> O Zarathustra,
> grausamster Nimrod!
> Jüngst Jäger noch Gottes,
> das Fangnetz aller Tugend,
> der Pfeil des Bösen!

So far this is the sort of description we are used to. But then the address goes on:

> Jetzt—
> von dir selber erjagt,
> deine eigene Beute,
> in dich selber eingebohrt . . .
> Jetzt—
> einsam mit dir,
> zwiesam im eignen Wissen,
> zwischen hundert Spiegeln
> vor dir selber falsch,
> zwischen hundert Erinnerungen
> ungewiß,
> an jeder Wunde müd,
> an jedem Froste kalt,
> in eignen Stricken erwürgt,
> Selbstkenner!
> Selbsthenker!

93

And from now on truth and wisdom are burdens, or fetters, or bonds which constrict and imprison the poet, who is called later:

> steif,
> ein Leichnam—
> von hundert Lasten übertürmt
> von dir überlastet.

Again the contrast, between the lordly sovereignty and freedom of the eagles, who open and close the poem, and the deadness and maimed struggles of the poet who is devoured by his own wisdom—this contrast is the heart of the poem, and it is clear that these two are both symbols of the same thing, they are inseparable, the one conjures up the other, just as Nietzsche's Dionysian exultation cannot exist without the utter tragic isolation and self-communing which is self-destroying. The ambivalence which we mentioned at the beginning and which we saw so strongly expressed in the first poem, is even more clear and uncompromising here. Could one have a more negative and tragic image for the poet or prophet than this:

> Jetzt—
> zwischen zwei Nichtse
> eingekrümmt,
> ein Fragezeichen,
> ein müdes Rätsel—
> ein Rätsel für Raubvögel.

This was a poem about Zarathustra. The next 'Das Feuerzeichen' is a poem put into his mouth, though, as often in the whole cycle, there is continual shifting between the second person and the third, continual ambiguity as to who the speaker is at any moment. This is again part of the general ambivalence—the fictional speaker has no clear identity, shifts and merges continually from one mask to another. Here, in contrast to the previous poem, we have measured calm rhythms, a certain formal balance and a great degree of serene musicality—as though this mountain-top with its guiding beacon of fire, was a refuge from the wild turbulence we have witnessed, a rock of achievement, a haven towards which we have been steering through a storm. The mystical note, with talk of the 'siebente, letzte Einsamkeit' is struck here unambiguously, and in 'Die Sonne sinkt', which follows, we have a rare example of the perfect balance and stillness which Nietzsche could attain at blessed moments. This is what he meant when he spoke of the 'Heiterkeit' of Dionysos, this is the sun at midday, the ending of all questing and struggling, the timelessness when Pan sleeps. The ease and sureness of the writing here is impressive, the same type of experience as in the poem 'Venedig', but on a much larger scale. The play of colours, in the second section, as the sun sinks, and the blessed moment passes, is evocative

94

and expressive in a more direct way than anywhere else in Nietzsche. And the culmination is surely one of his most sustained and faultless passages:

> Heiterkeit, güldene, komm!
>   du des Todes
> heimlichster, süßester Vorgenuß!
> —Lief ich zu rasch meines Wegs?
> Jetzt erst, wo der Fuß müde ward,
>   holt dein Blick mich noch ein,
>   holt dein *Glück* mich noch ein.
>
> Rings nur Welle und Spiel.
>   Was je schwer war,
> sank in blaue Vergessenheit,—
> müßig steht nun mein Kahn.
> Sturm und Fahrt—wie verlernt' er das!
>   Wunsch und Hoffen ertrank,
> glatt liegt Seele und Meer.
>
> *Siebente* Einsamkeit!
>   Nie empfand ich
> näher mir süße Sicherheit
> wärmer der Sonne Blick.
> —Glüht nicht das Eis meiner Gipfel noch?
>   Silbern, leicht, ein Fisch,
>   schwimmt nun mein Nachen hinaus.

I have attempted to indicate a progression in these poems, a development in a clearly-conceived direction, so that each falls into its place in the developing pattern. And it would be tempting to present the culmination here as the end, the blessed state towards which all has been tending. In style and rhythm, in shape and imagery, there has been, has there not, a development in the same direction, from violence and turbulence towards harmony and simplicity and smoothness. It would be tempting to see the cycle as now ended. The fact that it does not end here, rather that this is a perfect moment surrounded by doubts, hesitations, wildness and suffering, is, it seems to me, entirely significant of Nietzsche's purpose. This achievement is short-lived and must pass, as must all poetic achievement, and there must be more tortured questioning before Nietzsche's consciousness is fully revealed. I do not propose to consider the remaining poems in detail. The 'Klage der Ariadne' has of course its particular significance in respect of Nietzsche's relationship with Wagner and Cosima, but this I leave on one side. I note that this poem is a plethora of questions. Through the mouth of Ariadne, the poet attempts to come at the majesty of the god Dionysus. The imagery is of torture, hunting, cruelty, self-abasement, of course with overtly sexual implications, and Nietzsche makes no bones about the more repellent aspect of his subject:

> Was willst du dir erfoltern,
> du Folterer!
> du—Henker-Gott!
> Oder soll ich, dem Hunde gleich,
> vor dir mich wälzen?
> hingebend, begeistert-außer-mir,
> dir Liebe—zuwedeln?

And the words of the god at the end are quite uncompromising:

> Muß man sich nicht erst hassen,
> wenn man sich lieben soll?

With 'Ruhm und Ewigkeit' we are once again using the Zarathustra-mask, the first section describing him in violent terms, with images of lightning and thunder and the spreading of fearful awe, the last two sections being spoken by him, a sort of exultant declaration of his scorn for common humanity and the trivialities which occupy men, a proud emphasis on his mission to regenerate them; moving onward and upward from a scornful denunciation of the world's fame to the ecstatic address to 'Notwendigkeit' and 'Ewigkeit' which concludes the poem.

> Meine Liebe entzündet
> sich ewig nur an der Notwendigkeit.

The progression here is from lightning and storm in the mountains to the coin-clinking of the market-place, then on to the still silence of the night-sky, and finally to the star, shining alone in the eternal spaces, a symbol of necessity and eternity, in its cold radiance in every way antithetical to the wild flashes of the opening and yet once again referring ultimately to the same thing.

Finally, in the last poem of the cycle, 'Von der Armut der Reichsten', we have a long retrospect, a summing-up and balance-sheet of the Dionysian experience. This looking-back over life, weighing it all up in tranquillity and calm, is the key-note struck in the first lines:

> Zehn Jahre dahin—,
> kein Tropfen erreichte mich,
> kein feuchter Wind, kein Tau der Liebe
> —ein *regenloses* Land

The landscape is exactly that which opened the first poem of the cycle, and the governing image, of thirst-parched lips yearning for water, is carried on throughout the poem. We hear of udders, milk, the 'süße Tau der Liebe', and the images of ripening as a result of receiving water or sustenance, are piled up on one another:

> von der Sonne gesüßt, von der Liebe gebräunt,—
> eine *reife* Wahrheit breche ich allein vom Baum.

This leads to the notion of Zarathustra as the bringer of nourishment, and the general depiction of his creativity, his generosity, his over-spilling of himself:

> Wer sind mir Vater und Mutter?
> Ist nicht mir Vater Prinz Überfluß
> und Mutter das stille Lachen?

But in the middle of the poem there is a dramatic change of speakers, and this is of course entirely characteristic of this cycle. Zarathustra sees one of his truths approaching, and, in the hush which he commands, the truth speaks. The rest of the poem, spoken to, not by, Zarathustra, brings out the obverse of his splendour and serenity.

> Du möchtest schenken, wegschenken deinen Überfluß,
> aber du selber bist der Überflüssigste!
> Sei klug, du Reicher!
> *Verschenke dich selber erst*, o Zarathustra!

And the truth goes on, repeating the opening words of the poem, but adding its bitter comment:

> Zehn Jahre dahin—
> und kein Tropfen erreichte dich?
> kein feuchter Wind? kein Tau der Liebe?
> Aber wer *sollte* dich auch lieben,
> du überreicher?
> Dein Glück macht rings trocken,
> macht arm an Liebe
> —ein *regenloses* Land.

And the truth goes on to the final judgement, which is not a rejection of Zarathustra's claims but a repetition of the price which must be paid, the tragedy which must be faced.

> Du mußt ärmer werden,
> weiser Unweiser!
> willst du geliebt sein.
> Man liebt nur die Leidenden,
> man gibt Liebe nur dem Hungernden:
> *verschenke dich selber erst*, o Zarathustra!

> —Ich bin deine Wahrheit.

This is almost a return to the negations of the first poem 'Nur Narr! Nur Dichter!', but it is combined now with a total recognition of all that has been expressed in the poems in between, and it represents a crisis for Nietzsche, just as the first poem did, only now the way to surmounting it has been made clear. It seems to me important that it is this poem which ends the cycle, not the triumphant earlier ones, like 'Die Sonne sinkt'. We are moving in territory where there is no sure arrival, every conquest has to be yielded again and then made anew. The poet's achievement is no sooner expressed than it is called into question. This is why, I believe, Nietzsche battles his way through to the triumph of 'Die Sonne sinkt' but then cannot in honesty leave it there, but must add these three last poems, each exposing a piece of the remaining agony, the agony which can be held for an instant in strain, and yield a perfect sure joy, but remains a permanent underlying fundament to the poet's whole being.

Perhaps we may now attempt to see how Nietzsche's poetry stands in the development from the nineteenth century to the present day. I started by mentioning Heine, and I think it would be agreed that there are good grounds for considering Heine the first European poet whose sensibility is akin to that of our contemporaries. By which I mean that his work expresses the essential dissolution of fixed categories of feeling which is so prevalent in the twentieth century. The line runs, I suppose, from him through Baudelaire and on to the Expressionists, to Rilke and Trakl, and on to such men as Gottfried Benn. Nietzsche has a secure and important place in this development, not for technical reasons, not for the breaking-up of received forms, the stretching of the notions of imagery, the daring use of unexpected and discordant motives, and so on—though here too of course his originality should be remarked—but rather for a more fundamental quality which seems to me of great importance. I spoke earlier of poetry as allowing uses of language which are strictly non-representational, that is which do not try to convey any description, either of objects or of states of mind. Of course any use of language must willy-nilly convey a state of mind, but in lyric poetry it is possible for this not to be the prime consideration. Poetry can move towards the condition of being what one may call a linguistic artefact, or a piece of linguistic machinery, where the words themselves form a pattern (and I do not of course mean simply a musical pattern) which exists in its own right, independently of whatever sense may be read out of (or of course, into) it. Such poetry is analogous to non-representational art, and my main submission is that Nietzsche is at least moving strongly towards this. After him, both Trakl and Benn, and of course many others, have pushed this much further. Valéry erected a whole theory of this, and it is, I think, no accident that the most recent book on Nietzsche is in fact a very close and detailed comparison of him to Valéry.[3]

But Nietzsche saw, I think, more profoundly that many poets since, what this involves. It involves, does it not, ultimately the sacrifice of all claim that poetry has to do with 'truth'. Once any art becomes non-representational, then however carefully you define and refine your notion of artistic or poetic truth you are finally forced to abandon the claim to it. The important thing for Nietzsche, I think, who after all protests again and again that all our 'truths' are either convenient lies or else 'perspective valuations', is that at the ultimate poetry cannot claim truth, that Plato, that 'Feigling vor der Realität', as he calls him, was right (only of course for the wrong reasons). And if poetry is not truth, what is it? It is what the *Dionysos-Dithyramben* are—linguistic constructs which create a whole system of relationships which are not necessarily applicable to the real world, as a system of four-dimensional geometry can be perfectly consistent and satisfying without having any relationship to our three-dimensional world.

Whether for Nietzsche this is a triumph or a defeat one cannot say. Here as always his essential reaction is ambivalent. '*Nur* Narr, *nur* Dichter'. This is on the one side. But to set against that is his continual hankering after the condition of music. 'Sie hätte *singen* sollen, diese meine Seele—und nicht reden![4]

NOTES

1. Joh. Klein: Geschichte der deutschen Lyrik, p. 644.

2. H. Rehder: Leben und Geist in Nietzsches Lyrik (Dichtung und Volkstum, 37, 1936).

3. Edouard Gaède: Nietzsche et Valéry. Gallimard 1962.

4. Vorrede to *Geburt der Tragödie* (1886).

Discussion

Thomas, *Salinger* and *Allemann* raised questions concerning Nietzsche's relations with other writers, and especially his admiration for Heine—its causes, duration and beneficial or harmful effects on his (Nietzsche's) writing. The speaker maintained that it had brought Nietzsche to grips with the question of poetry and truth.

Replying to *Mainland*, the speaker thought Nietzsche's use of parody was his reaction to writings which had touched him closely.

Replying to *Brooke*, the speaker agreed that some of Nietzsche's prose could be regarded as 'poetic', but thought the poetic passages, where language had taken command, spoilt the prose work.

Allemann stressed the modernity of Nietzsche. He also described Nietzsche's poetry as 'Gedankenlyrik', thoughts clothed in imagery.

Closs referred to the Klage der Ariadne and the idea of sacrifice in Nietzsche's 'Der Zauberer'. Ariadne cannot bear the God's brutal onslaught, yet in her loneliness she longs for him: 'Mein Henker-Gott!—Nein! Komm zurück, mit all deinen Martern!' . . .

Brockes and the limitations of imitation

by

WILLIAM F. MAINLAND

Not Chaos-like together crush'd and bruis'd,
But, as the world, harmoniously confus'd:
Where order in variety we see,
And where, tho' all things differ, all agree.

(Alexander Pope, *Windsor Forest*)

WHAT I am to say about Brockes has its own narrow limits. I am not concerned, or concerned only in passing, with the poet's emulation of an old, traditional mode of expression. The quarrel of the ancients and the moderns is to interest me only in that new guise suggested by Professor Allemann's paper: in contrast to poetry which is 'nicht mehr Lyrik' I shall have to adduce examples of verse which is *perhaps* already lyrical. What I should like to do, in turning to a period a little more remote than any other within the scope of our Symposium is to listen with you to the response of a poet to the *things* around him. What I have to put before you is a brief study of his individual observation, which involved him in the selection of objects and aspects and obliged him to devise an idiom to communicate his reflections. The interest of the enquiry has been, for me, threefold: the patterned variety of the poet's work; the limits fixed by his personality, his intention and the epoch upon the manner of his observation and the idiom of his response; and the shifting limits of appreciation in later times.

Let me now suggest from the resources of English poetry certain rough contours round my theme:

> But noble Muse, proceed immediately to tell
> How Evsham's fertile vale at first in liking fell
> With Cotswold, that great King of Shepheards; whose proud site
> When that fair Vale first saw, so nourisht her delight
> That him she only lov'd: . . .
>
> Where little purling winds like wantons seeme to dally,
> And skip from Bank to Bank, from Valley trip to Valley.
> Such sundry shapes of soyle where Nature doth devise
> That she may rather seeme fantasticall then wise.

(Michael Drayton, *Poly-Olbion*, 1613)

101

> ... At once array'd
> In all the Colours of the flushing Year
> By Nature's swift and secret-working Hand,
> The Garden glows, and fills the liberal Air
> With lavish Fragrance; while the promis'd Fruit
> Lies like a little Embrio, unperceiv'd,
> Within its Crimson Folds ...
>
> (James Thomson, *The Seasons, Spring*, 1728)

> The sunset tipped with gold St Michael's Church,
> Shouts of boys bathing came from Highgate Ponds,
> The elms that hid the houses of the great
> Rustled with mystery, and dirt-grey sheep
> Grazed in the foreground; but the lines of verse
> Came out like parodies of A. & M.
>
> (John Betjeman, *Summoned by Bells*, 1960)

From Drayton's paramyth we move to the emotionally tinged presentation of sensory detail in Thomson and then to the contemporary poet's retrospect upon his impressionistic period—'My urge was to encase in rhythm and rhyme / The things I saw and felt (I could not *think*)'—with its faintly ironical reference to the traditional religious undertone.

Within this essentially modern imitation of nature from early seventeenth to mid-twentieth century Brockes takes a notable place. Our perception of the place he holds and our response to him have been hampered chiefly by three things. The first of these is the laborious, pedestrian nature of some of his verse. ('Many there are that can fall, but few can arrive at the felicity of falling gracefully,' as Pope has his Martinus Scriblerus say in his study of the art of bathos). The second is Lessing's essay on the demarcation of the arts, *Laocoon*, which was held a little too long as canon of taste instead of being regarded merely as remedial in its own time. The third is the promotion of the poet Günther in Goethe's retrospect on his own poetic education. It would be interesting to note the number of literary histories, down to our own time, which have dealt with Günther in the paragraph immediately before or immediately after Brockes. And how Brockes has suffered! Richard Benz (*Deutsches Barock*, 1949, p. 292) makes this juxtaposition with maximum contrast of characterization; but while he suggests (p. 293) that Günther is more modern, much nearer to us, because 'die Geschichte seines Inneren der einzige Inhalt seiner Kunst gewesen ist' he has this to say of Brockes (p. 291): 'Sein Großes ist vielleicht gerade, daß seinem Naturerlebnis die lyrische Ich-Bezogenheit fehlt, die immer nur die eigne Stimmung an Schmerz oder Freude in der Natur wiederfindet—er steht mit der Ergriffenheit des erstmals Schauenden vor der Natur, erschüttert und anbetend ...' Benz sees Brockes as illustration of a religious habit of thought in his time: God is revealed in Creation rather than in any dogmatic formula; 'aber das Ganze von Brockes' Leistung war das nicht; sie beruhte in der wirklichen Andacht und Erhebung durch eine neue künstlerische Schau' (p. 291).

What was new in Brockes's artistic perception? When we ask such a question we are thinking historically, not only of what went before, but of what was to follow, what was heralded by this particular innovation. Most widely characteristic of Brockes, I think, is his ecstatic exploration of the physical world, animate and inanimate, its structure, its colour, its activity. The previous century had bequeathed a fairly wide scheme of references to the objects in man's environment; but the scheme was very largely an elaborate convention for the supply of metaphors and similes. Brockes accepted the bequest of mineralogical and botanical vocabulary, but behind his use and vast extension of it there was a different impulse. A new 'Weltweisheit', less harassed by the thought of disastrous change, induced him and others not so famous in his time—Drollinger, Heräus—to set up a sort of poet's specimen cupboard and, taking delight in things as they are, to enjoy some fore-taste of that pleasure which later and greater collectors were to experience—Goethe, Stifter. This intellectual enquiry, this almost static interest, no longer obsessed by thought of decay, nor as yet committed to a philosophy of evolutionary change, was perhaps necessary before the great new thrust of organic theory could gain force, and natural phenomena could be freshly integrated in the poet's world of feeling.

> Nasturtium, die Sonnen-Wende,
> Die schöne Bluhm' aus Africa,
> Die Ritter-Spor, Calendula,
> Bedeckt die Betten itzt fast ganz
> Mit einem gleichsam güldnen Glanz.
>
> (*Ird. Vergn.* VII, 426, cit. Pfund, p. 137)

and again

> Für Verwundrung ward ich stumm,
> Als ich jüngst dein Feur erblickte, funckelndes Geranium.
>
> (cit. Pfund, p. 138)

are very far removed from:

> Dieses Baums Blatt, der von Osten
> Meinem Garten anvertraut,
> Gibt geheimen Sinn zu kosten,
> Wie's den Wissenden erbaut.
>
> Ist es ein lebendig Wesen,
> Das sich in sich selbst getrennt?
> Sind es zwei, die sich erlesen,
> Daß man sie als e i n e s kennt?
>
> Solche Frage zu erwidern,
> Fand ich wohl den rechten Sinn:
> Fühlst du nicht an meinen Liedern,
> Daß ich e i n s und doppelt bin?
>
> (Goethe, *Gingo Biloba* in *Westöstlicher Divan*, Sept., 1815)

Yet, from the verse of Brockes speaks to us 'der Wissende'—in a different idiom, it is true, from that of the scientist Haller—but, like Haller, Brockes knew the remedy for himself and for his age against the fetid imagery of poets who had grasped the symbols conjured from Nature in order to body forth their own imperilled lust for propagation. Then there were the precious stones used by poets of the Baroque as icons to analyze the beauties of the loved one. Brockes, looking at a 'Goldkäfer', admires 'sein wandelbares Grün, / Das bald wie Gold, bald wie Rubin, / Und bald aufs neu Smaragden, schien.' (*Ird. Vergn.* I, 99, cit. Pfund p. 144). This is transference of visual perception from one part of nature's realm to another, and the poet is involved as one who seeks and observes, defines and admires. Sometimes, especially in the latest parts of the *Irdisches Vergnügen*, there is over-anxious enquiry into the composition of stones and minerals, even into the genuineness of gems:

> Manche Schönheit wird entdecket
> Auch im Jaspis, dessen Schein
> Muß grün und mit Roth geflecket,
> Wenn er anders echt ist, seyn.

> (*Ird. Vergn.* IX, 75, cit. Pfund 143)

He is led by observation to philosophic conclusions, as, for example on a day in a garden when he and two friends are surprised by the recognition that the petals of flowers are not green. (The prevalence of green in external nature, and its appeal to the eye no doubt brought quiet satisfaction to the contemplative mind of Brockes's generation; as we may read in David Hartley's *Observations on Man*: 'Green, the middle Colour of the Seven primary ones, and consequently the most agreeable to the Organ of Sight, is also the general Colour of the Vegetable Kingdom. . . .' Brockes was himself impressed by the immense range of shades of green in Spring —'in tausendfärbgem Grünen' is his phrase in *Frühlings Gedancken, Ird. Vergn.* VIII, and for him, as for others of his time, the daylight in the woods is 'grüne Nacht'). So the three gentlemen in the garden wonder a little that no flowers share in this most agreeable of colours. Thereupon 'des schönen Gartens Herr und Pfleger' quietly presents to them a flower with green petals; it is of course one which had often been mentioned by poets of the previous century but was now being seen as a thing interesting in itself—the anemone. So these amiable collectors of naturenotes reach happy agreement in a matter relevant to the philosophy of their time and even to literary theory:

> Hierüber stimmen wir zuletzt der Meynung bey,
> Daß alles, was in der Natur
> Sowohl an Farben, als Figur,
> Nur möglich, auch vermuthlich wirklich sey.

> (*Ird. Vergn.* Auszug, Hagedorn u. Wilckens, ed. Hamburg 1763, p. 59)

The teasing of these matters into verse is not unfamiliar to the student of the classics, who can follow the tradition through to the neo-Latinists of the seventeenth century labouring in metre to describe intricate processes such as the detail of paper-making (J. Imberdis, S. J., *Papyrus sive ars conficiendæ papyri* (1693), tr. E. Laughton, 1952). English contemplative writing of the early eighteenth century shows clear kinship. It is a very different use of verse from that of the bardic poets, or the men of gloomy Ossianic persuasion, the rhapsodists, the neo-Hellenists of the later eighteenth century. The use of the term 'philosophical poetry' or, more pointedly 'Gedanken-lyrik' to describe it bring us up sharply against the formulations of those who claim that the lyric is non-informative. By such restrictive definition Brockes and many of his generation would be deprived of the bulk of their vast store at the frontier of the lyric territory and be allowed to enter with only a very few personal effects. It might be hard to claim concession for Brockes by appeal to another formula, and to say that he had in his own way been anticipating the use of poetic form 'zu begreifen was uns ergreift', and sharing this understanding. Yet it is probably easier now to make this claim than it was in the late, lingering twilight of romanticism. I think we may now see Brockes, revealing something of the spirit of certain early members of the Royal Society and pointing, a little uncertainly, sometimes with very clumsy gesture, towards that confluence of science and imagination which Goethe achieved in his *Faust II* and in his *Farbenlehre*.

Breitinger thought of Brockes as the 'Historikus': 'er bringe auch die unbedeu-tendsten Dinge mit der Sorgfalt eines Naturforschers'. (In passing, we may say that for Brockes nothing was unimportant). Quoting this from Breitinger, Ermatinger (*Deutsche Lyrik seit Herder*, I, p. 8) suggests that Brockes is the first Impressionist in German literature, 'nicht nur weil er vor keiner Schranke des Stoffes haltmacht, sondern vor allem weil er auf peinliche Genauigkeit in der Wiedergabe der Wahr-nehmungen hält'. In this there is, I am afraid, the inaccuracy of terms insufficiently confined. The exact rendering of visual perception would apply equally well to Turner, to the pre-Raphaelites, and to the French Impressionists. Mention of the *Farbenlehre* which I made a moment ago may help us towards a clearer notion of what Brockes was about in his recording of colour-perception. We recall Goethe's exact and purposeful method of analyzing colour-effects in a landscape at certain (for the artist) critical times of day. We may now turn to a piece of landscape description by Brockes:

> Da aber, wo das Licht der Sonne selber strahlt,
> Scheint alles, nicht so sehr gefärbt, als wunderschön
> In einer bunten Gluth zu stehn.
> Im grünen Feuer glüht das Laub, das Kraut, das Gras
> In tausend-färbigem, wann es bethaut und naß.
> Ein gelber angenehmer Brand
> Bedeckt den gelben Kies und Sand,
> Ein röthlicher das jüngst gepflügte Land.
> Es glänzt die reine Luft, es glüht die glatte Fluth
> (Wenn da, wo sie sich reg't, viel gold'ne Blitze schwimmen,

Und, wie geschür'te Kohlen, glimmen)
In einer weißlich-blauen Gluth.
In dunkel-blauer stehn entfernte Hügel,
In einer rothen, rothe Ziegel,
So wie in einem grauen Schein
Beschilfte Hütten, Holz und Stein.
In den bestrahl'ten Blumen flammen
Gluth, Farben, Glanz und Schein zusammen.
Die schwarzen nicht so sehr, als bunt-gefärbten, Schatten
Erheben die beflammte Pracht,
So wie das schwarze Heer der Schatten, bey der Nacht,
Stern, Mond und Licht, daß sie noch einst so schön,
Durch ihren Gegensatz, erhöh'n.

(*Ird. Vergn.* Hagedorn u. Wilckens, ed. Hamburg 1763, p. 73)

Here we are asked to note the incidence of strong, direct light on a variety of objects. There are some individual references such as 'dunkel-blau' for the distant hills, which might be followed up profitably in relation to painterly vision of the time. The general conclusion we draw is that Brockes saw, in such lighting, an *effulgence* of local colour. But, leaving aside the fascinating and characteristic insistence upon 'Glut', 'Feuer' and 'Brand', we may find that the most interesting lines relating specifically to colour are: 'Die schwarzen nicht so sehr, als bunt-gefärbten, Schatten . . . erhöh'n'. This passage shows that Brockes, at least on that occasion, did not see shadow as an area of darkness: his reference to 'bunt-gefärbt' might indicate early painting convention of using a deeper tone of local colour for the cast shadow; but, in conjunction with the mention of contrast, it may suggest that he was anticipating a much later convention—the painter's use of complementary colours for shadow-tones.

Brockes, with many of his contemporaries, was eloquent in his thankfulness for the bounty of light—light shining upon a world infinite in its promise of things to see, to study, to adore.

> . . . so exquisitely fram'd
> Is this complex, amazing scene of Things.
> But tho' conceal'd, to every purer Eye
> Th' informing Author in His Works appears;
> His grandeur in the Heavens: the Sun, and Moon,
> Whether that fires the Day, or falling this
> Pours out a lucid softness o'er the Night,
> Are but a Beam from Him . . .

(Thomson, *The Seasons*, *Spring*)

It was a natural and happy conclusion to his life's work that Brockes applied himself to the translation of Thomson's *Seasons*, for much of his meditation was in harmony with that of the English poet. Perhaps less readily allured than Thomson or Haller by the varied aspects of the social scene or by the challenge of ethical problems, Brockes indulged his wit and imagination in speculation, at times naive, about the phenomenal world. And the phenomenal world exists by virtue of God's gift of light. Where the moralist of the previous century posed the question: 'Was ist dieß Leben noch?' and answered it by a series of emblems of transience, Brockes applied the form of the question to the consideration of colour: 'Was sind die Farben doch?' His answer was again an echo of the Baroque, but in a different universe of discourse: 'Nichts, als ein bloßes Nichts', since colours exist only if there is light.

> Alles auf der Welt erbleicht,
> Wenn die güldne Sonne weicht.
> Allen Körpern, die wir kennen,
> Flößt dein Licht das Leben ein.

At this point we may think that Brockes is on the point of expressing something as profound as the words of Mephistopheles convey (Faust I, 1355–56):

> Von Körpern strömt's, die Körper macht es schön,
> Ein Körper hemmt's auf seinem Gange...

But Brockes's guileless insistence on the particulars of experience leads him into somewhat shallow water:

> Wenn sich nun dein Wunderschein
> Von den Kreaturen scheidet,
> Sieht man, wie der Körper leidet.

> In den Wunden kann man's spüren,
> Wenn wir deinen Strahl verlieren,
> Daß bei deinem fernen Schein
> Alle Schmerzen größer sein.

> (see DNL XXXIX 2, p. 316)

An impressive thought on cosmogony has shrunk suddenly to a hint on heliotherapy.

It seems inevitable that in anything that is still written about Brockes there will be some reference to his physico-teleological deism. This precise phrase is not always used, but the meaning of it is almost always conveyed with varying degrees of pity or of acrimony. For later generations, with their own brand of complacency or envy, the distich *der Teleolog* from the Goethe-Schiller *Xenien* has no doubt proved very attractive:

> Welche Verehrung verdient der Weltenschöpfer, der gnädig,
> Als er den Korkbaum schuf, gleich auch die Stöpsel erfand.

Page after page of Brockes's verse provides material to illustrate his recognition of God's intricate and elaborate provision for man's needs:

> Haben wir ein Wildpret nötig, wird ein Falk, ein Hund geschickt,
> Welcher sonder unsre Mühe das, was man verlangt, berückt
> Und in unsre Küche liefert. Ändert sich die Jahreszeit,
> Und wir wollen uns zum Schutz und zur Zier ein ander Kleid,
> Zinst das Schaf uns seine Wolle, zollet das Kameel sein Haar,
> Und es spinnt der Seidenwurm uns ein leicht und schön Gewand.

> (see DNL XXXIX 2, p. 369)

It seems to me irrelevant to criticize the making of such statements. The matter which does concern us is the use of 'gebundene Rede' to express them. Enquiry into this must lead us further than Brockes's own *apologia* (see Fulda, DNL XXXIX 2, p. 283): 'Wann ich aber gar bald gewahr ward, daß die Poesie, wofern sie keinen sonderlichen und zwar nützlichen Endzweck hätte, ein leeres Wortspiel sei . . . als bemühete ich mich, solche Objekte meiner Dichtkunst zu erwählen, woraus die Menschen nebst einer erlaubten Belustigung zugleich erbauet werden müßten'.— This is merely a remedial intensification for Brockes's own time, of the old recipe 'delectare prodesse'. What was it, we must ask, that induced him to express these thoughts about God's bounty, and about the gift of Reason which makes man master of all he surveys, in rhythm and rhyme, interspersed with modifying words and phrases—'fast, gleichsam, so zu reden'—which, by post-romantic convention at least, are called 'prosaic'? Brockes, eagerly interested in the study of variant pronunciation in Niedersächsisch, had a keen ear for spoken sound, and could conjure up as pleasing a jingle of rhyme as any 'Pegnitzschäfer' had ever contrived:

> Geflügelte Bürger beblätterter Zweige,
> Befiederte Sänger, ihr preiset, ihr rühmt,
> Da alles belaubet, da alles beblühmt,
> Die Güte des Schöpfers, und ich schweige? Nein:
> Dieß, durch die Geschöpfe gerührte Gemüthe
> Lobsinget des Schöpfers allmächtige Güte.

(*Singgedicht, Ird. Vergn. Ausz.* Hagedorn u. Wilckens, ed. Hamburg, 1763, p. 5)

A. Closs (*The Genius of the German Lyric*, 1962, p. 139) has rightly drawn attention to the setting of Brockes's works by noted composers; the association of poetry and music was part of Brockes's early interest in the work of Marino. Many of Brockes's poems show a most careful adjustment of words with obvious auditory intention. The poem probably most frequently quoted to illustrate this—*Die auf ein starkes Ungewitter erfolgte Stille*—may be set side by side with Klopstock's *Frühlingsfeier*:

Ein fürchterliches Braun färbt die erzürnte Flut,
Die Luft ein gräßlich Grau. Man sieht das Wasser schäumen,
Die Wellen heben an, erschrecklich sich zu bäumen;
Es wütet, wallt und wankt die ganze Wasserwelt,

Der Donner rollt' und knallt', Blitz, Ströme, Strahlen, Schlossen
Vermischten ihre Wut, die roten Flammen flossen
Und wallten überall als wie ein feurig Meer
In der geborstnen Luft entsetzlich hin und her.

(see DNL XXXIX 2, pp. 326–27)

Such confluence of effects of sound and sight was admired in the poet's own day, and Weichmann (*Poesie der Niedersachsen*, 1721–) cited Brockes to illustrate 'wie groß die Wirkung dieser vereinigten Künste' (Mahlerey, Music) 'in der Tichtkunst sey, und wie derjenige, so in der letzten was tüchtiges zu leisten gedenket, wenigstens überhaupt von den beiden ersten einige Kenntniß haben müsse' (cit. B. Markwardt, *Geschichte der deutschen Poetik*, I, 1937, p. 336; cf. also in reference to close association of poetry and music the preface by B. H. Brockes Jun. to Herrn B. H. Brockes *Harmonische Himmels-Lust im Irdischen*, Hamburg, 1741). Brockes was able on occasion to devise all the appropriate sounds to accompany the visual presentation in painterly terms of the period. The poem quoted shows a precise, if conventional, succession of detail, and it is evocative. Eric Blackall, in one of the best-informed and most sensitive essays on Brockes which one may ever hope to read (*The Emergence of German as a Literary Language*, 1959) says: 'Brockes's use of language is rarely poetic. It is at most precise, rarely evocative. Precision is a prose quality' (op. cit. p. 254). This last statement raises an old question, and one which I do not think can be answered once and for all, because the very meaning of it will probably continue to vary in the irregular succession of times of emotion and times of cerebration in the progress of our poesy. I hope, on the other hand, that it will be possible to answer the question which I myself have just put, and which I should now like to extend: Why does this poet, who proves at times that he can be evocative by precise visual imitation and appropriate adjustment of sound, at other times, by equally careful description of objects in a rhythmical and rhymed composition, become as Blackall puts it (op. cit. p. 262) 'flabby almost to the point of tastelessness'? This must be seen to have some bearing on that problem which I regard as central in an enquiry into early eighteenth century poetry: the problem of the limitations which arose to restrict the effective effort towards imitation.

I think we may look for an explanation, as far as Brockes is concerned, firstly in his over-zealous attempt to communicate sensory data and secondly in his analysis of the faculties of the poet. I will be especially brief in dealing with the first of these, drawing attention in passing to the wealth of material ably analyzed by Harry W. Pfund (*Studien zu Wort und Stil bei Brockes*, New York, 1935; see also my review in *M.L.R.*, vol. XXXII, 1937, pp 482–484). We have noted a progress in Brockes's system of descriptive reference from one realm of external nature to another. But there are obvious limitations in the effect. These seem to be particularly noticeable when he uses, as he is so fond of doing, a comparison drawn from his ever-ready collection of minerals and precious stones bequeathed by the Baroque. It may be a useful and accurate guide to a painter when he reads in a poem that there is emerald in the landscape, sapphire in the sky, silver on the river; but for other readers associations of size and particularly surface quality, even a wayward thought of economic value, will distort the view. Brockes's equally keen awareness of the scent and taste of things tempted him over-much to describe this most evasive of all our perceptions; Blackall quotes a spectacular example from *Irdisches Vergnügen* I (op. cit. p. 253):

> Mich deucht . . .
> Es sey darin der Duft und Kraft vereint zu finden
> Von Honig, Mandel-Milch, Most, Pfirsich-Kern, Zimmet-
> Rinden,
> Und daß mit holder Süßigkeit
> Ein wenig säurliches und bitt'res sich verbinden
> In solchem Grad, der Herz und Hirn erfreut.

The object described is a violet. This kind of description will almost surely fail in its purpose unless wit in its brevity comes to the writer's aid, as I think it does in an English lexicographer's definition of a banana (for mention of which I am grateful to Professor Isaacs): 'a banana is a kind of vegetable sausage with the flavour of a pineapple'.

I move to the other matter—the analysis of the faculties of the poet. May I remind you of what Schiller wrote concerning the didactic poet in *Über naive und senti-mentalische Dichtung*:

> Dasjenige didaktische Gedicht, worin der Gedanke selbst
> poetisch wäre und es auch bliebe, ist noch zu erwarten . . .

and

> Der gewöhnliche Fall ist, . . . daß der abstrakte Begriff
> herrschet und daß der Einbildungskraft, welche auf dem
> poetischen Felde zu gebieten haben soll, bloß verstattet
> wird, den Verstand zu bedienen.
>
> (Säkular–Ausg. XII, 2, p. 207)

The question may properly be raised: Was Brockes a didactic poet? If we say that he was, are we perhaps confusing teaching with preaching? Yet I think there is clear evidence for the didactic in such poems as *Der Regen, Betrachtung der Sonne,* and *Die Luft* (see *Deutsche Lit. in Entwicklungsreihen, Aufklärung* 2. pp, 274–303); here, as in many other poems, Brockes is teaching the reader to observe, examine, under-stand and respect the indispensable environment of his life. Sometimes, as we have seen, and as we shall see, again he makes a rapturous escape from the palisade of the didactic. But when he is teaching, does he not invite the criticism which Schiller expresses? In the last book of *Irdisches Vergnügen* Brockes considered 'Verstand, Gedächtniß, Phantasey' as 'ein gedrittes Eins' which must rule the poet's pen:

Was wäre doch die Phantasey, wenn sie zugleich nicht überlegte
Und durch die Wirkung des Verstandes der Vorwürf' Unterscheid erwägte?
Sie wär ein bloßer todter Spiegel . . . ,
     . . . Einfolglich sonder Phantasey
Wär der Verstand auch anders nichts, als eine Handlung sonder Schranken:
Ohn' Absicht, sonder Zweck und Vorwurf, sich bloß bewegende Gedanken,
In einer stetigen Verwirrung ununterschieden, zu geschweigen,
Daß, bey verwirrter Phantasey, sich noch verwirrte Schlüsse zeigen
Und falsche Sätze folgen würden. So wird auch kein Gedächtniß können,
Von einer Kraft, was vorzustellen, sich jemals scheiden oder trennen.

(ed. 1744, IX, p. 467)

I think we may see, faintly pre-figured in this clumsily woven damask of theory of the elderly Brockes, Schiller's notion of 'die ruhige Gegenwart des Objekts.' In Brockes's poetry the thought is constantly associated with objects conjured up by memory and present in the imagination of the poet.—But Schiller's notion of the co-operation of the artist's faculties diverges widely from that of Brockes. It may be said that whereas in Schiller the unison was aesthetic, in Brockes it was moral. The intervention of Klopstock brought a vast change from the concepts and idioms of Brockes's generation to those of Schiller's. The unique amalgamation of thought and expression realized by Klopstock was a vivid new experience for those who followed him, and it was probably only because of Klopstock that Schiller was able to say with assurance and depth of conviction that the thought in a poem should be itself poetic. It often seems that for Brockes poetic expression meant a regular, orderly statement in verse of thoughts which were themselves concerned with the admired order of God's Universe, devised for man's benefit and pattern for man's behaviour. To us it must appear unnecessary and somewhat superficial to prolong, as he does, a kind of metrical recitative, working his way through a disquisition in rhyme, which, because the lines are often much too long, ceases to be an aide-mémoire; nor is the prosodic structure as yet moulded and modulated for a sudden quickening of the senses that they may apprehend more than the words in any other order could convey. Thus, very often the verses which Brockes has laboured or delighted to make may weary us, and the things he is presenting, imitating, will lose their contour, and the sense will be lost with it.

I have used the word recitative, distorting its meaning. Yet I hope, that as it may be more aptly applied to some of Brockes's compositions of musical intention, perhaps my use of it is not quite unpardonable. In some of the longer poems I note on the one hand the discursive parts, on the other either the closely-knit moral pronouncement with its clearer rhythm and its more effective mnemonic rhyme, or those verses where, sometimes quite unexpectedly, Brockes as I have said escapes from the palisade.

There is still, I think, a prevalent notion about him which tallies more or less closely with what Fulda wrote in his introduction in DNL XXXIX 2: 'es ist eigentlich nur das Kleine in der Natur, was er zu schildern sucht' (op. cit. p. 288). Fulda admits a slight modification, making special reference to the poem on calm after

111

the thunder-storm. But this is not enough. Brockes was interested not only in the frost on the window-panes, the blossom and the eerie shadow of the cherry-tree in the moonlight, the feathered atom that poured forth its song in the night, the forget-me-not, the midges born of worms on the pond, or 'the green myriads in the peopl'd grass'. He marvelled at all these things; but, schooled in the large and gloomy horrors of the Baroque, he found new amazement in the contemplation of space, of light, and of fire. The problem of light and the flame in Goethe's *Faust* has not yet, I think, been solved. It might be well to look to Brockes and his analysis of fire, at times pedestrian, at times curious:

> Viele neue Weisen meynen,
>   Daß fast alle Körperlein,
> Ob sie gleich nicht helle scheinen,
>   Voller Feuer-Theilchen seyn.
> Wenn die gnugsam kleinen Theile,
>   Nun in gnugsam schneller Eile,
> (sprechen sie) nur sind bewegt,
> Wird unfehlbar Feuer erregt.
>
> (*Ird. Vergn.* Hagedorn u. Wilckens, 510)

Thus the Brockes who doubtless knew about Becher, the phlogiston and other theories. In the same context there is Brockes, anticipating lines in Schiller's *Lied von der Glocke*:

> Schrecklich ist die Macht der Flammen,
>   Wenn sie wütet, anzusehn.
> Wenn sich Dampf und Feur zusammen
>   In verwirrte Kreise drehn,
> Sich mit Prasseln aufwärts schwingen,
> Sich gebähren, sich verschlingen,
>   Gleichet die geschwärzte Luft
>   Eines Feur-Ofens Gruft.
>
> (op. cit. 498)

At last the inevitable, disingenuous confession follows, confirming, so it would seem, the still common prejudice against Brockes:

> Mehr, als daß, vom Feur zu sagen,
> Steht in meinen Kräften nicht.

But let the prejudiced reader linger a little over the next half-dozen lines:

> Weil, wenn wir zufern es wagen,
>   Das durchdringendste Gesicht
> Doch auf die Natur erblindet.
> Keiner lebt, der sie ergründet,
>   Und wir scheinen bloß gemacht,
>   Zu bewundern ihre Pracht.

Of light, and of Brockes's painterly vision of its play upon colour, I have already spoken. What now of the early eighteenth century poet's exploration of space? 'So tritt das Raumgefühl im Verlauf der deutschen Lyrik bei Brockes plötzlich als eine Fragestellung von tiefgreifender Bedeutung auf. Der Eigenwert des Raumes tritt überall spürbar heraus . . . Er wird hier als von einem göttlichen Endzweck durchdrungen vorgestellt; von einem Zweck, der fast durchweg nicht auf den Nutzen für die Menschen zielt, sondern, ruhend in sich, das Universum trägt'. In an impressive monograph, only slightly marred by statistical zeal (' . . . der erste Band des *Irdischen Vergnügens*, der doch zu 16,5 Prozent sich mit dem neuen Raum beschäftigte . . .'!) Christof Junker made this significant claim for Brockes (*Das Weltraumbild in der deutschen Lyrik von Opitz bis Klopstock*, Germanische Studien, 1932, p. 45). For a twentieth century consideration of Brockes as poet it is of some importance to note that in the contemplation of space the somewhat fussy attempt to demonstrate the kindly intent of God's domestic economy in field, herbarium, and fishpond should give way to a sense of awe. We shall not, of course, expect to find in Brockes's expression of this new sense an entirely new pattern. In the poem *Die Sonne* from which I have quoted ('Allen Körpern, die wir kennen / Flößt dein Licht das Leben ein') he imagines for a moment the universe deprived of light: 'Welch ein Abgrund voller Schrecken . . .' From this beginning one might for a moment expect some intimation of the sudden impact of darkness, as in Milton: 'so thick a drop serene hath quench'd these orbs' which to a fantastic eighteenth century critic, born out of his time, seemed to convey the *sound* of darkness. Brockes was not born out of his time. He had to draw upon the shapes which poets of macabre imagination had conjured up in the century of his birth:

> Schwärzer als des Abgrunds Rachen
> Wär die Welt ohn' deinen Strahl,
> Ein entsetzlich Nest der Drachen,
> Ein verwildert Mörderthal . . .

(see DNL XXXIX 2, p. 317)

Instead of the 'nirgends nichts' through which Faust later had to find his way to 'die Mütter' Brockes had to people his lightless chaos with lurid shapes. But then suddenly he uses a word that carries us back to ancient legend:

> Nichts als ew'ge Wüsteneien,
> Wo nur Eulen würden schreien,
> Wo Gespenster Bürger sind,
> Blinder Larven Labyrinth.

(loc. cit.)

'Eulen'—there is the doleful cry of the screech-owl dwelling in the wilderness among the spirits of the dead—Lilith who brought terror to children in Old Testament times.

But much, much more impressive is the poem *Das Firmament*, on which Blackall (op. cit.) has made very valuable comment.

> Als jüngst mein Auge sich in die Saphirne Tieffe,
> Die weder Grund, noch Strand, noch Ziel, noch End' umschränkt,
> Ins unerforschte Meer des holen Luftraums senkt',
> Und mein verschlungner Blick bald hie bald dahinlieffe
> Doch immer tieffer sank: entsatzte sich mein Geist,
> Es schwindelte mein Aug', es stockte meine Seele
> Ob der unendlichen, unmäßig-tieffen Höle,
> Die wol mit Recht, ein Bild der Ewigkeiten heißt,
> So nur aus Gott allein, ohn' End' und Anfang, stammen.
> Es schlug des Abgrunds Raum, wie eine dicke Flut
> Des Boden-losen Meers auf sinkend Eisen thut,
> In einem Augenblick, auf meinen Geist zusammen.
> Die ungeheure Gruft des tieffen dunklen Lichts,
> Der lichten Dunkelheit, ohn' Anfang, ohne Schranken,
> Verschlang so gar die Welt, begrub selbst die Gedanken;
> Mein ganzes Wesen ward ein Staub, ein Punct, ein Nichts
> Und ich verlor mich selbst.
>
> (*Ird. Vergn.* I; see Blackall op. cit. p. 246)

This is, I think, the kind of imagination which Schiller may have been looking for in Klopstock and did not find. It expresses even in its strong negation of plastic terms the panic state which we recognize in lines towards the end of *Der Spaziergang*:

> Wild ist es hier und schauerlich öd'. Im einsamen Luftraum
>   Hängt nur der Adler und knüpft an das Gewölke die Welt.
> Hoch herauf bis zu mir trägt keines Windes Gefieder
>   Den verlorenen Schall menschlicher Mühen und Lust.
> Bin ich wirklich allein?

The fear of solitude gives way to the solace of nature's presence:

> ... In deinen Armen, an deinem
> Herzen wieder, Natur, ach! und es war nur ein Traum.

From the 'bodenlose Tiefe' in which the 'Phantast' may lose himself, the poet of the *Spaziergang* is saved by the knowledge that through the millennia nature is constant. The poet of *Das Firmament* makes known his goal, his haven, in the paradox of his final words addressed to the void and to God:

> Allein, o heylsams Nichts! glückseliger Verlust!
> Allgegenwärt'ger GOTT, in Dir fand ich mich wieder.

Thus his faith itself sets a limit from which his anguished imagination draws back in wholesome assurance. The God in whom he believes has placed him in a world of articulate order and has endowed him with senses to perceive its myriad perfections. The other part of his endowment is intelligence and the gift of articulate speech. With an active vocabulary probably richer than that of any contemporary poet, and an intricately modulated syntax, Brockes set himself to convey to others what his senses told him of the divine order of things. Recognizing again and again the limits of his power, he yet persevered, and with genial unconcern for logic, he longed for the limitless delight of the blessed spirits who, he supposed, must have complete perception:

> Welch ein Seelen Lust muß sel'ge Geister rühren,
> Wenn sie mit geistigen verkläreten Gesichtern,
> Und nicht mit Augen nur; nein ganz,
> Den Strahlen-reichen Morgen-Glanz
> Von so viel tausend Sonnen-Lichtern,
> In hundert tausend Welten spüren!

> (*Ird. Vergn.* Hagedorn u. Wilckens, p. 79)

Brockes's pre-occupation with imagined chaos was inevitably restrained by his belief in an intelligent order in physical matter and in life. By this belief he was shielded from the conjecture that an extension of perception would reveal only more discord, more suffering, more evil than man comprehends. Therefore he could happily imagine the perfectibility of perception and could not even share the vision which Vondel had known in the middle of the previous century: man in his innocence and in the limitation of his sphere envied by celestial spirits:

> Geen Engel, onder ons, zoo zoet een adem heeft,
> Gelijck de frissche geest, die hier den mensch bejegent,
> Het aengezicht verquickt, en alles streelt, en zegent.

> (Joost van den Vondel, *Lucifer*, 1654)

What baffled Brockes in his eager study of phenomena was not awareness of the illusion of his senses but awareness that they were incomplete. He was possessed by a notion of quantity. Incompleteness he found also in the instrument of expression. There were 'infinite Numbers, Delicacies, Smells, / With Hues on Hues Expression cannot paint'. Again and again in Brockes's verses the stones and the flowers and the insects, all the great and little wonders of God's Creation are declared, 'unbeschreiblich'. But his efforts to articulate his response to the things he saw and heard and smelt and tasted reveal a limitation of which he was perhaps never fully conscious. He trusted language over-much to provide him with integers of meaning, and could not trust himself for long on the other planes of language to which later generations of poets have been pursued. At times we see him as the amateur scholar, limited by the zeal of his age to clarify and explain, at other times as precursor of poets in the romantic age, lost in a wonder more confused than his and murmuring in melancholy amazement: 'unaussprechlich, geheimnisvoll'.

Did Brockes, and some of his contemporaries, perhaps find a way among other ways of recognizing that that half-sentence which has been echoing in our ears since this morning's discussion cannot ever be completed, since its form requires an intelligible correlative beyond the conception of mind and therefore beyond the formulation of syntax: 'Die Wirklickheit ist etwas, das . . .'?

SHORT BIBLIOGRAPHY
(see also titles in text)

Works of Brockes:

Irdisches Vergnügen in Gott, 1721–48.

Auszug der vornehmsten Gedichte, Hagedorn u. Wilckens, 1763.

Harmonische Himmelslust, 1741.

Beurtheilung einiger Reim-Endungen . . . absonderlich in Ober- und Nieder-Sachsen, in C. F. Weichmann's *Poesie der Nieder-Sachsen*, 1721.

Herrn B. H. Brockes . . . übersetzte Jahreszeiten des Herrn Thomson, 1745.

Critical and comparative material:

CLOSS, A., *The Genius of the German Lyric, An Historical Survey of its Formal and Metaphysical Values*, 1962.

COLLEVILLE, M., *La renaissance du lyrisme dans la poésie allemande*, 1936.

JUNKER, CHR., *Das Weltraumbild in der deutschen Lyrik von Opitz bis Klopstock*, 1932.

MAACK, R., *Über Popes Einfluss auf die Idylle und das Lehrgedicht in Deutschland*, 1895.

PFUND, H. W., *Studien zu Wort und Stil bei Brockes*, Ottendorfer Memorial Series of Germanic Monographs, New York, 1935.

POPE, A., *Works* in 6 vols., London, 1764.

THOMSON, J., *The Four Seasons*, crit. ed. O. Zippel, Palaestra LXVI, 1908.

TILLOTSON, G., *Pope and Human Nature*, 1958.

Discussion

Asked by *Closs* what link there was between Brockes's verse and lyrical poetry, the speaker said the link was to be found in Brockes's 'escapes' from his usual framework; Brockes's occasional irrational response was akin to our modern experience.

Böckmann spoke of the poet's different view of his calling in different centuries. Opitz regarded himself as a (lyrical) poet, but no modern reader would agree.

Böckmann also referred to the 'Neujahrsgedichte', which showed how Brockes had discarded the geocentric view of the universe and was very occupied with the idea of many worlds in space, and the question whether Christ must redeem all these worlds as well as our own. Böckmann compared Brockes's factual statements to the recitative, and his praise of God to the aria in a cantata.

Mainland agreed and pointed out that behind Brockes's anxious enquiring there was always the assurance of ultimate harmony.

FOURTH SESSION

Chairman: Professor J. ALER

Professor **P. BÖCKMANN**: Eighteenth century German hymnic verse.

Chairman: Professor **W. F. MAINLAND**

Professor **H. B. GARLAND**: Schiller the Revisionist—The poet's second thoughts.

Eighteenth century German hymnic verse

by

PAUL BÖCKMANN

In the eighteenth century a profound change in German Lyric poetry took place, which had its effective influence far into the nineteenth century. This change appeared to exercise no favourable influence on hymnic verse. Even more, one can say that since that time hymnic poetry has appeared only occasionally. It could expand only as long as man found himself in a close relationship with a stronghold of faith so that he could worship the divinity. But the conditions for this were lacking so long as the findings of science had their influence upon the concept of life. Thus it seems only natural that the lyric poetry of modern times moved away more and more from the ecclesiastical-Christian hymn-poetry, using completely different means of expression. When, nevertheless, hymn-poetry was revived by certain poets, it could throw light not only upon the understanding of the problems and possibilities of lyric poetry, but also clear up its relation to religious traditions and experiences.

Originally the word 'hymn' denoted a song of praise of a god, corresponding to the Greek lexical meaning of hymnic (ὑμνέω)—similar to laud, extol, praise. Thus the old Christian songs of praise to the trinitarian God could at the same time be called hymns and, in the sense of the psalms, could turn thanking and praising to the Creator. The apostrophe to Christ, as the Lord and Saviour of lost mankind, in the form of a prayer of thanksgiving and petition or of praise, remains the determining factor for the diction and mode of expression. This is the case in the hymn of Ambrosius:

> Intende, qui regis Israel,
> Super Cherubim qui sedes
> Apare Ephraem coram, excita
> Potentiam tuam et veni.

> O höre, König Israels
> Der über Cherubim du thronst,
> Erschein dem Ephraim, richte auf,
> Dein Reich der Herrlichkeit und komm!

Throughout all the centuries of Christianity this tone has lived on, and since Luther has also been taken over into the Protestant Hymn:

> Aus tiefer Not schrei ich zu Dir!
> Herr Gott erhör mein Rufen,
> Dein gnädig Ohren kehr zu mir
> Und meiner Bitt sei offen!

Accordingly, for Optiz, the songs of praise which we 'should sing to our God' are still called hymns. Only in the eighteenth century was this connexion with the Christian tradition of church-song lost, so that Gottsched scarcely used the word 'Hymn' and only spoke of 'Odes or Songs' which celebrate the fame of heroes. Then, however, the humanistic tradition made its presence felt and by the time of the paper of Longinus 'Concerning the Sublime', the longing for a new dithyrambic or rhapsodic style is awoken, which takes Horace as its model and soon looks back also to Pindar. Through the efforts of Klopstock it once more became possible to unite this enthusiastic tone—determined as it was by the classical ode-strophe—to the world of Christian belief and to give the office of Poet a particular dignity. He referred as much to the image of the Greek sibylline poet, the Vates, as he did to that of the psalmist, in accordance with the double vision of his lyric creation, which on the one hand attained its particular status and effective strength through his odes, and on the other hand, sought once again in his 'Geistliche Lieder' to meet the needs of the protestant divine service. According to the discovered list of his books, Hölderlin was in possession of Klopstock's 'Geistliche Lieder' with the introduction on 'hymns' and 'songs' (*Gesang* and *Lied*). Here he not only found the remark that 'the imitation of the Psalms is the highest aim which a poet can set himself to attain and which the reader is permitted to demand of him', but also a distinction between the 'sublime style' of the canto and the 'more gentle manner' of the song. Both should move the heart and have as their content thanksgiving and adoration. With this, expectations are expressed which remain important for Hölderlin. This extolling and thanksgiving in the sublime form of the canto not only gives the subject to his lines but also that tone peculiar to him, which distinguishes his manner from the expression of experiences and emotions which is found in Goethe's poetry. At the same time he certainly sees himself faced with the task of testing anew the claim and possibilities of such an act of thanksgiving. Whereas Klopstock could content himself with animating the traditional doctrines and values of Christian belief in revealed religion with his own power of feeling, and reconciling them with a new knowledge of nature, gained as it was from Physics and Astronomy, Hölderlin had to seek new paths for himself.

Klopstock distinguished between 'Oden' and 'Geistliche Lieder'. When Hölderlin published his first poems in the 'Swabian Poetical Annual for the Year 1792', the 'Musenalmanach', he labelled them 'Hymns'. These are the only verses which he expressly called hymns and which personify and address the ideals of human endeavour as Goddesses. At the beginning is the 'Hymne an die Muse' which is followed by the hymns 'An die Freiheit' and the 'Göttin der Harmonie' and further yet in the 'Poetische Blumenlese fürs Jahr 1793', the 'Hymnen an die Menschheit', the 'Schönheit', the 'Freundschaft', the 'Liebe' and the 'Genius der Jugend'. These titles ignore all Christian topics which still remained decisive for Klopstock, particularly for the great poems in free rhythms of 1758/59. Titles such as 'Dem Allgegenwärtigen', 'Das Anschauen Gottes', 'Der Erbarmer' but also the 'Frühlingsfeier' make this clear. Referring to Klopstock's odes, Herder said: 'Most of his lyrical works approach the hymn'; he termed them 'monologues of the heart' in which 'sentiments' flow forth until a new series of ideas stirs us with a 'sweet pensive narcosis'.

The hymn is regarded here as that type of poem, which is distinguished by its heightened sensibility, its particular emotion or by intensity of pathos. It should give the utmost facility of emotional expression and is therefore on the same level as the 'Erlebnisgedicht' in Goethe's sense of the word; and Goethe's hymns also match up to these demands: not only in 'Wanderers Sturmlied' or 'An Schwager Kronos', but also in 'Prometheus' and 'Ganymed' is a heightened self-reliance presented in a form taken up completely with the portrayal of personal emotions which according to its essence was intended for different purposes, referring to another world and thereby to the distancing of veneration and sanctification. One may certainly interpret Goethe's hymns in Herder's sense of 'monologues of the heart' as if they were determined by Herder's commentaries to Klopstock's odes. But Klopstock's own language has a purpose other than the expression of sensibility; and also the early hymns of Hölderlin appear as inadequate when compared with those of Goethe, if the attitude of praise is disregarded. Therefore it is necessary to follow more precisely the path which leads from Klopstock's enthusiastic ode via a few informative connecting links to Hölderlin's early hymns in order to characterize the intellectual conditions of his later lyrics. Hölderlin's 'modus operandi' is only too often insufficiently recognized as standing in a close relationship to the endeavours of other poets of his age. This is particularly obvious with regard to a hymnody of nature, which after Klopstock appeared above all in Stäudlin's 'Schwäbischem Musen-Almanach', which leads from Stäudlin via Conz to the young Neuffer, but had also already been prepared for by the Count Friedrich Leopold zu Stolberg. There are the stanzas 'Der Dichter an die Natur' by Stäudlin, but also a 'Hymne an die Schönheit' (about 1788) and a poem 'An die Ruhe' (1782). There is a poem by Conz 'An Klopstock', that was composed immediately after his visit to the poet in 1792, and culminates in the lines:

> In seinen Liedern lernt ich mich selbst verstehn;
> Hier lebten meine Träume, mein namenlos
> Verfliessendes Gefühl fand Sprache,
> Stand in Gestalt mir vorm trunken Blicke.

Neuffer's first poem had already appeared in the 'Almanach' for the year 1787 about which Stäudlin, as editor, remarked that he hoped readers would approve his publishing this ode 'as the work of a seventeen-year-old youth'. This forms perhaps the most visible connecting link between Klopstock's language in his odes and Hölderlin's beginnings, all the more so since Neuffer clung to these lines his whole life through, prefacing his 1816 edition of poetry with them—admittedly in a revised form—under the title 'Naturweihe' and concluding the edition of 1827 with them in a newly revised form. Neuffer in his later 'Hymne an die Natur' takes up the subject once more. This concept of nature became a leading one, and ousted the traditional concept of God to an ever-increasing degree so that the only 'traditional hymnic elements' left are those of celebration and thanksgiving. Behind these various endeavours lies the one basic question of whether the glorification of God can be transferred to nature or whether subjective expression of emotion must take its place.

This question is not only important for the German development, but is closely related to the contemporary European intellectual climate, and the new perception of nature founded by Newton. In 1755 Kant had treated his 'Allgemeine Naturgeschichte und Theorie des Himmels' 'in accordance with basic Newtonian principles' enclosing verses not only by Albrecht von Haller but also by Pope and Addison. From Haller's 'Ode über die Ewigkeit' (1743) he quotes the verses:

> Unendlichkeit! Wer misset dich?
> Bei dir sind Welten Tag und Menschen Augenblicke.

He uses Pope's 'Essay on Man' in a translation of Brockes (1740):

> Welch eine Kette, die von Gott den Anfang nimmt . . .
> Von dem Unendlichen zu dir, von dir zum Nichts!

> Vast chain of Being! which from God began . . .
> . . . from Infinite to thee,
> From thee to Nothing . . .

Addison's verses (quoted in Gottsched's translation) also praise God as the creator of infinitive nature:

> O Herr so gross bist du,
> Dich nach Würdigkeit zu loben, reicht die Ewigkeit nicht zu.

There is even a 'free imitation' of Pope's 'Universal Prayer' in the 'Blumenlese' for the year 1793 edited by Stäudlin, an ode, published in 1738 as a sort of explanation of the 'Essays on Man', discussing the relation between man, Nature and God with regard to the infinite space of the world. Here the veneration of God seems only possible 'within the boundless temple of nature'—as it is translated in the German version:

> Dir schallen tausendfach der Wesen Chöre,
> Dir wallt der Opferduft von jeder Flur;
> Dir brennen alle Sonnen als Altäre,
> Im grenzenlosen Tempel der Natur.

This corresponds with the stanza:

> To thee, whose Temple is all Space,
>   Whose Altar Earth, Sea, Skies.
> One Chorus let all Being raise,
>   All Nature's Incense rise!

The hymnic mode of address asserts itself in all these cases, but only so that nature can appear as the only real force moving mankind, and the only force to be explored

by him, a force in which patterns of legitimacy and necessity prevail and everything is interrelated. Only from this standpoint can reference be made back to God
as the Prime Mover, the Soul who fills the body of Nature—as Pope says:

> All are but parts of one stupendous whole,
> Whose body Nature is, and God the soul.

This change in religious ideas is clearly of decisive importance for hymnic poetry
and the manner in which it can even turn to a personal divinity in petition, thanksgiving and praise.

At first Klopstock's procedure of celebrating God as the creator of nature remains
effective but only by replacing—in accordance with modern science—the geocentric concept by a cosmic one. The ode 'Dem Allgegenwärtigen' speaks with the
attitude of the man adoring and giving thanks, addressing the Father as the Infinitive and Omnipresent, recognizing Him as the Creator in His creation and in all
manifestation, in the mighty rushing of the gale, as in the flower—'Gott machte
sie'. To him the following praise is due:

> Halleluja dem Schaffenden!
> Ich hebe mein Aug' auf und seh'
> Und, siehe der Herr ist überall!
> Sonnen, euch, und o Erden, Euch, Monde der Erden,
> Erfüllet rings um mich des Unendlichen Gegenwart!

The apostrophe to the suns, earths and moons is only justifiable because the infinite
is present in them. And against these worlds—'incalculable even to the angels'—
man's soul possesses a particular dignity, since through Christ it gained a belief in
its own immortality. Thus the apostrophe to the Father is carried on to the Son:

> Ohn ihn wär der Gedanke deiner Gegenwart
> Grauen mir vor dem allmächtigen Unbekannten.

This theologically based order is re-established, because it recognizes man as man
and does not surrender him to an overwhelming nihilistic nature. At the same time,
however, nature as an organ of the Creator determines the whole range of presentation; the poets accompany it, as in the Wingolf-Ode:

> Aus allen golden Zeiten begleiten dich, Natur, die Dichter.

Count Friedrich Leopold zu Stolberg goes further; he writes a hymn 'An die
Sonne' (1778) and one 'An die Erde' and now expressly selects the title 'Hymne',
apparently as a result of translating Homeric Hymns to the Gods; this being further
strengthened by the fact that he also uses the hexameter. Here the celebratory
address to natural phenomena is carried out on a wide front, as if the sun could be
evoked as a mythical force and as if the powers of the 'heavenly youth' were to
become worthy of praise:

LIBRARY

> Segnend strahlst du herauf, und bräutlich kränzet die Erde
> Dir die flammende Schläfe mit tauendem Purpurgewölke.

It has been justly pointed out how close such verses already come to the solemn language of Hölderlin. Here one's attention is drawn to the forms which determine the life of nature, to the mutual relations between the ancient elements, between light, earth and sea:

> Sonne, lächle der Erd, und geuss aus strahlender Urne
> Leben auf die Natur!

But then however Stolberg returns to the tradition established by Klopstock. The natural existence does not lie in itself but has to be interpreted with reference to the Creator. He stands above the suns which he hurled like a sower of seeds— 'millions at once'—like a judged eciding their fate: 'God's judgement awaits you, God's mercy'. The hymn to nature therefore changes into a moral lesson, in which mankind is reminded of its transitoriness. The peculiar problem of hymnic language emerges clearly. The Christian concept of life forbids any hymnic elevation of that which is of this earth and prevents an approach to the mythical word of antiquity, and perception of the basic patterns of nature calls into question the traditional concepts of the creation and robs the utterance of thanksgiving of the other world.

With Gotthold Friedrich Stäudlin, editor of the 'Schwäbischen Musenalmanach' since 1781, new intermediary forms appear in which the hymnic tone becomes still more independent of the evocation of God the Creator. It is the poet's wish to rise to the dazzling heights of the German 'Bardenchor' and to be 'Liebling der Natur': the 'divine nature' together with the 'goddess of beaming beauty' may consecrate him, so that he becomes a 'Singer of God', who 'tears the soul heavenwards in the fervent heat of devotion' ('Mein Wunsch', 1788). He evokes the 'fiery souls of youth' in the Ode 'An die Jünglinge meines Vaterlandes' referring to Kepler as the predecessor of Newton, as Hölderlin on his part will do in his Kepler-Ode of 1789. Hymnic style and the Law of Gravity enter into a peculiar correspondence. Nature is evoked as the basis of personal existence; the conditions of its intellectual efficacy are to be found in its beauty. The poet implores it:

> Die du mir mehr als Mutter bist, . . .
> Vernimm . . . des Sohnes flehenden Gesang.

He extols it:

> Schön bist du, Bildnerin Natur!
> Schön ist dein Himmel, deine Flur.

She communicates to him 'peace of soul' and 'beauteous simplicity'. With this the celebration of nature leads on to the celebration of those intellectual forces which are characteristic of it, as similarly occurs in Stäudlin's 'Hymne an die Schönheit'.

Admittedly the old conception of God the Creator is still active in the background, when beauty is evoked as 'first daughter of the Creator'; but it is more important that the beauty should be raised as a spiritual sun above the sensuously visible and be honoured itself as a goddess:

> Dich lobzusingen waget der Erdensohn ...
> Heil dir, der Schönheit Göttin ...
> Du überstrahlst die Sonne dort oben! Du
> Bist selbst die schönre Sonne der Schöpfung!

She has co-operated with her 'heavenly friend', wisdom, ever since 'the myriads of worlds sprang out of the revolving womb of chaos'. Thus the attempt occurs in the case of Stäudlin to relate the celebration and address to a 'Du', to an active intellectual force in nature. The personification of beauty or wisdom as goddesses, a correspondence to which is to be found in the 'the goddess of melancholy' or 'Peace' in other odes, has its origin in the embarrassment caused by the disappearance of God the Creator as an 'object' (the 'Du') of praise and thanksgiving. With Conz the first result of this situation is a return to a personal inner world. But even with him the heart is not merely satisfied with expression of feeling; the hymnic language is addressed rather to his own mind as a 'thou' which as a 'divine spark' has to earn the praise for itself in order to comply with its exalted vocation. At the same time there is a threat of a complete loss of contact with the world, as if the poet can no longer raise himself above his personal distress but only demand of himself that he struggles for immortality, whether through heavenly or earthly fame. The poem 'Sein oder Nichtsein' inquires after the Ego, in the face of the 'great puzzle of Nature', in order to gain a support against transitoriness. Time after time it gets lost in the labyrinth of questions and finally ends with the utterance which sounds as Christian as it does pantheistic: 'There is no death in the Creation'. This type of poetry is more suited to reflexion on the disquieted self than that incantation which directs the self beyond itself and—in giving thanks—turns upon the greater 'Thou'. It is only a natural consequence of this that a later poem published by Conz in 1803— 'Das Wort der Natur'—no longer ventures to address nature but lets nature speak to the poet, and refers to the unity of man and nature. Now nature speaks thus:

> Eines bin ich und du bist mit mir Eines! ...
> Meinen Geist erfasset der Geist allein!

This, too, is then an utterance based on reflexion, which leaves no room for the voice of enthusiasm. Apparently a revival of hymnic language—in the Klopstockian mode—could only be successful so long as the turning to nature and her sublimity could still be related to the old conception of God as Creator of the world, so that the apostrophe of the 'Du' might retain its specific meaning and justification. The more, however, that mankind sought a conception of itself exclusively within its association with Nature, the more it saw itself referred on the one hand to concrete perception, and on the other to the subjective reality of his feelings without being able to attach himself to a 'Du' to which thanks were due.

Even Hölderlin's friend Neuffer from Tübingen was not successful in escaping this contradictory situation, although he had a poetic talent of his own and appropriated the hymnic tone even before Hölderlin in the poem 'Die Natur'. His 'Loblied' has as its aim the praise of 'God's miracles', confessing to the amicable union of souls and condemning all aggressive action, for nature awakes 'a feeling of goodness'. The moral undertone is joined here with the inclination towards the Idyllic and makes questionable the sublime tone of the beginning:

> Hier, o Natur! In deinem Tempel
> Höre des glühenden Jünglings Loblied,
> Den du begeisterst.

The antithesis between the highly-strung tone of inspiration and the practical sense involved in middle class solidity is intensified still more in the later drafts of the poem. The result is that the hymnic forms of address act more as a poetic embellishment, which, by appealing to 'Mother Nature', transfigures patriotic self sacrifice, marital fidelity, feeling for nature, piety and consciousness of duty. The last draft, which was published forty years after the first, is completely satisfied to equate nature with that voice of the heart which man bears within him as the 'Holy pledge of the Godhead'. From those poetic impulses which grew up out of the collaboration and confrontation of the Christian belief in a revealed religion and modern natural science, only a general striving towards harmonization remains, which uses the hymnic style more out of tradition than out of any inner necessity.

It is only when one surveys these different endeavours towards a revival of the sublime style in the lyric as a song of praise, that Hölderlin's achievement in its singular greatness becomes truly manifest. He is the only one who bursts out of these mutually exclusive alternatives and at the same time, therefore, substantially extends and modifies the basic lyrical attitude which Goethe had achieved. He does not content himself with an expression of personal experience but perseveres in a kind of poetry which is concerned with thanksgiving and celebration. He too has to learn by experience that this celebration, this naming, no longer fits into a commensurable order of things and is not related to a firmly defined object. He sees himself banished from the Christian belief in revealed religion and is no longer able to fulfil his task through the glorification of God the Creator. Nor is he content to celebrate the elemental forces of life as such, although apostrophes to Father Ether, Mother Earth, to the God of the Seas and the God of the Sun are frequently interwoven into his verses. And also the intellectual forces of peace, truth or beauty, friendship or love, do not form the subject of his poems as mythical figures as if they could objectify themselves in the form of stories and incidents. Hölderlin's true daring shows itself rather in the fact that his utterances of thanksgiving and glorification are not able to be directed as they were, to any firmly defined object. The 'Du' to whom he speaks denies itself to him even while he addresses it. This signifies two things. On the one hand this form of language affirms that man is not able to leave the self–thou-relationship as an interlocutory relation. The language—by its very nature—forces him into the 'Du'-apostrophe. This relationship is not bound by the answer of the Du, but continues when man, as the being on whom life places claims, and who is searching for himself, is urged to speak. On the other hand this form of speech makes clear that the hymnic apostrophe always regards this relation as a mere relation and not as an object beyond experience or as a mere hypostasis of feeling. Hölderlin's poetry neither tells of a world of gods nor creates any form of myth; he neither revives an old one nor invents one of his own. The mythical name as a holy name does not signify anything existing, but has its reality in the function of evocation and naming of that which is only real in the relation of the self to its world and as a relationship. Just as love to another person can affirm itself by the calling of their name, the loving participation in the existence of this relation is assured by its name. It is not language as an empty sound but as a force of designation which determines Hölderlin's utterance of thanksgiving and adds weight to the hymnic form of speech.

The decisive step which took him beyond the Klopstockian manner followed by his fellow-poets manifests itself in the poem 'Der Wanderer', which he sent (together with the poem 'An den Äther') to Schiller for the 'Horen' in June, 1797 and which in the summer of 1800 he once more treated, so that by comparing both versions the path he took in three years can be surveyed. The really illuminating thing is the manner in which the apostrophe to nature plays an eminent part. He is content neither with a general praise nor with the accentuation of spiritual forces or moral expectations but aims at the inner relationship of man to his world. He experienced it as an elemental connexion which he could not leave. Thus it is not sufficient just to give expression to subjective emotion or to be content with an objective description; the only possibility remaining is to assure himself of the relationships in which man finds himself in an address of praise. The wanderer returning to his native land no longer portrays his feeling for landscape, since the peculiar intercourse of man and nature only takes form in the apostrophe. The utterance of thanksgiving impresses itself on the form of the language and becomes the main aim of the poem, but in such a way that it apprehends the living fullness of existential relations. 'Nature' no longer appears as just the keyword which leads to an understanding of life but as 'homelike nature' which constitutes the concrete reality of the individual. Thus the poem culminates in the evocation of this 'homelike nature', or more precisely, of the 'Native Earth' and 'Native Sun':

> Wie Aurora den Tithon umfängst du in lächelnder Blüte
> Warm und fröhlich, wie einst, Vaterlandserde, den Sohn ...
> Und die Pfade rötest du mir, es wärmt mich und spielt mir
> Um das Auge, wie sonst, Vaterlandssonne! dein Licht ...
> Heimatliche Natur! Wie bist du treu mir geblieben!

The fervour and solemnity of the apostrophe become audible, since all native figures are at the same time 'witnesses of the eternal, beautiful life of the world' and the homecomer knows himself to be a son of this land, linked in love to it and relates it as a 'Du' to himself. The frequent verbal compounds with 'um', 'umfangen', 'umspielen', 'umarmen', 'umsäuseln', etc ..., reflect that peculiar participation of man in an existence related to him, in which and through which the 'ego' comes to know itself. All arousal of emotion can only be understood in the context of the relationship with the 'Du' of the living world, so that the sorrows of separation are still reflected back on it and make the unity perceptible as something lost or to be regained. A nature which appertains closely to mankind has taken the place of something factual and objective.

In the ultimate version of 'Der Wanderer' this attitude to language has an even more definite effect, above all in the closing stanza which heightens the tone of celebration still more, since the isolated ego only continues to find consolation and refuge in the apostrophe to the Gods. Above all the individual manifestations of life, the elemental forces remain the trusted escorts, to whom man knows himself to be attached:

> Und so bin ich allein. Du aber, über den Wolken,
> Vater des Vaterlands! Mächtiger Äther! Und du
> Erd' und Licht! ihr einigen drei, die walten und lieben,
> Ewige Götter! Mit euch brechen die Bande mir nie.

No longer are only 'homelike nature' or 'heavenly Homeland' mentioned but the eternal Gods are referred to and with that the concept of the 'present Olympus' from Hyperion is taken up once more. The Ether as 'Father of the Fatherland' signifies a still more extensive realm than the 'native earth' and corresponds to the 'Homeland of Nature' which includes all existence and thus also all life within the homeland and 'blooms eternally young amidst all your senses'. Thus the mentioning of the gods has no intention of turning the elements into myth but of referring the attitude of evocation to the widest sphere of existence and of recognizing the living connexion between the particular and general. For these elements have always accompanied the wanderer:

> Ausgegangen von euch, mit euch auch bin ich gewandert
> Euch ihr Freudigen, euch bring! ich erfahrner zurück.

Remembrance and Thanksgiving are fulfilled in the evocation, through which the relationship of man to existence, which has already been found is affirmed. But at the same time it is important that both versions are not satisfied with the apostrophe to the forces of nature—be they patriotic and homelike or elemental and divine—but only find life and fulfilment in celebrating the alliance of all being by arousing the individual phenomena. The solemnity of the verses arises not only through the express form of address but above all through the naming of multifarious things with which mankind is concerned and to which he bears a loving relationship. The country with mighty river and mountain range, plants and animals appears as a living entity, to which belongs the village with the mill and the house with the garden where the wanderer grew up and which now receives him back again. Nature and mankind belong together as hand and tree when the former plucks the fruit. Man grows out of the nature which nourishes him, and remains subject to her. The verses evoke this connexion by the manner of their naming. The way leads from the broad to the narrow, from the countryside into the house, to the window and back once more into the broader picture. The use of domestic imagery turns into an act of thanksgiving, since it only affirms the connexion of man with his world.

> Und am glänzenden See, wo der Hain das offene Hoftor
> Übergrünt und das Licht golden die Fenster umspielt,
> Dort empfängt mich das Haus und des Gartens heimliches Dunkel,
> Wo mit den Pflanzen mich einst liebend der Vater erzog ...
> Schwer ist worden indes von Früchten dunkel mein Kirschbaum
> Und der pflückenden Hand reichen die Zweige sich selbst.

The interplay of all life, in which man participates and which determines him is evoked and gives a new sphere to hymnic language. Thus the basic element is found which gives Hölderlin's poetry its particular tone. But this language of praise and thanksgiving belongs to a contradictory and sorrowful dynamic of life and therefore remains attached to a peculiarly elegiac approach. No essence of life as such can guarantee secure possession; there is no ultimate target for human activity nor any objective world of gods reigning over mankind. This existential unrest belongs to the determining basic experiences. The constant element appears only in continual flux and in the respective limitation of relationships.

In order to preserve the claim of this celebratory naming it must remain connected to the elegiac lament, the subject of which is the unity which is either lost or continually being questioned. Thus the unification of thanksgiving with the expression of sorrow is only the clearest sign that all mythical names within the poem remain directed towards the correlation between man and his world.

For this reason it may be understood that praising and thanksgiving become more subordinate in Hölderlin's later poems and lose in explicitness and exactitude. The turning towards the gods arises rather from the attitude of a deserted or an expectant man, who sees in them members of a past or a future world. The address to those forces of life which move men is concealed or deflected in a peculiar manner. Admittedly the Archipelagus-poem gains its solemn ring through the extensive apostrophe of the 'God of the Seas', the 'Father', the 'Mighty One', the 'Divine One', the 'Mourning God' who pervades the world of the Ionic Islands and communicates with all other elements. But those men who sang their gratitude to him have passed away and the present race leaves the Divine Ones unsung; it is a lonely man who looks back to the past in order to prepare for the future, uttering those words of praise which celebrate the 'God of the Seas'. It is only in this context that the evocation preserves its claim. In 'Brod und Wein' the laudatory expression is almost completely concealed by the elegiac contemplation, as if the poet could no longer say it himself but only evoke it in the name of the Greek past:

> Vater Äther! So rief's und flog von Zunge zu Zunge.

The evocation is preserved for a past or future humanity and becomes effective only in the attitude of expectation:

> Denn wir sind herzlos, Schatten, bis unser
> Vater Äther erkannt jedem und allen gehört.

The more the celebration of the divine becomes limited by the distress of man, or is called into question, the more the attitude of questioning replaces that of evocation, as if these unanswered questions were the proper condition for any hymnic inspiration:

> Aber die Thronen, wo? die Tempel und wo die Gefäße,
> Wo mit Nektar gefüllt, Göttern zu Lust der Gesang? . . .
> Warum schweigen auch sie, die alten heil'gen Theater? . . .
> Und wozu Dichter in dürftiger Zeit?

The evocation retreats behind a questioning which leaves room for contemplation and enables a gnomic-proverbial manner of speech to be adopted. The poem only aims more secretly at the evocation and emphasizes in its place its own position in time between the 'no longer' and the 'not yet'. Thus the peculiar state of suspense in which mythical names in Hölderlin find themselves is merely reinforced and the dialogical form of speech is still more directed at the correlation of man and world.

For Hölderlin the expression of self can always be traced back to the 'Du' apostrophe. In this way therefore he not only confronts his poem with all the traditions of religious poetry but at the same time plunges into profound altercations with modern poetry. He not only wishes to write how he feels, but to render thanksgiving feasible in poetic utterance. He is, however, also aware of the difficulties which such a demand entails, and mentions them quite often, particularly decisively in the elegy 'Heimkunft' which was composed on the return trip from Hauptweil in Switzerland in 1801. He calls to the intermediaries of the 'Great Father', the 'Angels of the Year' or the 'House', who, as the 'Heavenly Ones' brings joy to 'all veins of life'. But then, instead of the hymnic utterance, only the elegiac question remains for him:

> Wenn wir segnen das Mahl, wen darf ich nennen und wenn wir
> ruhn vom Leben des Tags, saget, wie bring ich den Dank?
> Nenn' ich die Hohen dabei? Unschickliches liebet ein Gott nicht,
> Ihn zu fassen, ist fast unsre Freude zu klein.
> Schweigen müssen wir oft; es fehlen heilige Namen,
> Herzen schlagen und doch bleibet die Rede zurück?

There is no room left for a God as Creator moving the world from outside; nor does a pantheistic equation of God and world remain; it is in living nature that man meets those realities of the soul which determine his relations with the attendant sphere of life and cause him to speak of the Godhead. Thus Hölderlin says: 'Weder aus sich selbst allein, noch einzig aus den Gegenständen, die ihn umgeben, kann der Mensch erfahren, daß mehr als Maschinengang, daß ein Geist, ein Gott ist in der Welt, aber wohl in einer lebendigen, über die Notdurft erhabenen Beziehung, in der er stehet mit dem, was ihn umgibt.' (Man can learn neither by questioning himself nor merely by the surrounding objects, that beyond mechanism there is a spirit, a God within the world but in a connexion, however, which is signified by a more lively relation being elevated above the basic necessities and in which he finds himself with all that surrounds him.) With this statement the conditions are explained which enabled him to understand poetry as thanksgiving to the Gods and to test the interlocutory character of the language used in the hymnic mode of address, without having to return to a world of myth.

For a long term the German lyric remained based on the example and model of Goethe. This meant poetry was brought into as close a relation as possible with personal experience and that the poem was understood as an immediate expression of feeling. The language bore the imprint of subjective experience and change of mood; the rhythm of the lines and their imagery sought to express a tone of perceptive feeling. With this, the 'song' became the predominant genre. Those so much more inventive, or artificial, forms that the humanistic tradition had taken over from Classical Antiquity—that is, above all the Ode, the Elegy and the Epigram—retreated into the background or were themselves forced to serve desire for subjective expression. Not until the modern lyric, with its emphasis on symbolism, has poetry moved further away from the expression of experience and atmosphere, and given a new meaning to poetic language by a more experimental creative process. Consequently there is a new interest to be found in those epochs of tradition in which the lyric distinguished itself above all by heightened linguistic artistry, or in those in which poets approached the limits of emotional expression and were familiar with a different relationship to language, different from that of the subjective desire for expression. In this context, a consideration of the hymnic style of the eighteenth century and particularly of the language of Hölderlin can be fruitful for an understanding of the lyric.

For in Hölderlin we can recognize the manner in which modern poetry can take language beyond the expression of emotion. Even though the view that poetry does not simply convey ideas, thoughts or emotions but rather effects a linguistic achievement of its own has grown more forceful: since Mallarmé it remains difficult to determine what it is doing with language. Mallarmé said: 'Ce n'est point avec idées, que l'on fait des vers. C'est avec des mots'. F. R. Leavis, too, is convinced of this when he turns against the Romantic tradition of the lyric and its most direct expression of simple emotions. The poet should distinguish himself rather by his relationship to the language. 'He is a poet because his interest in his experience is not separable from his interest in words'. Still, the question remains to what extent poetic language differs, and in what way, from the prose of everyday communication. This has been answered in various ways. Hofmannsthal spoke of the symbols by which poetry acts, of the mysterious figures which signify only themselves and can not be deciphered. Valéry paid more attention to the linguistic process, to the figure of speech as a magic formula which cannot be reduced to its communicative sense. 'La poésie tend à se faire reproduire dans sa forme'. T. S. Eliot speaks

133

of 'the music latent in the common speech of its day' and which acts together with the ambiguity of meaning in words and characterizes it as a 'musical pattern'. In Hölderlin's case, one might say that such symbols, figures or patterns are closely bound up with definite modes of expression. The interlocutory manner of speech proves to be just as determinative of form as is in other cases the expression of the 'Ego'. The word of praise in the apostrophe testifies to a linguistic action which at the same time bears witness to an intellectual activity and remains associated with concrete intellectual situations. The manner of utterance accentuates man's relationship to his world; it is here that the productivity of the poet is determined, as is at the same time his connexion with concrete intellectual situations. Thus must the poetry of our epoch also be characterized in its development of a 'modus dicendi' in which our unresolved questions can be given expression.

Discussion

Aler asked if Spinozism had not acted as a catalyst intensifying the discussion of how Theism and Science could be reconciled.

He also stated that Newton described 'Räume' (i.e. 'Räumlichkeit' or 'extensio' in Descartes' sense) as 'sensorium dei'. *Aler* thought this indicated an attempt even in Newton's day to solve the problems which Böckmann had mentioned.

Böckmann replied that Hölderlin was familiar with the letters 'Über die Lehre des Spinoza in Briefen an den Herrn Moses Mendelssohn' (1785) by Friedrich Heinrich Jakobi which were a decisive source of the Spinoza-conflict of the eighteenth century, but they had not changed his outlook fundamentally.

The discussion was broken off owing to shortage of time.

Schiller the Revisionist—the poet's second thoughts

by

H. B. GARLAND

IT is no doubt unnecessary to point out that the first half of the title of this paper is devoid of political significance. If 'Revisionism' was a heresy as yet unrecognized in Schiller's day, Schiller was nevertheless one of the most notable exponents of and experts in revision, performing it truly as 're-vision'; and for want of a better word in English I have therefore ventured to label him a revisionist. The second part of my title is, of course, a simplification. The printed poem is already the result of a complex process which would be very crudely summarized if it were described as the poet's *first* thoughts. Nevertheless, publication of a work is a landmark, and not only because it brings about the impingement of the work upon the wide and unknown circle of readers. For the poet it brings a sense of crossing a threshold as clearly demarcated as the frontier between gestation and birth. It is the aim of this paper to show that with Schiller, as with some other poets, this subjective feeling can be illusory. The poem is often not the finished thing the poet has imagined, and the process of becoming, far from ending suddenly, continues spasmodically to function; it can be revived by similar experiences, by chance external pressures, or by an intermittent ferment of the mind which remains unfathomable to the outside observer.

This process of continuous or intermittent fermentation is revealed in the many examples of successive versions of poems in the oeuvre of Hölderlin. They offer a fascinating study in poetical metamorphosis; but they are, however, mostly unaffected by a crucial phase of publication, and it is indeed likely that the failure to publish was a predisposing factor in Hölderlin's protracted inspirational process. Publication operating as a chance factor may be seen in a famous poem of François de Malherbe. There is a well known and probably authentic anecdote that lines 15–16 of *Consolation à M. du Périer* read in the poet's manuscript:

> Et Rosette a vécu ce que vivent les roses,
> L'espace d'un matin.

The carelessness of a compositor rendered the line as:

> Et rose elle a vécu ce que vivent les roses,[1]

a reading which was at once adopted by the poet. Malherbe's instant recognition of the superiority of the printed text to his manuscript was a poetic response, a functioning of the process of creation through the critical discernment.

There is a wide-spread tendency to regard the original version of a poem as imbued with some kind of inherent authenticity, which must, it is claimed, be lacking in later versions, the product of revision.

In Deutschland (says Gerhard Storz) hat sich nämlich eine merkwürdige Neigung ausgebildet: Werden frühe Entwürfe, Erstfassungen eines Werkes bekannt, das in der Gestalt letzter Hand klassisch geworden ist, so beliebt man den älteren Wortlaut gewissermaßen für echter zu halten und ohne weiteres in ihm die frischere, reinere Verwirklichung der dichterischen Absicht zu sehen.[2]

The cult of the 'Urtext' of Bruckner's symphonies is perhaps an example of this trend in the musical field. What losses may ensue if the earliest known text is to become canonical may be seen in Wordsworth's *Prelude*, in the 'Urtext' of which the lines on Trinity College Chapel end with:

> The Antechapel, where the Statue stood
> Of Newton, with his Prism and silent Face.

The superb conclusion:

> The marble index of a mind for ever
> Voyaging through strange seas of thought alone

is an addition of the D Text, written down some twenty years later,[3] a remarkable instance of the poet's mind rising to heights not compassed in the original version.

Poets, of course, differ in the degree in which their creative process endures beyond the publication of the poem. With some, publication is symbolical of an alienation of the poem. Handed over to the world at large, it ceases to be a part of themselves; something analogous to a callous forms over the experience and with the completion of this seal that particular phase of creative activity is at an end. But there are other poets in whom the experience may subside, but does not die. It lies beneath the surface, perhaps dormant for many years, and emerges again upon some fortuitous occasion.

Schiller, more than most poets, could not leave well alone. A perfectionist trend, cognate with the ambition which is so clear a feature of his early years, drove him to re-handle and to improve his poetry. To Wilhelm von Humboldt he wrote:

> es ist mir unmöglich etwas unvollkommen
> zu lassen, solange ich es noch besser machen kann.[4]

But he could not have done this with success if the experience had not still been alive within him. Inspiration rekindled because there was still fire concealed in the embers. Not all Schiller's revisions, of course, were happy. The early poems were for the most part too remote from him; and his alterations to them consisted largely in devastating excisions which, in *Das Geheimnis der Reminiszenz* look remarkably like bowdlerization. *Freigeisterei der Leidenschaft*[5] lost not only two thirds of its length, but its title as well. Schiller was particularly ruthless in his treatment of poems which had an intimate personal significance and expressed, often in crude terms, a strong sexuality.[6] His operations on these poems (and operation may well be taken here in its surgical connotation) took the form of the amputation of stanzas and the excision of words felt by him in his maturity to be offensive.

Not all his revisions of early poems, were, however, of this kind. 'Meine Blumen', when published in *Die Anthologie auf das Jahr 1782*, had combined roguishness, comedy and half-concealed sensuality with a gracefulness which alone appealed to Schiller when he came to appraise the poem for his collected edition of 1800. Stirred by this one quality and so inspired anew by his own poem, as it were, he has transformed this minor work into a poem in which grace predominates, eliminating what he felt to be disturbing elements, and yet producing, in his full classical period, a rococo poem, though in another mode. The metrical structure and strophic lay-out are unchanged, though only four lines out of thirty survive intact, whilst a further five, though modified, are recognizable. Yet this poem, the title of which Schiller significantly depersonalized into 'Die Blumen', is an unmistakable counterpart of the original.

The most interesting examples of Schiller's protracted creation in the field of poetry are, however, to be found in poems written from 1788 onwards. I propose to examine three of these in some detail, all of them extremely well known, beginning with 'Die Götter Griechenlands',[7] which is unique among Schiller's poems in its double form. Many of his poems appeared in two versions, but in all other cases the later form suppressed the earlier. 'Die Götter Griechenlands' alone appeared both in original and final shape in Schiller's Gedichte. Schiller himself obviously preferred the later version and expressed his liking by including it in the first volume, relegating the 'Urtext' to the second. This inclination towards the one form does not deprive the duplication of its significance. It can be assumed that Schiller, though he had evolved a new form of the poem, could not entirely repress a certain longing, a kind of grudging respect, for the original version. It is no doubt significant that the revision of this poem took place in 1793,[8] six years before the editorial work upon the collected poems. Schiller had therefore outlived the poem in both its forms; indeed in 1795 he had betrayed occasional feelings of revulsion from it,[9] without specifying either version. This distance enabled him to see his two forms of 'Die Götter Griechenlands', not as a draft succeeded by a definitive version, but as two distinct poems on one theme. It affords a tacit confirmation by Schiller himself that the poetic process, from which these poems grew, far from being halted at the stage of first publication, continued for some years after.

According to Schiller, 'Die Götter Griechenlands' was composed under pressure to gratify a request from Wieland for copy for *Der teutsche Merkur*—'da machte ich in der Angst—ein Gedicht'.[10] Haste and urgency expedited creation, and in his emergency Schiller drew upon an element in himself which he had been tending to eliminate from his work. He revived indignation. The hostile criticisms of the poem, of which Friedrich Stolberg's is the best known,[11] were directed at the inimical attitude to Christianity explicit in the poem. The phobia was, in fact the survival of an unresolved complex of Schiller's middle twenties, and 'Die Götter Griechenlands' is thus a work which, in one important respect, was out of date for the poet when it was written. We may assume that Schiller's subject lay close to a dormant, but not yet extinct, focus of activity which had aroused resentment, animosity and indignation in Schiller. The poem thus created was at once hard hitting and gently resigned, mordant and nostalgic; the satirical and the elegiac poets of 'Über naive und sentimentalische Dichtung' here rub elbows. Schiller was but indifferently aware of a discrepancy of style, for the manner of his own youth had rested upon such harsh conflicts of opposites. That he could not at first see himself in this poem as others saw him is proved by his words to Körner in 1788:

> Mir gefällt diß Gedicht sehr, weil eine gemäßigte Begeisterung darinn athmet, und eine edle Anmuth mit einer Farbe von Wehmut untermischt.[12]

This is a recognizable description of the then unwritten second version, but not of the first, to which it refers. And Schiller's alterations, made some five years later, convert the first form into what he had once imagined it to be already.

Let us examine in detail the changes. The most obvious outward feature is the reduction in length. The poem has shrunk from 200 lines to 128. Eleven of the twenty-five original stanzas[13] have disappeared, two have been condensed into one[14] and two new ones have been added.[15] It seems unlikely that these Draconian measures were taken merely to reassure the faithful and to avoid offence, for they go far beyond what was necessary for this purpose; and on the other hand stanza 20 of the original, with its emphatically contemptuous:

> *Einen* zu bereichern unter allen,

is retained.

I have no doubt that Schiller's reasons were not theologico-political, but aesthetic. The genius of the blue pencil was in his happiest mood. The pruning knife was an essential counter to the luxuriance of growth of which Schiller was always conscious but which he often could not avoid; for it was the first and most vital stage in his method of creation. But he used his critical faculty for a second and almost as important creative phase.

Some of the forfeited stanzas have clearly lost their place because of the proliferation of classical examples—the seventh, eighth and ninth, for instance, threatened to turn the poem into an abridged (but not so very much abridged) Lempriere. Their omission has allowed greater significance and weight to those allusions which survive. The sacrifice of a compendium of nine references in these three stanzas leaves one, for instance, readier to appreciate the allusive tenth stanza which, without naming him, is solely devoted to Bacchus. These deletions move in the direction of simplicity, and their primary aim is unity. But others seek to achieve a harmonious and smooth movement (which indeed is another accessory to unity). So stanza 4 with its roughness and obscurity, and stanza 11 with its heavy emphasis and involved expression have also vanished.

It was remarked many years ago by Bellermann[16] that with the disappearance of some of these stanzas a whole sequence of comparatives is also effaced. The eleven stanzas expunged have taken eighteen comparatives with them, eleven of which were concentrated in the two stanzas 8 and 9. The incidence of so many comparatives in so short a space was obviously open to stylistic criticism, but I do not think that repetitiveness is Schiller's principal ground for objection. Indeed other comparatives, occurring in isolation, have also been rejected in the later version. The third line of the original poem contained, for instance,

> Glücklichere Menschenalter,

which in the later form has been changed to

> Selige Geschlechter.

The second part of stanza 14, which contained a comparison has also been eliminated.

It seems probable that Schiller felt that the frequent recurrence of *comparison*, though it indicated duality in the poem, at the same time only ineffectively reflected the *contrast* which was its basis. In the second version the comparatives are reduced to three only. The function of the rest is performed by implication. Schiller now realized that the plain statement of lost beauty made clear, without need for constant prodding by comparison, the inadequacy of what had replaced it. The poem gained in harmony; that was the criterion which guided Schiller in his rehandling.

The striving for unity of manner and harmony between the parts is made manifest also by the two new stanzas of the later version. They both treat of the beauty and serenity of ancient mythology; and each contains in a single line a reminder of contrast. Stanza 6 begins with

> Finstrer Ernst und trauriges Entsagen;

but it deliberately refrains from openly identifying these with the present, for it continues

> War aus eurem heitern Dienst verbannt.

And the sixteenth stanza weaves into its texture of nostalgic regret the one line

> Und uns blieb nur das entseelte Wort,

which by the irregularity of its rhythm subtly implies the contrast, while avoiding any explicit pointing, underlining or emphasis.

The many alterations in detail are of equal interest and significance. Two changes of tense in the first stanza smooth the verse and accentuate the 'pastness' of the Ancient World. 'Der Dichtung zauberische Hülle' give a gentler sound and a truer view of poetry than 'Der Dichtkunst malerische Hülle' with its explosion of consonants and its out-dated descriptive epithet.

> Ach umsonst! dem schönen Freund

in stanza 4 conforms metrically whereas,

> Ach vergebens! ihrem schönen Freund

had, by its extra foot, dissented from the pattern of the stanza in the first version.

> Und des Wirtes braune Wangen
> Laden lustig zu dem Becher ein

gains in simplicity, as well as achieving a characteristic Bacchic epithet, in contrast to the colourless awkwardness of:

> Und die Wangen des Bewirters laden . . . etc.

The harsh crudeness of

> Blieb nur das Gerippe mir zurück

with its stumbling rhythm, gives way to the smoother

> Blieb der Schatten nur zurück.

By severe cutting, by delicate pruning, by judicious alteration of detail and by the creation of entirely new components Schiller has transformed a poem of his middle years, which looked back to his youth more than it looked forward, into a poem of his later period, of classicism, harmony and serenity. Yet the elements of the earlier work, its harshness, abruptness and occasional stridency were not defects; they were, for the most part, the genuine and appropriate expression of an experience different from that which Schiller incorporated in the later version. This is what he himself recognized by incorporating both as autonomous poems in his collected edition. Perhaps the divergence between them may be symbolized in antithetic form by one small alteration in line 21:

> Eine Dryas starb mit jenem Baum

has become in the new version

> Eine Dryas lebt in jenem Baum.

The shift of accent from death to life parallels the change from anger to harmony,
  The two versions of 'Die Götter Griechenlands' also afford a striking example of Schiller's power of creative compression. Stanzas 14 and 15, to which I have already briefly referred,[17] are reduced in the second version to the single stanza 9. It

appears to be a simple piece of joinery; the last four lines of one stanza and the first four of the next are deleted, and the surviving parts of the two stanzas have been fitted together to form a new one. They did not fit exactly, since the fourth line of 14 flowed into the fifth:

> Still und traurig senkt' ein Genius
> Seine Fackel.

And so, to make a perfect join, the sentence had to be shortened making

> Seine Fackel senkt' ein Genius.

It may seem at first sight that merely mechanical processes are here taking place. But let us consider more closely this simple alteration. The preceding lines read:

> Damals trat kein gräßliches Gerippe
> Vor das Bett des Sterbenden. Ein Kuß
> Nahm das letzte Leben von der Lippe. . . .

Schiller mentions, only to dismiss, the medieval and baroque skeleton, the accent is on harmony and serenity; and that impression persists in the new:

> Seine Fackel senkt' ein Genius

in which a simple yet eloquent gesture symbolizes death in a reverent and harmonious fashion. To attain the shortening necessary to make the perfect join, Schiller has removed 'Still und traurig'; the first of these adjectives was not vital to his purpose, the second emphasized precisely what he was concerned to remove. Schiller had no wish to deny the sadness of death, but at this point he was not concerned with it, and the removal of 'traurig' augments the cogency of his thought. Furthermore, the eight line stanza, as Schiller conceived it in 'Die Götter Griechenlands' is articulated into two groups of four lines, so that a pause of variable weight intervenes in the middle of each stanza. Schiller does not adhere with absolute rigidity to the division of the strophes; five stanzas of the original twenty-five had neither full stop nor semi-colon at the end of the fourth line. Nevertheless, all but two of these five have at any rate a pause at that point. Only two stanzas run without any interruption from the fourth line into the fifth. One of them, stanza 26, has been deleted. The other, the stanza under discussion, has been converted into a completely regular one by the reorganization of the fourth line. Schiller has therefore achieved by his alteration, not only a satisfactory join with the new second part of the stanza, but an enhancement of his meaning and an improvement in the verse structure.

What of the eight lines omitted? They read as follows:

> Schöne, lichte Bilder
> Scherzten auch um die Notwendigkeit,   (110)
> Und das ernste Schicksal blickte milder
> Durch den Schleier sanfter Menschlichkeit.

142

> Nach der Geister schrecklichen Gesetzen
> Richtete kein heiliger Barbar,
> Dessen Augen Tränen nie benetzen,   (115)
> Zarte Wesen, die ein Weib gebar.

The two lines which speak of the veil of humanity softening the sombre look of fate were not only entirely at home in the original poem, but equally in keeping with the unity and harmony which Schiller aimed at in the second version. Their disappearance is perhaps a loss. But by the exclusion of the rest Schiller achieved an undoubted gain. 'Scherzten auch um die Notwendigkeit' is one of the least happy of Schiller's figurative uses; one of those occasions when he employs seriously combinations of words which are only tolerable in irony. As for the four lines that follow they contain harsh and crude contrasts which belonged to the violent dualism of the first version, but were no longer appropriate to the harmonious form of the second.

The second half of stanza 15, which now concludes the new stanza 9, adds in measured tone two classical allusions making a perfect link with the classical figure of the spirit with extinguished torch.

In 'Die Götter Griechenlands' Schiller created a new poem without disavowing the old. With 'Der Spaziergang' the final form of 1800 replaces the 'Elegie' of 1795 because the poem, though subject to many alterations of detail, remains essentially unchanged. Several utterances of Schiller indicate the high value he set upon this poem,[18] and though these all belong to the months following its first publication there is no reason to suppose that his high estimation of it underwent any marked change. Nevertheless Schiller's ceaseless self-scrutiny discovered imperfections. As early as January 1796 he wrote to August Wilhelm Schlegel:

> Seitdem z.B. die Elegie gedruckt ist, habe
> ich schon über 40 corrigenda darinn entdeckt,
> den bloßen Versbau betreffend.[19]

The business of correcting what he regarded as faults stimulated the creative process. This Wilhelm von Humboldt recognized as one of the characteristic activities of Schiller's mind.

> Denn ich weiß schon, [he wrote] daß
> Sie selbst leichter zur Arbeit gereizt
> werden, wenn Sie etwas vor sich haben,
> daß Sie bloß corrigieren wollen.[20]

Self-criticism stimulated creation, but since Schiller's conviction of the poem's excellence persisted, the re-forging and re-creating takes the form of a large number of detailed amendments which, in re-shaping single or half-lines, or substituting one epithet for another, give individual parts of the poem greater fluency, simplicity, cogency or clarity, without sacrificing the virtues of the original.

Schiller's alterations to the 'Elegie' number forty-one, or forty-two if we include the change of title. This is a formidable total. They are divisible into two groups: deletions and re-shapings. Sixteen lines have been struck out, all of them 'clean' erasures of one or more distichs. Direct evidence of the reason for their removal is not available, but an examination suggests that a combination of two or more factors was usually responsible: dubious scansion, obscurity, intellectual over-elaboration and over-obviousness. So lines 67/68, with the inappropriate use of 'Staude' and the false caesura in the pentameter, have disappeared. The recondite allusion to Astraea in the first line and the cramped thought of the second have led to the dropping of lines 157/158.[20b] And a cleverness, which was here out of place, has probably excluded lines 185/188:

> Weit von dem Menschen fliehe der Mensch! Dem Sohn der Veränderung
>   Darf der Veränderung Sohn nimmer und nimmer sich nahn,
> Nimmer der Freye den Freyen zum bildenden Führer sich nehmen,
>   Nur was in ruhiger Form sicher und ewig besteht.

Lines 177/178 probably too greatly retarded and congested a period which was already heavily burdened.[20c]

Since with 'Der Spaziergang' we are dealing with a poem which Schiller, in his view, improved, and not with one which he transformed, as he did 'Die Götter Griechenlands', and since his own and his friends' estimation of the original was already high, the exact reasons for his omissions must remain more or less plausible speculations. Fine and delicate judgements of taste were involved. Nevertheless the process of reading the later version first and then comparing it with the original at no point leads to a sense of greater enlightenment, fluency or power in the older form; indeed the later version, as a result of the deletions is slightly clearer and more cogent. And we are therefore justified in seeing in these omissions the subtle functioning of a critical faculty which was in the service of creation.

Some thirty of the changes consist in alterations of lines in which we can compare directly that which was first written and Schiller's 'second' thoughts. The most obvious feature of these amendments is the improvement of the scansion of the verse. Schiller defended himself [21] against certain detailed criticisms of his versifications by Wilhelm von Humboldt, but it is characteristic of him that he took the criticisms to heart, absorbed them, and in due course took up the poem again, re-shaping not only the lines to which Humboldt took exception but others as well.

Thus line 13:

Frei, mit weithin verbreitetem Teppich empfängt mich die Wiese

became:

Frei empfängt mich die Wiese, mit weithin verbreitetem Teppich,

in spite of the fact that Schiller had made a spirited defence of the former version as expressing 'distance'.[22] Lines 99 and 119 which Schiller also championed in the version in *Die Horen* were also subsequently modified. Few will maintain that Schiller's alterations, though at first reluctant, were not fully justified. The form:

doch nur der Ruhm kam zurücke

is inferior to:

doch der Ruhm nur kehrte zurücke

not because of the substitution of 'kehrte' for 'kam' (though the swallowing of 'kam' in consequence of its unstressed position was a fault), but because the new word order involves a slight pause after 'Ruhm', and this hint at a catch in the throat suits the elegiac tone of the passage better than the original.

In other instances Schiller saw in Humboldt's comments, as clearly as Malherbe[23] in his printer's proof, how completely the suggestion fulfilled what was his true aim. Thus he concurred immediately in the alteration of line 35:

Unter mir seh ich endlos den Aether und über mir endlos

into

Endlos unter mir seh ich den Äther, über mir endlos.

For, though the fault was a fault of scansion, the new form, in addition to removing that defect, expressed more completely Schiller's meaning:

Daß der ganze Hexameter zwischen den beiden *endlos* eingeschlossen wird, macht hier, wo das Unendliche vorgestellt wird, keine üble Wirkung. Es ist selbst etwas Ewiges, da es in seinen Anfang zurückläuft.[24]

Moreover Schiller did not blindly accept Humboldt's critical comments.

Teilst du mit deiner Flur fröhlich das enge Gesetz

remained unaltered in spite of Humboldt's objection, which Schiller gently but firmly rejected with the words:

Den Vers:
Theilst du mit deiner Flur
lasen Sie anders als ich.

The process was not one of subordination. Criticisms from a respected source were a means of arousing Schiller's own self-critical faculty, which in turn revived and stimulated creative activity. With 'Der Spaziergang' this led to a number of detailed improvements in an already excellent poem. The analogy of the file, so often applied to Schiller's revision of this poem is inappropriate. What occurs is a re-moulding. However small the scale may be, the fire is re-kindled, and a process of re-creation ensues.

In 'Der Tanz' the hand of Wilhelm von Humboldt is also perceptible, but at an earlier stage. Schiller sent his manuscript to his friend at Tegel in the summer of 1795 and three prosodic criticisms expressed in Humboldt's letter of 18 August[25] met with immediate response from Schiller. The re-shaping at these three points is mentioned incidentally by Schiller in his letter to Reichardt of 28 August,[26] and the amended forms are embodied in the first printed text of the poem in *Der Musenalmanach auf das Jahr 1796*.

'Der Tanz' then reappeared in the *Gedichte* in 1800, but in a form so much altered as to make it one of the most remarkable instances of Schiller's revisionary activity. The whole poem has been subjected to a process of re-forging so extensive and intensive that it might be expected to yield an entirely different poem on the same basic theme. Of the thirty-two lines of the original only nine survive intact;[27] seven of the remainder have undergone an alteration of one significant word. No less, therefore, than half the poem has been subjected to a process of thorough re-creation. When we consider that this is an elegiac poem composed of distichs, the transformation appears even more remarkable, for only two of the sixteen distichs are retained in their original form. The truly significant aspect of this process of re-casting (in the full sense of the metaphor) is the identity of the two versions. 'Der Tanz' remains recognizably the same poem, and all its parts retain the same articulation in both versions.

In striking contrast to 'Die Götter Griechenlands', and even to 'Der Spaziergang', the blue pencil has played no part. Not only are place of departure and destination of the poem unchanged, but the whole route and every point by which it passes are the same. It is clear that the articulation of the original version was already perfect in Schiller's eyes, and that the poem stood in no need of the tautening process which he achieved so brilliantly and unerringly by deletion. Every line of the later version corresponds, notwithstanding the mutations, to its equivalent in the original text. Even when a line is so changed as to be unrecognizable, its function is perceptibly the same. Thus the question in the 'Gedichte' version:

Schlingen im Mondlicht dort Elfen den luftigen Reih'n?

corresponds exactly to:

Ist es Elysiums Hain, der den Erstaunten umfängt?

That the later version is superior in its rhythmic organization is obvious, but it is also perceptible that it avoids the momentary confusion as to the identity of 'den Erstaunten' and simultaneously provides a pictorial image greatly superior to the colourless 'Elysiums Hain'.

The superiority of the revised text is indeed striking at all points. The first line had begun with a pronominal subject and a serpentine image:

146

Sieh, wie sie durcheinander in kühnen Schlangen sich winden.

In the final form this has given way to:

Sieh, wie schwebenden Schritts im Wellenschwung sich die Paare
Drehen!

achieving precision in the subject, a double and much more appropriate image
for the movement of the dance and, finally, the boldest of enjambements, thus
perfectly implying the impetuous momentum of the dance. The second line sacri-
fices 'auf schlüpfrigem Plan', which is more than compensated by 'Den Boden berührt
kaum'; the third drops 'von den Leibern geschieden', and substitutes the more
graphic 'befreit von der Schwere des Leibes'. So the process of melting down and
re-casting continues throughout the poem, achieving precision where there was
vagueness, relief where there was flatness, vivid colour where there were neutral
tones. Two further examples of transformation must suffice:

Daß mit Herrscherkühnheit einher der einzelne wandelt,
    Keiner ihm sklavisch weicht, keiner entgegen ihm stürmt?

was a characteristic Schillerian distich, with its energetic, yet congested, hexameter
and its parallelism in the pentameter. It is replaced in 1800 with:

Jeder ein Herrscher, frei, nur dem eigenen Herzen gehorchet
    Und im eilenden Lauf findet die einzige Bahn?

in which the energy, freed from congestion, is enhanced, and the parallelism, become more subtle, no longer impedes the dancing impetus. And the last line:

Handelnd fliehst du das Maß, das du im Spiele doch ehrst?

which had brought the poem to an end without bringing the rhythm to a halt, is by
a simple, but inspired inversion brought to a full close in the later version:

Das du im Spiele doch ehrst, fliehst du im Handeln, das Maß.

Here the indetermination of the question has been transformed into the terminal
full stop, the rallentando before the final note is conveyed by the pause with comma
before 'das Maß'; and this word, which may be said to be the tonic of the poem,
appropriately achieves emphasis as the last word, continuing to ring in our ears
after we have put the book down.

Other poets have revised their poems, and through the preservation of their
papers it has become possible to compare two or more versions. Goethe's 'An den
Mond' and 'An Schwager Kronos' are well-known instances. A famous one in
English literature is Gray's 'Elegy', of which the Eton College manuscript and the

printed text of 1758[28] reveal differences achieved by deletion and re-shaping, after the fashion of several of Schiller's poems. But in these examples the process of revision precedes publication.

Few poets, however, have revised so often and so extensively as Schiller. We may well ask ourselves, why? For with Schiller, as much as with Beethoven, the first process of creating had a startling affinity to primal chaos. Petersen records his state of inspiration thus:

> In ihrer äußeren Wirking war die Begeisterung bei Schiller in der Tat korybantischer Art. Wenn er dichtete, brachte er seine Gedanken unter Strampfen, Schnauben und Brausen zu Papier.[30]

Similar symptoms are recorded by Streicher:

> Während dem er im Zimmer, das oft bloß durch das Mondlicht beleuchtet war, mehrere Stunden auf und ab ging und nicht selten in unvernehmliche, begeisterte Laute ausbrach.[31]

These are the marks of poetry emerging from the depths of the mind under stress, strain and suffering. And the alleviation which Schiller in these moments of unendurable tension experienced from the impact of music on his ears[32] or the smell of over-ripe apples on his sense of smell[33] confirms his spontaneous yet difficult process of poetic generation. Yet this primitive, eruptive creation is only one side of his creative activity. If Schiller was at first inarticulate and rapt, he was later alert and self-conscious. His critical faculty quickly awoke, and together the two impulses of creation proceeded hand in hand. Unfortunately for us, he took no steps to preserve the various stages through which the interaction of generation and judgement led his various works before publication, but we can gain some inkling of it from the 'Demetrius' manuscript and the poetic fragment called by Suphan 'Deutsche Größe'.

What happened after publication has, in some of its manifestations, been the subject of this paper. Undoubtedly publication was a landmark for Schiller as it is for other poets. When his poems were printed he felt a glow of pleasure and approval. But the process which had made them was not finished. The critical faculty had not abandoned its duty of judgement nor renounced its alliance with the process of creation. And so, many of Schiller's poems underwent substantial transformations, and who is to say that their final shape is truly final? So persistent was Schiller's urge to re-model and re-create that we may feel justified in presuming that, had he lived the human span of three score years and ten, some of the poems might have undergone a further phase of creative revision, I repeat, of re-vision. Be that as it may, Schiller is probably unique among poets in his creative exploitation of his critical ability. His ceaseless revisionary efforts, his second and later thoughts, remind us that a principle of 'Werden' is active, not only in Goethe, but in Schiller also.

NOTES

1. ALLEM, M., Notes to *Les Poésies de Malherbe*, ed. P. Martinon (Classiques Garnier), p. 311.

2. *Der Dichter Friedrich Schiller*, 1959, p. 136 f.

3. DE SELINCOURT, E., '*The Prelude*' *of William Wordsworth*, 1932, p. 256.

4. 7 September 1795 (Jonas 4, 254).

5. *Der Kampf* in *Gedichte I*, 1800.

6. The personal significance of these poems, denied by R. Buchwald. *Schiller*, New Edn., 1954, I, 333, has rightly been reasserted by B. von Wiese, *Schiller*, 1959, p. 226 f.

7. First published in *Der teutsche Merkur*, March 1788. A comparison of the two versions from the standpoint of 'Geistesgeschichte' appears in B. von Wiese, *Die deutsche Lyrik*, I, 196.

8. Letter to Körner, 5 May 1793 (Jonas 3, 311).

9. Letter to W. von Humboldt, 29 November 1795 (Jonas 4, 333).

10. Letter to Körner, 17 March 1788 (Jonas 2, 30).

11. In *Das deutsche Museum*, August 1788.

12. 12 June 1788 (Jonas 2, 75).

13. Stanzas 6, 7, 8, 9, 11, 13, 16, 17, 23, 24, 25 of the original.

14. Stanzas 14 and 15 of the original into stanza 9 of the later version.

15. Stanzas 6 and 16 of the later version.

16. *Schillers Werke*, 1895, I, 321.

17. See above p. 140.

18. See e.g. letters to Körner, 21 September 1795 (Jonas 4, 273) and to W. von Humboldt, 29 November 1795 (Jonas 4, 333).

19. 9 January (Jonas 4, 385).

20. Letter to Schiller, 2 February 1796 (*Briefwechsel zwischen Schiller und Wilhelm von Humboldt*, 1830, p. 418).

20a.   Unbemerkt entfliehet dem Blick die einzelne Staude,
            Leyht nur dem ganzen, empfängt nur von dem Ganzen den Reiz.

20b.   Ihren Schleier zerreißt die Scham, Asträa die Binde,
            Und der freche Gelust spottet der Nemesis Zaum.

20c.   Biß, verlassen zugleich von dem Führer von außen und innen,
            Von der Gefühle Geleit, von der Erkenntnisse Licht

21. Letter of 29 November 1785 (Jonas 4, 335 ff.).

22. 'drückt das Silbenmaß selbst das Weite aus' (Jonas 4, 335).

23. See above, p. 136.

24. Jonas 4, 336.

25. Op. cit., p. 137 f.

26. Jonas 4, 245.

27. ll. 6, 8, 14, 18, 23–25, 29, 30.

28. *The Poems of Thos. Gray*, ed. L. Austin Poole, 1917, pp. 89–97, 181–187.

30. HARTMANN, J., *Schillers Jugendfreunde*, 1904, p. 203.

31. STREICHER, A., *Schillers Flucht von Stuttgart*, New Edn., 1959, p. 147 f.

32. STREICHER, op. cit., p. 147; C. v. Wolzogen, *Schillers Leben*, 1830, II, p. 70 f; J. Petersen, *Schillers Gespräche*, 1911, p. 340.

33. ECKERMANN, J. P., *Gespräche mit Goethe*, ed. H. H. Houben, 1908, p. 518.

Discussion

Questioned by *Fowler* on the importance he attached to the original version of a poem which had later undergone revision, the speaker said that the original version must not be regarded as binding. Revision could greatly alter a poem. This occurred when the poet had passed 'the point of no return' and could not recapture the mood in which he had composed the original.

The effects of Schiller's revisions of his own poems were then discussed, with special reference to 'Die Götter Griechenlands', 'Der Tanz' and 'Der Spaziergang'.

Garland emphasized the important musical element in Schiller's works, and said that scholars had neglected this.

Closs compared the 'Spaziergang' in which there is no single symbolic image supporting the comprehensive social-cultural canvas, with the 'Tanz' in which a single basic image is the poem's active force and vision.

Garland concluded by showing that in Schiller's revision was a re-vision and that the critical judgement can be an auxiliary to creation when, as in Schiller especially, aesthetic creation is inseparable from aesthetic judgement.

FIFTH SESSION

Chairman: Professor W. I. LUCAS

Dr. S. S. PRAWER: Reflections on the numinous and the uncanny in German poetry.

Chairman: The Hon. W. R. S. BATHURST: President, Colston Research Society

RICHARD THOMAS CHURCH, C.B.E., F.R.S.L.: A writer in the modern world.

Reflections on the numinous and the uncanny in German poetry

by

S. S. PRAWER

Tor, wer glaubt zwischen Sohle und Scheitel
Sei alles beschlossen, was Mensch genannt wird!
Des Herzens unauslöschlicher Drang, die Geisterarme,
Die hinausgreifen nach den Ringen an den Pforten Gottes!

Wilhelm Klemm: Erscheinung

Der nordische Aufseher for 1759 lists in its table of contents a poem entitled: *Eine Ode über die ernsthaften Vergnügungen des Landlebens*. Such a title raises certain expectations: one looks to find something akin to the contemplative poetry of Brockes, say, or Haller—to the kind of descriptive verse that issues, explicitly or implicitly, in the physico-theological proof dear to eighteenth century deism. If one turns the poem up (in No. 94, dated 2 August 1759) one finds it accompanied by a prefatory note that goes some way to confirm such expectations: 'Dann erst', we read amongst other things, 'ist der Schatten recht kühl, der Wald grün, die Luft erfrischend und wohltätig, der Mondabend recht still; wenn die ruhige und schönere Seele als jenes alles ist auf diesen Stufen zu dem allgütigen Vater der Schöpfung emporsteigt.' But then comes the poem itself:

Nicht in den Ocean
Der Welten alle
Will ich mich stürzen!
Nicht schweben, wo die ersten Erschafnen,
Wo die Jubelchöre der Söhne des Lichts
Anbeten, tief anbeten,
Und in Entzückung vergehn![1]

When Klopstock, after some slight changes of wording and rhythm, gave this poem the title *Die Frühlingsfeier*, he merely shed the egg-shells of the *Aufklärung*. He acknowledged the shift, hardly prepared for by his original prefatory note, from calm contemplation to ecstatic celebration; from a reasonable assessment of the use and beauty of this world—as seen from the standpoint of man—to an impassioned recognition of forces that bring ecstacy and terror and at whose existence language can only hint.

Mit tiefer Ehrfurcht schau ich die Schöpfung an,
Denn du!
Namenloser du!
Schufest sie!

153

With these short lines, in which language seems to recede before that which cannot be named, in which exclamations seek to convey directly what cannot be said discursively, Klopstock opens a new chapter in German literature. He makes a new attempt to push lyric poetry to the very frontiers of human experience, to speak of what Rudolf Otto and C. G. Jung have taught us to call the 'numinous' or 'wholly other': of strange, awe-inspiring, sublime forces whose influence has been felt by religious natures throughout the world and at all times, but before which human speech has always seemed less than adequate.

What happened in Klopstock's *Frühlingsfeier* was paralleled, some fourteen years later, in a different though related field, when the *Göttinger Musenalmanach* published a poem based on a Low German folksong that recalls, in many of its features, the familiar ballad *Sweet William's Ghost*. This poem—Bürger's *Lenore*—may well have aroused in its first readers expectations different from ours: for the *Bänkelsänger* tone in which much of it is couched had been frequently used for comic purposes in the eighteenth century; not least by Bürger himself in such comic 'ballads' as *Ein Ritter ritt wohl in den Krieg*. And if *Lenore* was not—as surely the movement of its opening stanza must have proclaimed to all but the most insensitive—a comic skit, then might it not be a cautionary tale, a 'lehrreiches Wunderbares' in Breitinger's sense? Did it not in fact inculcate, in a cracker-barrel motto, the importance of patience and stoic acceptance of the decrees of providence?

> Geduld! Geduld! Wenn's Herz auch bricht!
> Mit Gott im Himmel hadre nicht!

But these words, it will be remembered, are roared out by fiends; and in *Lenore* the cautionary, moralizing element is even less relevant to the final effect than the 'physico-theological' element in Klopstock's great Odes. In responding to the nocturnal ride of Wilhelm and Lenore we are not primarily concerned with questions of crime and punishment; we are caught up in a ghostly terror, a secularized apocalypse, new in sophisticated German poetry; we experience an irruption of forces that can best be designated by such terms as *unheimlich*, demonic or uncanny.

Klopstock and Bürger alike start with the idiom and the intellectual conceptions of their day and break through into new realms; or rather, ultimately, into the same realm, for the numinous and the uncanny are—as Rudolf Otto has shown in a classic study—intimately related.

> Auch wo der Dämonen-glaube sich längst zum Götter-glauben erhöht hat, behalten die 'Götter' als numina für das Gefühl immer etwas 'Gespenstisches' an sich, nämlich den eigentümlichen Charakter des 'Unheimlich-furchtbaren', der geradezu mit ihre 'Erhabenheit' ausmacht oder durch sie sich schematisiert.[2]

Paul Tillich too, in his *Religionsphilosophie* of 1925, seeks to link the Holy and the Taboo, what inspires awe and what inspires fear:

> Dadurch, dass das Heilige positiv und negativ die unmittelbaren Bewusstseins-formen transzendiert, wird es für das Bewusstsein einerseits die Erfüllung, zu der

es hinstrebt, andererseits der Abgrund, vor dem es zurückschaudert, und beides ist eins. Das erste macht das Heilige zum *Beseligenden*, d.h. zu dem, worin das Bewusstsein seine unbedingte Erfüllung findet, das zweite macht das Heilige zu dem *Unantastbaren*, dem sich das profane Bewusstsein nicht nahen darf.[2a]

No wonder, then, that both Klopstock and Bürger should invoke the terminology of the German Bible and hymn-book to their aid, and that Bürger should point, in an essay significantly entitled *Zur Beherzigung an die Philosophunculos*, to the connexion between his own mode of transcendence and that of religion. 'Wieviel', Bürger asks in that essay, 'soll man nun von Eurem Glauben an Religions-Geheimnisse halten, wenn ihr die anderen, weil ihr sie nicht verstehet, für Undinge ausgebet?[3]

The realms reopened to German poets, with the help, above all, of German Pietism, have since been widely and intensively explored; notably by Goethe, Hölderlin, the Romantics, Mörike, the later Rilke, Trakl, the Expressionists and certain poets of our own day. The need to do so has, of course, been felt more at some times than at others—more during the Romantic period and the last five decades than in the age of Jung Deutschland, Poetic Realism and Naturalism; but it has always been there. In this paper, I shall try to examine some of the many ways in which it has found expression; some of the ways in which German poets of the last two hundred years have sought to adumbrate experiences for which, they often felt, no adequate language existed.

Here we come face to face with our first paradox. 'Wovon man nicht sprechen kann', said Wittgenstein, 'darüber muss man schweigen';[4] and Stefan George, for one, learnt to resign himself, however sadly, to finding no 'thing' where there was no word.[5] Klopstock, however, in a memorable snatch of dialogue, expressed a different faith in the power of poetry.

Der Dichter kann diejenigen Empfindungen, für welche die Sprache keine Worte hat, oder vielmehr nur (ich sage dies in Beziehung auf den Reichtum unserer Sprache) die Nebenausbildungen solcher Empfindungen, er kann sie, durch die Stärke und die Stellung der völlig ausgedrückten ähnlichen, mit ausdrücken.

Oder auch wohl nur darauf deuten.

Freilich, wenn die ähnlichen nicht stark genug sind, und nicht an der rechten Stelle stehn; wenn beides nicht so beschaffen ist, dass es das Feuer in der Seele weiter ausbreitet.

Mich deucht, dass auch das Silbenmass hier und da etwas mitausdrücken könne.

Überhaupt wandelt das Wortlose in einem guten Gedicht umher, wie in Homers Schlachten die nur von wenigen gesehenen Götter.[6]

Hölderlin too—of all German poets the one who sought most consistently to preserve and convey an intuition of the transcendent—recognized and overcame this paradox in four lines of *Heimkunft*:

> Schweigen müssen wir oft; es fehlen heilige Namen,
>   Herzen schlagen und doch bleibet die Rede zurück?
> Aber ein Saitenspiel leiht jeder Stunde die Töne,
>   Und erfreuet vielleicht Himmlische, welche sich nahn.

'Es fehlen heilige Namen'—the divine has receded, no terms are adequate to express the ineffable experience, the apprehension of the Holy; but 'ein Saitenspiel leiht jeder Stunde die Töne', poetry can adumbrate, if not directly then through signs and symbols, whatever man is capable of feeling.

Such signs and symbols are offered, everywhere and always, by the visible world around us, and poets have not been slow to seize upon the sights and sounds of nature in order to make them speak what Blake called the language of 'divine analogy' and the German Romantics the language of the 'hieroglyph'. Eichendorff's forests are real forests, remembered from his childhood at Lubowitz; but they are also signs of supernatural lures and threats.

> Wie rauscht schon abendlich der Wald;
> Die Brust mir schaurig schwellt!
> Die Fremde fern, der Wind so kalt,
> So tief und weit die Welt!
> Es lockt so tief, es lockt so fein
> Durchs dunkelgrüne Haus,
> Der Jäger irrt und irrt allein,
> Find't nimmermehr nach Haus.
>   (*Ahnung und Gegenwart*, III, ch. 23).

As in Klopstock—but with what different means!—we are here given a sense of vast spaces receding before us ('So tief und weit die Welt'); and the hunter of the final lines is seen at once in the forest and in this greater cosmic setting which gives the words 'nach Haus' a powerful symbolic resonance. Eichendorff himself, it will be remembered, saw poetry as religious in its essence ('in ihrem Kern selbst religiös') because it is born, ultimately, out of a feeling of the insufficiency of this terrestrial world ('ein unabweisbares Gefühl von der Ungenüge des irdischen Daseins') leading to a desire 'das Diesseits an ein Jenseits anzuknüpfen'.[6a] This clearly does not apply to all poetry; but it helps us to understand Eichendorff's own hieroglyphs and to feel better the force behind those famous lines from Matthias Claudius's *Abendlied* in which the word 'wunderbar' has to be taken quite literally:

> Der Wald steht schwarz und schweiget,
> Und aus den Wiesen steiget
> Der weisse Nebel wunderbar.

Forest and meadow, river and sea, sky and wind can all become symbols for other orders of reality; and the depths of a well or a cave serve as signs for other, more unfathomable depths in poem after poem from Goethe to Hofmannsthal. The works of man, too, can be made to speak of the divine or demonic; the Romantics like to use the image of mining to suggest exploration of such mysteries, and in the poetry of Georg Heym or Paul Zech the modern city itself gives birth to devils or suggests

> Gottes Bannfluch: *uhrenlose Schicht.*
>
> (Zech: *Fabrikstrasse Tags*)

Mörike is particularly successful in making us apprehend exactly some familiar sight or sound and feel behind it, within it, something strange, some other force which the poet himself describes as 'fremd' or 'feenhaft' or 'dämonisch', or once— in *An eine Christblume*—as 'mystische Glorie':

> Primel und Stern und Syringe, von einsamer Kerze beleuchtet,
> Hier im Glase wie fremd blickt ihr, wie feenhaft her!
>
> (*Nachts am Schreibepult*)

> . . . da drang aus dem nächsten Gebüsche
> Hinter mir Nachtigallschlag herrlich auf einmal hervor,
> Troff wie Honig durch das Gezweig und sprühte wie Feuer
> Zackige Töne; mir traf freudig ein Schauer das Herz,
> Wie wenn der Göttinnen eine, vorüberfliehend, dem Dichter
> Durch ambrosischen Duft ihre Begegnung verrät.
>
> (*Wald-Idylle*)

> Die Sonne kommt—sie scheucht
> Den Traum hinweg im Nu,
> Und von den Bergen streicht
> Ein Schauer auf mich zu.
>
> (*Früh im Wagen*)

The word 'Schauer' used by Mörike in the last two examples I have quoted is a favourite one with poets who speak this language of 'divine analogy'—it is easy enough to find examples in Eichendorff; for it is a word that describes an event in the natural world (something the wind does, or the rain), man's physical reaction to such an event, and a feeling of awe before forces that are felt to be beyond the visible and tangible. When Mörike speaks of the 'Schauer' that comes from the mountains, or Hölderlin (in *Der Archipelagus*) of 'schaurige Lüfte', all three of these meanings are co-present, and an evocation of the natural world becomes at the same time an evocation of the *mysterium tremendum*. There is an obvious semantic link between such 'Schauern' and the 'Schaudern' which Goethe—whose attitude to such phenomena was profoundly ambivalent[7]—makes his Faust call, at one point, the best part of our humanity because it keeps our spirit from growing rigid:

> Doch im Erstarren such ich nicht mein Heil,
> Das Schaudern ist der Menschheit bestes Teil;
> Wie auch die Welt ihm das Gefühl verteure,
> Ergriffen, fühlt er tief das Ungeheure.

'Divine analogy' is not the only means German poets have found helpful in their endeavour to point beyond the limits of our normal conceptual world. They have also travelled along what theologians call the *via eminentiae*: piling up attributes, heaping Pelion on Ossa, in order to show how far the divine transcends them all. Klopstock employed such means on occasions; but in doing so he only revived a tradition that goes back to the great religious poets of the Baroque, to Quirinus Kuhlmann and Gryphius.

> O Feuer wahrer Lieb! O Brunn der guten Gaben!
> O Meister aller Kunst! O höchste Heiligkeit!
> O dreimal grosser Gott! O Lust, die alles Leid
> Vertreibt! O keusche Taub! O Furcht der Höllenraben!
>
> O Weisheit ohne Mass! O reiner Seelen Gast!
> O teurer Gnadenquell! O Trost in herber Last!
> O Regen, der in Angst mit Segen uns befeuchtet!
>
> (Andreas Gryphius: *An Gott den heiligen Geist*)

Through the multiplication of such attributes of praise the poet suggests to us that none can fully describe his ineffable vision.

The *via eminentiae* thus runs into another way which seems, at first glance, far removed from it; a way shown once again by Klopstock and one which becomes increasingly important to the poets who follow him:

> Ehre sei dem Hocherhabenen, dem Ersten, dem Vater der Schöpfung,
> Dem unsere Psalmen stammeln,
> Obgleich der wunderbare Er
> Unaussprechlich und undenkbar ist.

In *Das grosse Halleluja*, from which I have just quoted, and in the inappropriately effusive ode entitled *Das Schweigen*, Klopstock is adding—as Professor Paul Böckmann has shown in his *Formgeschichte der deutschen Dichtung*—the dimension of silence to poetry and pointing to what may be called the *via negationis*:

> Aber ich lege die Hand auf den Mund. Denn werden mir auch
> Morgenröte die Worte, so fehlt es doch stets an etwas
> Dem Gedanken von *ihm*, fehlt dem Gefühl—ich schweige.

In face of the numinous and the uncanny, poets have felt again and again inclined to follow the lead of Isaiah and St. Paul and suggest their experience through negatives: 'But as it is written, Eye hath not seen nor ear heard, neither have entered into the heart of man the things which God hath prepared for them that love Him. But God hath revealed them unto us by His Spirit: for the Spirit searcheth all things, yea, the deep things of God.' (1 *Cor.* 2, 9). In German poetry the great master of this *via negationis*—of suggesting the 'deep things of God' through negatives—is

Novalis; we need only consider for a moment such phrases as 'unendlicher Geheimnisse schweigender Bote' in *Hymnen an die Nacht*, or look at the famous hymn to the Virgin which ends *Geistliche Lieder* and which makes its most powerful effects through the negative terms 'keins von allen' and 'unnennbar'.

> Ich sehe dich in tausend Bildern,
> Maria, lieblich ausgedrückt,
> Doch keins von allen kann dich schildern
> Wie meine Seele dich erblickt.
>
> Ich weiss nur, dass der Welt Getümmel
> Seitdem mir wie ein Traum verweht,
> Und ein unnennbar süsser Himmel
> Mir ewig im Gemüte steht.

Hölderlin, too, had found himself constantly face to face with the unutterable:

> Dreifach umschreibe du es,
> Doch ungesprochen auch, wie es da ist,
> Unschuldige, muss es bleiben
>
> *(Germanien)*

and the poets of our own century, though unable to feel, all too often, that the 'deep things of God' are being revealed to them by the Spirit, have vied with one another in treading a kind of *via negationis*. One thinks of the later Rilke, exposed on the 'mountains of the heart', affirming again and again 'Alles / ist nicht es selbst' or 'dies . . . ist unbeschreiblich' (Fourth Duino Elegy); of Theodor Däubler, who declared in *Das Gleichnis*: 'Was niemand sagen kann, das bannt uns fest'; of Hermann Broch, who has been called, with some justice, deficient in a sense of the numinous (*Times Literary Supplement*, 29 March 1943, p. 210), but whose poem *Das Nimmergewesene* shows his reluctant sense of an ultimate mystery that can be expressed only through negatives:

> Gleichnis um Gleichnis versinkt
> Und es bleibt das nüchtern Unwirkliche,
> winterlich glühend,
> das Geheimnis.

One thinks, finally, of Ingeborg Bachmann, in whose *Früher Mittag* the Un-Speakable walks the land:

> Das Unsägliche geht, leise gesagt, übers Land;*

and of Paul Celan, whose latest volume of poems, *Sprachgitter*, sums up in three lines the paradox that his spare, mysterious verse had suggested from the first:

* Can we not hear Klopstock, in that Dialogue already quoted: 'Überhaupt wandelt das Wortlose in einem guten Gedicht umher wie in Homers Schlachten die von nur wenigen gesehenen Götter'?

> Das nicht mehr zu Nennende, heiss,
> hörbar im Mund.
>
> Niemandes Stimme, wieder.
>
> (Ein Auge, Offen)

One recent poet, Heinz Piontek, has issued a warning against what he called the orphic rumblings, 'orphisches Geraun',[8] of his contemporaries, suggesting—not without justification—that it might in many cases hide a fundamental emptiness, an ultimate lack of anything to say; but even Piontek ends his *Romanze vom Abschied* with a characteristic negative:

> Dem Unerfahrbaren geb ichs zurück.

Here, however, we have reached the very limit of our theme; for the numinous and the uncanny, however ineffable, however 'unsäglich', are by no means 'unerfahrbar'. They are, as mystics and poets have always testified, among the most powerful, if not among the most general, of human experiences.

It is therefore not altogether true to say that there are no words to describe such experiences. In most languages we find such terms as *anyad eva, samadhi, asura, kadosh, arreton, deinos, semnos, dirus, ineffabile, holy, uncanny, numinös, unheimlich* and so on; and religion and folk-belief offer a variety of traditional symbols which poets can use in their attempts to convey to their readers an experience that transcends, or appears to transcend, that of our everyday consciousness: an experience which is felt to be an encounter with the 'wholly other' as threat, as lure or as promise. German poets have not been slow to seize on the opportunities offered in this way. One might here adduce Klopstock's recourse to the vocabulary and imagery of the Psalms; Trakl's use of the sacramental symbolism of bread and wine; Hölderlin's rediscovery of the Dionysiac side of Greek mythology; Goethe's attempt to account for the 'Schauder' of *Ilmenau* by evoking images from fairy-lore and from Shakespeare; the Romantics' many adaptations of the *Tannhäuser* and *Belle Dame Sans Merci* myths; the figures of local superstition that haunt the ballads of Droste-Hülshoff and Mörike; the recurrent 'nixie' or 'mermaid' images in the poetry of Gottfried Keller; and the increasingly frequent appearance, in recent poetry, of the concepts of popular or classical demonology:

> Das Lenzgespenst, das Lenzgespenst geht um im Hage!
>
> (Theodor Däubler: Millionen Nachtigallen schlagen)

> Ich höre oft im Schlaf der Vampire Gebell
> Aus trüben Mondes Weben wie Gelächter
>
> (Georg Heym: Was kommt ihr, weisse Falter …?)

> Das Sonnenschiff im Hafen liegt bereit,
> und auf die Lippen der Galionsfiguren
> tritt unverhüllt das Lächeln der Lemuren . . .

> (Ingeborg Bachmann: *Die grosse Fracht*)

or, in a bold attempt, by a Catholic poet, to evoke the *mysterium tremendum*:

> wo Gottvater wie ein Werwolf haust

> (Christine Lavant: *Kreuzzertretung*)

The difficulty here is one of identification: for only rarely does the modern poet find traditional symbols entirely adequate to his purpose. He will therefore often distance himself through such *personae* as 'Bänkelsänger' (whose tone is adopted by Bürger in *Lenore*, and by many others); or children and simple country folk (Droste's *Der Heidemann*, Mörike's *Die Geister am Mummelsee*); or the sick (Heym's *Das Fieberspital*); or the mad (Stadler: *Die Irren*); or saints and visionaries (George's *Entrückung*). Another means of distancing is that employed by Goethe in *Ilmenau*, where a series of questions casts doubt not so much on the 'uncanny' experience, as on the symbols employed to convey it.

> Wo bin ich? Ist's ein Zaubermärchen-Land?
>
> ·   ·   ·   ·   ·   ·
>
> Ist es der Jäger wildes Geisterheer?
> Sind's Gnomen, die hier Zauberkünste treiben?
>
> ·   ·   ·   ·   ·   ·
>
> Soll ich Verirrter hier in den verschlungnen Gründen
> Die Geister Shakespeares gar verkörpert finden?

Often the poet finds that he has to adapt the traditional image to his purposes; the 'angel' of Rilke's *Duino Elegies* is a clear case in point, and so is Hölderlin's use of the figure of Christ in conjunction with figures of classical mythology:

> Wie Fürsten ist Herkules. Gemeingeist Bacchus. Christus aber ist
> Das Ende.

> (*Der Einzige*).

In a profound and thought-provoking study, Professor Eudo C. Mason has warned us against the danger of accepting such mingling of mythologies as religious revelation and the heresy of confounding poetry and prophecy.[9] But when Rilke speaks, in the poem *Imaginärer Lebenslauf* quoted by Professor Mason, of God leaping at man from an ambush ('Da stürzte Gott aus seinem Hinterhalt') he is surely recording an experience that has affinity with a certain type of religious experience; most readers will recall Moses' terrifying encounter with the hidden God, chronicled in *Exodus* iv 24–26. The poet allows us, in passages such as this, to sense the irruption of something beyond, something numinous and uncanny, into the 'Diesseitigkeit' and 'Hiesigkeit' fundamental to his work. This often happens in modern poetry, where apprehensions of the miraculous and supernatural have usually to be accommodated in a framework of unbelief. 'Wunder des Unglaubens sind ohne Zahl', Ingeborg Bachmann tells us almost programmatically in *Grosse Landschaft bei Wien*; and Paul Celan ends *Ein Tag und noch einer* with the lines:

> ich stürzte
> Alles in niemandes Hand.

This is the way the numinous (what Celan calls, in this same poem, 'düstere Wunder') returns to a world that has lost its transcendent orientation. It is a modern *via negationis*.

In recent poetry, then, we often have a sense of the 'return' of something which had been thought dead or put behind; and this should remind us that Freud—in a famous discussion of the *Doppelgänger* problem—has described a sense of 'return' as the main fountain-head of the Uncanny.

> Der Charakter des Unheimlichen kann doch nur daher rühren, dass der Doppelgänger eine den überwundenen seelischen Urzeiten angehörige Bildung ist... Der Doppelgänger ist zum Schreckbild geworden, wie die Götter nach dem Sturz ihrer Religion zu Dämonen werden. [10]

In support of his last statement Freud cites Heine's *Die Götter im Exil*; he might just as well have quoted Eichendorff, in whose poetry the old gods, the deities of Greece and Rome, return to bring 'Schauer' to the mind:

> Es rauschen die Wipfel und schauern
> Als machten zu dieser Stund
> Um die halbversunkenen Mauern
> Die alten Götter die Rund.
>
> (*Dichter und ihre Gesellen*, II, ch. 15)

In Oskar Loerke's *Wiederkehr*, however—the very title is significant in this context! —it is not the gods of Greece and Rome, but the Judaeo-Christian deity Himself, the God Nietzsche had declared dead, that seems to haunt the world:

> Auf brachem Feld, auf Bäumen und auf Balken
> Ruht Gottes Traurigkeit im Mond sich aus.
>
> Mein Gott, der nicht mehr ist, hier musst du wohnen,
> Hier hast du mich geboren und gewiegt,
> Und unser beider Atem rauscht in Kronen
> Der Weiden, die des Abends Zorn umfliegt.

Many poems, from Rilke's third Duino Elegy and *Eros* to Rudolf Borchardt's *Lust und Schauder*, speak of the return of forgotten gods or demons—the 'hidden guilty river-god of the blood'—in the love-experience:

> Dunkel war es aufgewacht
>   Aus dem ungewissen Grunde,
> Worte sprach's die ganze Nacht
>   Wundersam mit deinem Munde,
>
> Dunkel war es aufgewacht.
>   Sprich, o sprich, aus welchem Grunde!
>
> (Borchardt, *op. cit.*)

while Günter Eich's *Gegenwart* discerns within the immediately apprehended present a past that escapes the memory:

> Stimmen mehr und mehr in allen Lüften.
> Kein Erinnern reicht so weit,
> bis hinunter zu den Aschengrüften
> in die Nacht der Troglodytenzeit.

In the last-quoted poems we are asked to feel something transpersonal, something vast and mysterious, within our very self. This is something of which many poets have spoken in many different idioms and with varying degrees of directness; even Homer's invocation of the Muse or Caedmon's account of his inspiration might here be recalled. Hölderlin points to it in *Der Abschied*:

> Ach, wir kennen uns wenig,
>   Denn es waltet ein Gott in uns;

Annette von Droste-Hülshoff in *Das Spiegelbild*:

> Es ist gewiss, du bist nicht Ich;
> Ein fremdes Dasein, dem ich mich
> Wie Moses nahe, unbeschuht,
> Voll Kräfte, die mir nicht bewusst . . .

(the reference to Moses' approach to his God should be given due weight here!); and Hugo von Hofmannsthal—to quote an example in which the word 'unheimlich' is actually used—in *Terzinen über Vergänglichkeit*:

> Und dass mein eignes Ich, durch nichts gehemmt,
> Herüberglitt aus einem kleinen Kind
> Mir wie ein Hund unheimlich stumm und fremd.
>
> Dann: dass ich auch vor hundert Jahren war . . .

There are obvious links between this sense of the invasion of the self by vast, transpersonal forces, and the kind of feeling that has crystallized, in German literature, in the figure of the *Doppelgänger*. In *Doppelgänger* poems it is usually the repressed or hidden aspects of the personality, the Freudian Id or Super-Ego, the Jungian Shadow or Anima, that return to haunt the consciousness,[11] bringing uneasiness, fear or recoil.

> Seit ich selber mich gesehen,
> Hab das Antlitz ich verhüllt.
> (Brentano: *Jäger und Hirt, Schicksalslied*)

The depths of the 'I', externalized and confronting us, appear uncanny, alien, 'wholly other'. In contemplating them, we find old beliefs stirred up in us, beliefs we had thought long left behind—in the independent, almost bodily existence of the soul, in mirror and puppet magic, in demons that take on our own shape; and all these combine to produce a *frisson* that is anything but a *frisson nouveau*. We seem, at times, to penetrate beyond our individual consciousness, into realms of which the myths of all peoples speak, realms that Jung calls the collective unconscious, peopled by archetypes. Once again we have an uncanny sense of 'return'.

From the no-man's-land between poetry and religion our investigations have now led us to the no-man's-land between poetry, religion and psychology; and here we may call two very different guides to our aid. One of these is Paul Tillich who, in his famous New York sermon on *The Depth of Existence*, warned his hearers against supposing that the so-called 'psychology of depth' can guide men to the ultimate ground of their being and of all being, and who yet declared it meaningful to speak of God in terms 'of the depths of your life, of the source of your being, of your ultimate concern'. The other guide is William James. James was sceptical of many of the records he assembled in *The Varieties of Religious Experience*—he clearly thought that many of his visionaries, like Gibbon's dervishes, mistook the giddiness of the head for the illumination of the spirit; yet he insisted that within the subliminal depths of our mind we might come into contact with something beyond ourselves: 'If there are higher powers able to impress us, they may get access to us only through the subliminal door'.[12] It is, I believe, one of the functions of poetry to keep such doors open; to make us look into the depths of our own being; to remind us that 'it is the duty of the human understanding to understand that there are things which it cannot understand',[13] and at the same time to make forays into the hidden and unknown. By concentrating attention on the mystery that is an essential element of human experience, poetry reminds us continually of the limitations of language when measured, not only against a postulated or revealed eternal truth, but also against our own spiritual capacity:

> Die Rede geht herab, denn sie beschreibt,
> Der Geist will aufwärts, wo er ewig bleibt
> (Goethe: *Nimbus*)

By raiding the inarticulate[14] in order to overcome such limitations, poetry constantly extends the frontier of human consciousness and human speech.

It would, in fact, be possible—and the task might prove well worth undertaking, though one would have to guard against the danger of excessive schematism—to compile something like a rhetoric or grammar of the numinous and the uncanny in poetry. This would begin by showing the different ways in which the dimension of silence has been incorporated in verse—the difference, say, between Klopstock, who speaks effusively of the Unsayable, and Trakl, in whose work the Unsayable hovers between the lines. It would take account of the way in which the ancient tropes and figures of rhetoric have been pressed into the service of the transcendent; we know, for instance, that Charles Wesley regarded *chiasmus* as a verbal emblem of the paradox of the Incarnation and in that sense employed it frequently in his hymns.[15] It would go on to show the importance of *anaphora*, of conjuring repetition, from Klopstock to those modern poets of whom Walter Höllerer has rightly said in a *Transit* gloss: 'Der Dichter greift zur Anapher, um das Verborgene heraufzubeschwören';[16] and the equal importance of *aposiopesis*, the significant breaking-off which makes the end of Goethe's *Der untreue Knabe* so memorably uncanny and which combines with *apostrophe* or *invocation* to suggest a preternatural silence—a 'seltsames Verstummen'—in Trakl's *Das Gewitter*:

> Geduldige Stille odmen die Föhren,
> Die schwarzen Lämmer am Abgrund,
> Wo plötzlich die Bläue
> Seltsam verstummt,
> Das sanfte Summen der Hummeln.
> O grüne Blume—
> O Schweigen!

Apostrophe, and incantatory appeals of all kinds, can be used to conjure up the hidden and half-known (apostrophe combines, in the example that follows, with an interesting *hyperbaton*):

> Tritt aus dem Tor, Erscheinung, namenlose!
>
> (Walter Hasenclever),

interrogatives can produce a sense of uncertainty and mystery:

> Wer wohnte dort? Wessen Hände waren rein?
> Wer leuchtete in der Nacht
> Gespenst den Gespenstern?
>
> (Ingeborg Bachmann: *Nachtflug*)

while *amphibology*, and grammatical indeterminacy of all kinds, can produce in the reader a sense of strangeness and dream-like wonder that is not identical with a feeling for the numinous but is surely one of the pre-requisites for it:

> Schweigt der Menschen laute Lust:
> Rauscht die Erde wie in Träumen
> Wunderbar mit allen Bäumen,
> Was den Menschen kaum bewusst,
> Alte Zeiten, linde Trauer . . .
>
> (Eichendorff: *Aus dem Leben eines Taugenichts*, ch. 4)

The *impersonal 'es'-construction*—which is not always as impersonal as it seems!—has long been recognized, notably by Leo Spitzer, as one of the chief means of arousing the feelings that are our subject.[17]

> Da will sich's unten rühren
> Im stillen Göttergrab . . .
>
> (Eichendorff: *Das Marmorbild*)

or

> Und sieh! und sieh! an weisser Wand
> Da kam's hervor wie Menschenhand . . .
>
> (Heine: *Belsazer*)

or

> Es orgelt im Rohr und es klirret im Schilf . . .
>
> (Mörike: *Die Geister am Mummelsee*)

or

> Über die Heide hallet mein Schritt;
> Dumpf aus der Erde wandert es mit.
>
> (Storm: *Über die Heide*)

These are but four of the best-known examples from poems in which the 'impersonal' *es* becomes a numinous or uncanny presence. In the same way *abstract nouns* where we would expect concrete sometimes help to make the natural world transparent:

> Für *Einsames* ist eine Schenke da;
> Das säumt geduldig unter dunklen Bogen,
> Von goldenem Tabaksgewölk umzogen.
>
> Doch immer ist *das Eigne* schwarz und nah . . .
>
> (Trakl: *Ein Herbstabend* (my italics))

The *genitive linking of concrete and abstract*, which has been so consistently abused in recent poetry, often serves to make us apprehend the unfamiliar through the familiar, the unknown through the known, in such formulations as Rilke's 'Berge des Urleids'; *compounds* like Celan's 'Herzzeit' and 'Sterbegeklüft' are often employed for a similar purpose, as are *personifications* like Trakl's

> . . . anfällt ein knöchern Grauen
> Wenn schwarz der Tau tropft von den kahlen Weiden
>
> (*Der Herbst des Einsamen*)

Strange word-coinages or an unusual use of familiar words may also help us to break through our normal, prosaic conception of the world. The words 'fremde Fühlung', for instance, in Goethe's *Selige Sehnsucht*, suggest not only a feeling ('Gefühl') that overcomes us, but also the groping towards us of something other, something strange, something 'outside':

> In der Liebesnächte Kühlung,
> Die dich zeugte, wo du zeugtest,
> Überfällt dich fremde Fühlung
> Wenn die stille Kerze leuchtet.

Hyperbaton has already been mentioned; but all sorts of significant *dislocations of syntax* have served, ever since Klopstock, to direct the reader's attention in a forcible way to what is strange and 'other'. Thus Klopstock himself likes to interpose the name of the deity between a verb and its object, producing a grammatical and rhythmic shock which is like the irruption of God into the thoughts and affairs of this world:

> Ein stiller Schauer deiner Allgegenwart
> Erschüttert, Gott! mich . . .
>
> *(An Gott)*

while in Hölderlin's *Patmos* the words 'Gott' or 'der Gott' are made the subject of the sentence and then not uttered until the end, like a revelation long withheld:

> Nah ist
> Und schwer zu fassen der Gott

and again:

> Doch furchtbar ist, wie da und dort
> Unendlich hin zerstreut das Lebende Gott.

Hölderlin is particularly successful in conveying, through dislocations of normal syntax, the shock of being seized by the divine:

> Wenn aber einer spornte sich selbst,
> Und traurig redend, unterwegs, da ich wehrlos wäre
> Mich überfiele, dass ich staunt' und von dem Gotte
> Das Bild nachahmen möcht' ein Knecht—
> Im Zorne sichtbar sah ich einmal
> Des Himmels Herrn, nicht, dass ich sein sollt etwas, sondern
> Zu lernen.
>
> *(Patmos)*

As always in poetry, the *sound and rhythm* of the words are inextricably linked with their connotational suggestions, making us respond to the conquering deity of Hölderlin's *Patmos*; to the low breathings of the Lord of the Synagogue in Heine's *Prinzessin Sabbat*:

167

Durch das Haus geheimnisvoll
Zieht ein Wispern und ein Weben,
Und der unsichtbare Hausherr
Atmet schaurig in der Stille . . . ;

or to the silent apparitions that drag through Trakl's autumnal landscape:

Unter goldnem Gezweig der Nacht und Sternen
Es schwankt der Schwester Schatten durch den schweigenden Hain,
Zu grüssen die Geister der Helden, die blutenden Häupter;
Und leise tönen im Rohr die dunkeln Flöten des Herbstes.

(Grodek)

It is hardly necessary to point out the effect of the fricatives, and more especially the hushing 'Sch' sounds, in reinforcing those suggestions of darkness and silence that have always been among the chief means of inducing numinous and uncanny feelings. We might, however, at this point, let Maud Bodkin remind us of the connexion between the rhythm of poetry and the ritual dance out of which it may have grown: 'The body's enactment, through changes of speech-rhythm and intonation, of changes in the dramatic content of poetry, is the factor that links the reading of verse—even though silent, reduced to sub-articulation—with the ritual dance, conceived as the prototype of the arts. As the wild rhythms of the ancient dance tended to annul the participant's consciousness of separate personality, exalting him to union with his group and with its God, so, in fainter degree, the rhythms of poetry still serve to hold the reader apart from his everyday self and cares, caught up in the thought and feeling communicated.[18]

The nature of this survey has forced me to discuss, in the main, passages of verse isolated from their context; I would like, therefore, to end by looking briefly at a complete poem—a very short one, and for reasons which will become apparent, not one of the greatest—which continues a tradition that runs from Eichendorff's *Zwielicht* and *Waldgespräch* to Trakl's *In den Nachmittag geflüstert* and which seems to me in its modest way, despite some rather banal rhymes, successful in evoking feelings of the uncanny. It comes from Theodor Däubler's *Der sternhelle Weg* of 1915 and bears the title: *Winter*.

Geduldig ist der Wald,
Behutsamer der Schnee,
Am einsamsten das Reh.
Ich rufe. Was erschallt?
Der Widerhall macht Schritte.
Er kehrt zurück zu seinem Weh:
Das kommt heran wie leise Tritte.
Er findet mich in meiner Mitte.
Warum hab ich den Wald gestört?
Vom Schnee ward nichts gehört?
Hat sich das Reh gescheut?
Wie mich das Rufen reut.

The central image of this poem is a call into the forest, followed by—what? Is it just an echo? It feels like a threat, like the approach of something strange and alien[19] that is yet intimately connected with a 'lyric I' which seeks to assert, in line 7, its own centre of being and consciousness; an approach that follows, like pursuit and imprisonment in Kafka's *Der Schlag ans Hoftor*, from a simple, unpremeditated, apparently 'harmless' human action. At the very opening, the reader is shaken out of his accustomed world by the dream-logic of an unrelated positive, comparative and superlative: lines 5–7 show an unsettling alternation of anthropomorphic metaphor (Der Widerhall *macht Schritte*) and a simile that casts doubt on such anthropomorphization (Das kommt heran *wie* leise Tritte); the final couplets bring questioning, fear, uncertainty and regret. The uncanny is here a matter of structure, of sound and rhythm, as well as of connotational suggestion: it is reinforced by prominent questions, by the grammatical pause in the middle of the third line (which allows us to 'hear' the forest silence and re-experience the waiting for an answer), by the echoing feminine rhymes in the middle of the poem (Schritte—Tritte—Mitte) and the constantly shifting rhyme scheme, as well as by many other devices that it would be tiresome and pedantic to list in full.

The threat that informs Däubler's poem is felt to come from without; but since forest, snow and deer have been given, at the opening, human attributes, it is also a threat that arises within the soul of man. It is therefore possible to see in the poem either a response to nature (it is, after all, entitled *Winter*), to the outside world, even to a social situation in which men feel lonely and apprehensive; or a response to the Jungian Shadow or the Freudian Id within; or a response to something quite alien, supernatural and superpersonal, the unknown 'Das' of the ambiguous sixth line. Indeed, the force of the poem depends on our awareness of, and uncertainty about, all these possibilities. It is *unheimlich* in two senses of the word: 'un-homely', shaking us out of the familiar world, the world in which we can feel at home; and 'un-secret', throwing fitful rays of light into corners of the consciousness that usually remain dark and hidden.

In Däubler's *Winter* the feeling that predominates is one of the uncanny, of uneasiness before the alien and unknown; but in its essence the experience the poet here recounts is not unlike the recurrent experience of which Wordsworth tells in Book I of *The Prelude*, where human action within the world of nature is followed by

> Low breathings coming after me, and sounds
> Of indistinguishable motion, steps
> Almost as silent as the turf they trod,

or where a mountain seems to stride after the guilt-haunted boy 'with purpose of its own / And measured motion like a living thing'. In Wordsworth, however, as in Däubler's *Nordlicht*, what predominates is not a feeling of the uncanny as terror (though this too enters into Wordsworth's poem: 'the impressive discipline of fear' is an important factor in the child's education); *The Prelude* leaves us, rather, with a sense of awe and reverence before the numinous:

after I had seen
That spectacle, for many days, my brain
Worked with a dim and undetermined sense
Of unknown modes of being . . .

and again

No familiar shapes
Remained, no pleasant images of trees,
Of sea or sky, no colours of green fields;
But huge and mighty forms, that do not live
Like living men, moved slowly through the mind
By day, and were a trouble to my dreams.

I would like to offer this suggested comparison between Däubler's *Winter* and the (as literature undoubtedly greater) passage from *The Prelude* as proof that it is justifiable to treat, as I have done in this paper, the uncanny and the numinous together; but it should also serve as a warning, if warning were needed, not too lightly to equate the terror inspired by the one with the awe evoked by the other. Wordsworth, it may be remembered, talks not only of 'beauty that hath terror in it' and of a fear that 'fosters' the soul, but also of a 'soul-debasing fear' that he felt to be alien to his nature; and in the work of Hölderlin, too, we may distinguish between 'die Furcht, welche den Gott ansagt' (*An die Deutschen*) and 'Die gewurzelte / Ungestalte die Furcht' which divides men from the gods (*Der Abschied*). If we glance back at the two poems which started these reflections—Klopstock's *Die Frühlingsfeier* and Bürger's *Lenore*—we shall see that awe and terror[20] are present in both; but we shall also see that Klopstock's poem is numinous in its essence, while Bürger's is uncanny.

Seht ihr den neuen Zeugen des Nahen, den fliegenden Strahl?
Höret ihr hoch in der Wolke den Donner des Herrn?
Er ruft: Jehova! Jehova!
Und der geschmetterte Wald dampft!

(*Die Frühlingsfeier*)

Hoch bäumte sich, wild schnob der Rapp'
Und sprühte Feuerfunken;
Und hui! war's unter ihr hinab
Verschwunden und versunken.
Geheul! Geheul aus hoher Luft,
Gewinsel kam aus tiefer Gruft.
Lenorens Herz mit Beben
Rang zwischen Tod und Leben.

(*Lenore*)

What these quotations should make clear is that the numinous, with its apprehension of a transcendent good, tends towards the sublime, while the uncanny, with its apprehension of a transcendent evil, tends towards the grotesque.[21] Both have their dangers. Poets of the numinous sublime may lose the ground under their feet and beat their wings in regions where their readers cannot follow them:

> Hie und da bin ich auch auf Stellen gestossen (writes Matthias Claudius in his review of Klopstock's Odes), bei denen's mir ganz schwindlicht worden ist, und 's ist mir gewesen, als wenn'n Adler nach'm Himmel fliegen will, und nun so hoch aufsteigt, dass man nur noch Bewegung sieht, nicht aber, ob der Adler sie mach' oder ob's nur 'n Spiel der Luft sei. Da pfleg' ich denn 's Buch hinzulegen und mit Onkel Toby 'n Pfiff zu tun.[22]

Poets of the uncanny grotesque, on the other hand—and is not this, at least in part, the burden of Schiller's criticism of Bürger?—may become too enamoured of sensationalist 'effects', or teeter (as in the Däubler poem) on the edge of the ludicrous. But the poetry of the sublime and that of the grotesque, the poetry of awe and that of terror, are both important and necessary constituents of literature. Both may serve to convey feelings induced by specific social and historical situations—feelings such as that which Hegel termed *Entfremdung*, for instance, the alienation of man from his environment, which may lead to a heady sensation of belonging to other worlds as well as to Kafkaesque anxiety and depression. Both may tell of encounters with grandiose, solemn or apparently inexplicable phenomena of nature, and of encounters with depths of the self that lie below the normal consciousness. Both may take us to the very limits of possible experience and bring us up against transcendent principles at which the wisest of us can only guess. Such poetry has been well compared, by the Director of this Symposium, to the shield of Perseus, to 'Medusa's mirror', in which a poet 'imprisons a terrible reality'.[23] The head of the Medusa, awe-inspiring, terrifying and yet strangely beautiful, mingling the grotesque with the sublime, is surely one of the most powerful symbols poets have yet devised to express their apprehension of the uncanny and the numinous; and it is perhaps not irrelevant, in our present context, to recall that the Greeks granted it a place on the aegis shield of Pallas Athene, in whom they saw, not only the goddess of wisdom, but also the patron of all the liberal arts.

NOTES

1. I am grateful to Dr. H. T. Betteridge for letting me see a photostat copy of the first version of *Die Frühlingsfeier*. Of the many printed commentaries on the poem, the most useful for my purposes have been those of Gerhard Kaiser in *Wirkendes Wort* VIII, 1957–58, pp. 329–35, and in *Klopstock. Religion und Dichtung*, Gütersloh 1963, pp. 299–301 *et passim*.

2. OTTO, RUDOLF, *Das Heilige. Über das Irrationale in der Idee des Göttlichen und sein Verhältnis zum Rationalen*, 22nd edn., Munich 1932, p. 19.

2(a). TILLICH, PAUL, *Religionsphilosophie*, new edn., Stuttgart 1962, p. 73.

3. I owe this quotation, with much else that is relevant to an understanding of Bürger, to Albrecht Schöne's essays on *Lenore* in *Deutsche Vierteljahrsschrift* XXVIII, 1954, p. 324 ff. and in *Die deutsche Lyrik* (ed. B. v. Wiese), Düsseldorf 1956, I, p. 190 ff.

4. WITTGENSTEIN, LUDWIG, *Tractatus Logico-Philosophicus*, London 1922, Proposition No. 7.

5. 'So lernt ich traurig den verzicht
   Kein ding sei wo das wort gebricht'. (George: *Das Wort*).

6. *Über die Darstellung* (1799) in *Klopstocks Sämtliche Werke*, Leipzig 1855, X, p. 199 f.

6(a). EICHENDORFF, *Geschichte der poetischen Literatur Deutschlands, Werke und Schriften* ed. G. Baumann and S. Grosse, Stuttgart n.d. (1957), IV, p. 25.

7. e.g. *Dichtung und Wahrheit*, IV, 20, ' . . . er glaubte mehr und mehr einzusehen, dass es besser sei, den Gedanken von dem Ungeheuren, Unfasslichen abzuwenden'.

8. *Mein Gedicht ist mein Messer*, ed. H. Bender, Heidelberg 1955, p. 103.

9. MASON, E. C. *Der Zopf des Münchhausen. Eine Skizze im Hinblick auf Rilke*, Einsiedeln 1949.

10. FREUD, SIGMUND, *Gesammelte Werke*, London 1947, XII, pp. 229 ff.

11. Cf. TYMMS, R. V., *Doubles in Literary Psychology*, Cambridge 1949; and S. S. Prawer, *Heines Doppelgänger. Publications of the English Goethe Society*. N.S. XXXI, 1960/1.

12. TILLICH, PAUL, *Shaking the Foundations*, Harmondsworth 1962, pp. 63–4; William James: *Varieties of Religious Experience*, Lecture X.

13. KIERKEGAARD, *Journals*, translated A. Dru, entry for 1847.

14. ELIOT, T. S., *East Coker*, Section V.

15. Cf. *Representative Verse of Charles Wesley*, selected, edited and introduced by Frank Baker, London 1962.

16. *Transit. Lyrikbuch der Jahrhundertmitte*, ed. W. Höllerer, Frankfurt/Main 1956, p. 68.

17. in: *Festschrift für Karl Vossler*, Heidelberg 1923.

18. BODKIN, M. *Archetypal Patterns in Poetry. Psychological Studies in Imagination*, Oxford 1934, pp. 321–2.

19. Cf. LUCKA, E. *Verdoppelungen des Ich*, *Preussische Jahrbücher* CXV, 1904, p. 13.

20. It is, however, true to say that in Klopstock's poetry terror is not given quite enough weight, and that it is this fundamental optimism—more than anything else—which makes him appear somewhat remote to present-day readers.

21. Cf. MONK, S. H. *The Sublime. A Study of Critical Theories in XVIIIth Century England*, new edn., Univ. of Michigan Press 1960; and W. Kayser: *Das Groteske. Seine Gestaltung in Malerei und Dichtung*, Oldenburg 1957.

22. CLAUDIUS, MATTHIAS, *Der Wandsbecker Bote*, ed. F. Gross, Berlin 1912, p. 53.

23. CLOSS, A. *Medusa's Mirror. Studies in German Literature*, London 1957, p. 39.

Discussion

Mainland spoke of the contrast between Brockes and Klopstock. Brockes drew comfort from naming things, had no fear of being 'shut in by the word' and was perhaps an early pilgrim on the 'via negationis'.

Closs asked before whom a modern writer, to whom religion has lost its meaning, could cast himself down prostrate.

Allemann wondered how far it was possible to interpret that which the poet himself felt unable to say, and thought that what was left unsaid derived its whole strength from the poet's effort to say it.

Prawer quoted lines from Paul Celan's 'Ein Auge, offen?' Here something was said and felt, but it was not to be named. Statements cancelled each other out or were perhaps equally valid. The world had become more uncertain and uncanny than ever it had been to Klopstock. Poets like Celan were straining against the limitations of language.

A writer in the modern world

by

RICHARD THOMAS CHURCH

My title 'A Writer in the Modern World' is in itself sufficient instigation for a clinical enquiry. It is possible that such an enquiry could never have been asked for in any previous period of mankind's cultural history. Do we know, indeed, that any other period than our own was self-styled as 'the modern world'? That epithet 'modern' implies an intense, almost paralysing consciousness of the past. This is comparatively a new state of the mass mind. It is engendered by education, especially by education in psychology. Here is the culprit. Psychology, another term for organized self-consciousness. It has affected the whole way of life of mankind; our social principles and conduct, our manipulation of law, our attitude to religious doctrines, and to the arts. This last is what concerns us in the course of the Symposium in which I have the honour to share.

Attitude to the arts! It bears directly, for example, on the theme to be discussed by the Director of the symposium, Professor Closs. He is to talk on 'Concealment and Revelation in German Lyrical Poetry'. This contrast of two diverse impulses in our aesthetic would not have been so readily isolated, at any time, before the surgery of the psychologist was developed. Not even that subtle genius in the art of criticism, Gotthold Lessing, could work so deliberately. Nor could Aristotle in the first application of scientific method to the analysis of aesthetic principles, two thousand years ago. Lessing and Aristotle might have been contemporaries, with Lessing further refining the lines laid down by his master. But both were objective. Modern criticism is different. The X-ray of psychology has penetrated the organism of the human mind; and it has chosen to do so in a theatre of mirrors, so that the vivisectionist sees inside himself even while staring at the viscera of his neighbour's thoughts. We are all aware that we live in glasshouses, vulnerable and perpetually visible. If only it would make us stop throwing stones!

I think it was Jean Paul Richter (like Lessing a member of the Goethe entourage) who said that once the artist or the mystic had been touched by Revelation, he should instantly conceal it from the general public. That is both an important and a terrible saying, though it offers no new doctrine of aesthetics.

Based on past history, it followed both the precept and the practice of all hierarchies in priestcraft, in trade guilds, in Machiavellian politics. It goes deeper. It is based on the primitive and savage fear of the tribesman who, finding a treasure of food or ornament, at once conceals it. The esoteric in religion, in scholarship, in government, is based on that fear.

I believe that one of the most hopeful signs today is that our modern world, so far as it is beneficially democratic, is throwing down those barriers of secrecy. We are

174

crying with a loud voice, a national voice, a racial voice, 'Open Sesame' as we tear aside the curtains of the tabernacle within whose darkness the Ark of the Covenant has been secreted by the High Priest, by authoritarians, by bureaucrats.

But what are the conclusions? Has open diplomacy, has non-disciplinary education, has the throwing out of reverence for tradition in the arts, have these practices led us to the new Jerusalem? We know the answer.

But out of the confusion, and indeed the degradation of all our structures in these various aspects of civilization, out of this very confusion we begin to see our way to an enlargement of human relationships, and the arts by which those relationships are registered and promoted. And what is that way?

I think the answer is provided by a passage from Gilbert Murray's book on Greek religion. He says: 'The fact remains that man must have some relation towards the uncharted, the mysterious, tracts of life which surround him on every side. And for my own part I am content to say that his method must be to a large extent very much what St. Paul calls faith; that is, some attitude not of the conscious intellect but of the *whole being*, using all its powers of sensitiveness, all its feeblest and most inarticulate feelers and tentacles, in the effort somehow to touch by these that which cannot be grasped by the definite senses or analyzed by the conscious reasons'.

I would like to underline this quotation by reading a poem of my own, written many years ago, during the cynical decades between the wars. It is called THE MAN WITHOUT FAITH:

A Man without faith
Grows old before his years,
His world a wraith,
For whom the end nears
Like a winter mist
When the sun is cold
In the cold west.

His children about him
Are strangers, unknown,
The love that begot them
Cooled and gone.
If he get riches
They turn to rust,
And he can do nothing
With a handful of dust.
Life's miracle fails him,
Life's rapture, life's breath;
He has done with living,
He has forestalled death.

These two quotations bring us to the heart of the matter. It is this. Literature and faith cannot be divorced. A man may call himself an atheist or a materialist.

He may even be an inarticulate brute given up wholly to satisfying his appetites. Even such a man is groping for something, and in doing so is forced to a self-expression that is a definition of *some* kind of faith. So long as there is life in us, there is faith in us also. We cannot lift an arm or glance upward without some objective behind that elementary movement. And an objective is a faith; as primitive perhaps as some of the forms of life that are static on the dark beds of the ocean.

But when it comes to the use of words, and all the highly advanced organic structures which this implies, imagine what that means as a conveyance of faith, what *greater* gropings, what *nobler* aspirations! Still more is this process advanced when the use of words is *sustained* and made into a pattern of logic and a fabric of beauty. I believe indeed that we cannot construct the simplest piece of syntax without the motive behind it being an active demonstration of faith. We *have* to believe, even in order to *disbelieve*. The man who is calling out against God is the man who is worshipping Him most abjectly.

And this brings us to the problem of literary tradition, and the latter day attitude toward it. We can see in the history of literature how our poets and storytellers have perpetuated, deepened and added to those early religious concepts, giving them elasticity and a universal significance, so that they can be applied to the needs of even the most sophisticated society of man, such as this in which we live today. For several thousand years literature has carried these images of religion, all the time humanizing them and relating them more closely to the intricacies of human emotion and conduct. We need only to recall the mere themes of the poetry of Homer, Isaiah, and the Greek dramatists of the Golden Age, to realize how inter-dependent were religion and literature in their beginnings. Both sprang from the stark, human necessity of solving the mystery of life, of making the intangible concrete, and of binding chaos into some form of order that could support a standard of human values that might be extended into the society of man. Even in those processes by which literature looks upon the negative aspects of our human problem, the mere statement of them in a form of beauty brought a consolation, which was a sufficient tonic to conjure hope out of despair. The Hebrew prophet and poet says: 'As for Man, his days are as grass. As a flower of the field, so he flourisheth. For the wind passeth over it, and it is gone, and the place thereof shall know it no more'.

You see that in the mere expression of this idea of the insecurity of human life, literature achieves a paradox. It changes the humility of that statement into pride. The wind has indeed passed over it, but it is the wind of literature, which has changed the idea of fleetingness into something more permanent than a monument of stone. This is one of the great and basic values of literature: it is the preservative, the treasury of those moments when in height or in depth, the human mind touches the frontiers between experience and the mystery which lies beyond. When it does this in terms of an orthodox religious creed, it is only demonstrating its own superb efficacy as a medicine for the imagination of man, restoring even the most worn and ancient of dogmas and giving them new significance, new life.

I am not content to leave our explorations there. I believe that the expression of faith and belief through literature is an all-pervading activity that saturates the art of letters, just as rain penetrates into the soil and makes it fertile. Without faith and belief, the structures of our language are dried out and become barren rocks and caverns. I go further, and state my belief that indeed it is impossible for human language to remain intact and coherent, without this vivifying moisture of faith.

Here we come indeed to a consideration of the very sources of language, that instrument which multiplies our capabilities and has made us lords over the rest of living creatures. The genesis of those structures of language, the grammatical articulation of the syntax between words and the growth of words and sentences into the powerful rhythms and measures of poetry and the prose paragraph: these are an organic process in the realm of mind, a very real and tangible world, comparable to those in the physical world. I see no difference between the two, the ghost and the body. If we admit a difference, then we admit the devil of dualism and leave the door open for all those divisions to enter between matter and manner, time and space, body and soul, which have led the human race to the disastrous brink of the precipice where it now stands, hesitating.

So it is in literature. I believe literature cannot exist, whether in prose or verse, without its forms being articulated by faith and belief in the need and efficacy of the image. Much argument could be brought to a definition of this statement as a philosophic issue. General Smuts made some effort in this direction in his essay on the principle of Holism. But no statement of faith was ever advanced by argument; we know too well how true that is from the works of the Schoolmen, who made such a cat's cradle of theology in the Middle Ages. Our own age in particular is impatient of such logic chopping, and it is indeed one of the bitterest comments on the dogmatists of Communism today, that they strive to throw human society back into the clutches of the stiff, intellectual machinery of Sciolism, which has substituted labels in place of living realities.

The only way to advance upon that, to find the very source and ever-flowing power of the hopes and the vision that make possible any form of literature, is to give examples of the miracle of symbolical language in action. For it *is* a miracle, just as the other attributes of our universe are miracles; the sunshine, the manifest of flowers and animal life, the massive nature of stone, the mathematics of the night skies.

These images may seem fanciful to the materialist: but I would point out that they are part of those tangibilities of the mental world, to which I have already referred as powers that are both solid and authoritative. 'In the beginning was the Word and the Word was with God, and the Word was God. The same was in the beginning with God'. That familiar statement contains the whole potentiality of our human ascendancy over the rest of the universe. It is the poet's justification for claiming to be 'a legislator of the world'. It is indeed, so profound, so final, that it leaves nothing more to be said by way of definition, and can only be illustrated.

But when we come to illustrating, the field is infinite. We have the myriads of languages of the human race with their various conventions and historical structures in imagery and symbolism. Further, each individual person is equipped in some degree with a private treasury of such illustrations, all of them manifesting to a single truth, that without faith and belief there can be no literature. Some of these illustrations are crude and elementary, as in folk-song and in primitive sagas. Others

177

are decadent and tending to lapse into commercialized cynicism, such as we find in the crooning of our Wardour Street spirituals. The process is ever varied and ever fluctuating. It is like sunshine filtering down through the pollutions of our atmosphere bringing life and light, no matter how obscured it may be by the medium through which it percolates.

But what have I said so far? All I have done is to call it a process. What a word to use for this vast and universal power that commands everything we do and determines what we do. But surely we can feel with our *sixth* sense, that in this oblique approach toward a definition of the indefinable, our very failure is in itself a success. We have learned that faith and belief, the faith that is the mainspring of all creeds and all achievement, is something that we cannot circumscribe within a definition or a dogma. But we can *recognize* it. Indeed, without it, we sink into darkness and despair and the value goes out of all our possessions, material as well as mental. I can only say again, that literature without this foundation of faith is no longer literature. It is merely a coagulation of dead words, like lava spread round a volcano.

Human society is that volcano. It has erupted twice in the twentieth century and it is still rumbling, still throwing out minor streams of devastation. Optimists call this progress. They tell us we live in a progressive age, and in many respects they are right. Science helps us to master the austerity and indifference of nature. In spite of political setbacks, we at least believe in the humane rights of the individual.

But for the writer that cancerous overflow of lava is still a horror. It is also a challenge. He has to recover the very soil of civilized life, the soil fertile in understanding, in love, in beauty and in faith.

This is no age, then, for cynicism in letters, for persiflage and decadent toying with technical forms. We have to see this power of regenerative faith informing literature as it were in a judicial capacity. But we must not limit it to this, or we shall be in danger of confining it once again to the presentation of a dogma. Faith is capable of gaiety and of infinite surprise, those qualities of freedom which are perhaps the highest attributes of Godhead. A poem by W. B. Yeats will express what I mean. It is called THE WILD SWANS AT GOOLE:

> The trees are in their autumn beauty,
> The woodland paths are dry.
> Under the October twilight the water
> Mirrors a still sky;
> Upon a brimming water among the stones
> Are nine-and-fifty swans.

> The nineteenth autumn has come upon me
> Since I first made my count;
> I saw, before I had well finished,
> All suddenly mount
> And scatter wheeling in great broken rings
> Upon their clamorous wings.

I have looked upon those brilliant creatures,
And now my heart is sore.
All's changed since I, hearing at twilight,
The first time on this shore,
The bell-beat of their wings above my head,
Trod with a lighter tread.

Unwearied still, lover by lover,
They paddle in the cold
Companionable streams or climb the air;
Their hearts have not grown old;
Passion or conquest, wander where they will,
Attend upon them still.

But now they drift on the still water,
Mysterious, beautiful;
Among what rushes will they build,
By what lake's edge or pool
Delight men's eyes when I awake some day
To find they have flown away?

Each of those 'nine-and-fifty swans' may be taken as a symbol of the manifestations of faith and imagery embodied in literature—but embodied with wings. It is not without significance that we hear constantly of 'winged words'. The names of these wings are faith and the image. The flight which they sustain is perpetual. It reaches everywhere in our human estate.

I conclude on a note of resignation, knowing that I have failed, as every one must fail, to define the power of faith and the image in literature; knowing too that my illustrations of it are inadequate. For me the *word*, that elusive medium through which the poet works, is always sacred. May I end by quoting another of my poems, which is not inappropriate:

These daily words you listen to, are not
One man's invention, but the growth of time,
Seeded from nobility and crime.
Some are blemished fruits, destined to rot
And fall. Some revive that were forgot.
A few, like death in life, may faintly chime
Dropped from the belfry of a poet's rhyme
Upon the graves in history's burial-plot.
But all of them, long-lived or quickly gone,
Are active powers, the radium of thought,
The close-packed atoms of our human story.
Here then is need for caution. Be admonished
To use these daily words as though God-wrought,
Magical master-keys to light and glory.

This, I suggest, is the theme of the Symposium on the text of Reality and Creative Vision. It is being tested by learned speakers against the touchstone of German lyric poetry. But it is also of universal significance toward the restoration and survival of a truly civilized way of life amongst men of every race, creed and colour.

SIXTH SESSION

Chairman: Professor McCAUSLAND STEWART

Professor J. ALER: Mythical consciousness in modern German poetry.

Chairman: Professor S. KÖRNER

Professor R. PEACOCK: Factors in literary judgement.

Mythical consciousness in modern German poetry

by

JAN ALER

Wer fragt, der ist gerichtet!
Hier wird nicht kommentiert,
Hier wird an sich gedichtet.
('Morgenstern')

As you know, our chairman has asked me to introduce the subject of 'mythical consciousness in modern poetry'. It is an honour I am glad to accept. I am going to assume that we do not need to bother ourselves about the terms 'modern' and poetry'. I say, do not *need* to, though actually I mean: do not *want* to. For they are, after all, open to discussion.

On the contrary, I shall have to spend some time on the concept of 'mythical consciousness'. This subject is usually discussed in such lofty and extravagant terms, that a more precise approach will do no harm. Moreover, also Beda Allemann has spoken about modern poetry and in a sense our addresses complement each other. This means that it is necessary to make the difference between our subjects clear. I shall try to do so by means of stating and explaining a number of fundamental concepts, the connexion between them . . . and the distinction between them. With a view to this, I would like to draw your attention to: consciousness—myth—mythology—the mythical—. These will provide us with the instruments required to sort out and interpret a store of poetry. The scholar seems to have been destined more than any other, to demonstrate the truth of that teasing definition: 'Man is a classifying animal'. However, I shall draw up only a sketchy inventory of the subject matter, so that we will have more time left for analysis and discussion of the general viewpoints. Having arrived that far, we will then take leave with a more general look at mythical consciousness and end by linking up our remarks with the general subject of our Symposium: the relation between reality and creative vision.

The combined term 'mythical consciousness' assumes (1) that there are other types of consciousness and (2) that these different types can be distinguished from one another on the basis of the products which make them apparent, in our case: myths —in other cases theories or technical functions. Whoever formulates the matter in this way shows at the same time what is his concept of consciousness, in the most general sense of that word. In consciousness he sees a capacity. He does not consider it a mere reservoir of impressions. He considers it a productive factor, and he means it quite literally when he says: 'Man *makes* himself conscious of reality'. Consciousness is concerned with reality, it is an *activity* within reality, an attitude to reality, an attitude to life. If one sees it like this, it automatically changes the concept of reality itself as well. We may return to this point later on.

If this first approach is correct, we must distinguish mythical consciousness from consciousness of myth. This last expression means that one is aware of myths. One knows they exist, one may even know what they are, or at least presume so; in any case, attention has been paid to myth. This may, perhaps, indicate an attitude of mind that is related to the mentality represented by myth, but it need not do so, and, anyhow, it is not the same thing.

So the term 'mythical consciousness' characterizes a subjective mental attitude by relating it to objective data. These data are stories. What sort of stories? We were already familiar in childhood with an inexhaustible miscellany of strange and wonderful stories. In addition to fairy-tales, sagas and legends, this conglomeration also included myths, mainly of a classical origin, and these myths were more particularly concerned with gods. Our acquaintance with myth so early in life, permits us to agree almost unanimously with Hermann Hesse's well-known overture to the novel *Peter Camenzind*: 'Im Anfang war der Mythus'.

Later on, the Greco-Roman tradition proved a rather one-sided introduction to this world. Thus we were of the opinion that there was a fundamental difference between pagan myth and Jewish–Christian revelation, a difference like that between fiction and fact. Admittedly, there are differences between 'myth' and 'revelation', but not to such an extent that the Bible would completely lack mythical fantasy. In that case the entire problem of 'Entmythologisierung' would be non-existent, and the Bishop of Woolwich (to be honest to him) would have no need to bother with the preparation of a new impression of a 100,000 copies of his book. Only recently Klaus Ziegler gave a clever survey of all the attempts which have been made to reconcile myth and revelation, and surely these attempts prove that the impressions gathered in our childhood have been equally shared by adults for a long, long time.

But well, that was far too high-brow for us in our youth. It was to take quite a while before we were going to get a clearer picture. This involved also a notion about the function of myth in the objective structure of religion. We began to understand something of the relation between these stories and certain devotional observances (ceremonies, rites). 'Myths must be lifted from their flat existence on paper, and placed in the three-dimensional reality of full life', to use the words of your distinguished Bronislaw Malinowski.

We shall speak further of 'myth' in this technical meaning of the term, ignoring the popular misuse of the word. In everyday language the term has become synonymous with an 'unfounded prejudice'. We often dispose of an opinion by dubbing it a 'myth' and sometimes even mean that a deliberate attempt to mislead is involved. Used in this way, myth indicates highly colourful, rather primitive, in any case striking untruths. Certain 'overtones' then take on an independent existence and supersede the original meaning of the word. There has been, indeed, a definite cause for the word to develop this shade of meaning. By the grace of language, these stories of the gods constitute a reality of the imagination. To this extent one can agree with Paul Valéry when he defines myth as 'ce qui n'existe et ne subsiste qu'ayant la parole pour cause'. Thus in the derogatory use of the word 'myth', its verbal and fantastic character has become absolute. But if *we* were to accept this, the expression 'mythical consciousness' would begin to mean that a thing such as 'consciousness' only seemingly exists, that it is nothing but an invention, lacking any foundation. We prefer to leave sour jokes of this kind to the Behaviourists. In contrast to this, 'mythical consciousness' in this paper indicates an attitude to life which appears in such stories, promotes them, and in its turn, is promoted by them.

The myths which have enthralled us from our early youth onwards, are stories by anonymous authors. They are set in a primeval era, which is so long ago that they have completely lost their relation to time. In fact, they have become timeless. (Here, by the way, lies the difference between myth and revelation. In the latter the former tends to be taken for history.) They are concerned with supernatural beings, their relations with each other and with human beings. By virtue of the intervention of these supernatural beings, the events in these stories acquire a strange and wondrous character. Yet the audience to which they are addressed nevertheless regard these happenings as true. For them they have a fundamental significance even. For they render many a thing comprehensible, they confer meaning on certain actions. Very often these actions suit a purpose, a purpose of a utilitarian or pedagogic-anthropological character. The farmer sows his corn, the farmer's wife does her weaving, somebody enters into obligations, an adolescent is initiated in nubility. Acts of this kind help to keep man going. He gets practical results with them. Myth, however, does not make its audience aware of the purposefulness of all these actions by means of causal analysis. It confers meaning on such actions as repetitions of fundamental events in the distant past which it records.

In this way myth renders man more conscious of himself and his place in the world. Myth gathers him up into a cosmic whole which displays an evident order. In this way nature becomes a real 'Umwelt', which shelters man. There is an eternal fluctuation of impressions, but in this fluctuation phenomena also return regularly. To this rhythm of nature corresponds man's own rhythm of life, acquired by regular repetitions of a type of their own. This temporal order is being protected by consecration. At first the gods lived this way, now man lives thus after their example. He performs his acts like observances, with awe and confidence. There is no need for logical arguments—there is an order and it is established by authority. The order is watched over revengefully. It is not to be infringed. But then this order protects man. As Malinowski puts it: 'Myth is not an intellectual explanation or an artistic imagery, but a *pragmatic charter* of primitive faith and moral wisdom'. Man is at ease now about his fate, he will be completely free from agoraphobia in the universe. The origin of life, the destination after death, all this is told you in myth, from now on you know it. Also the negative influences that might threaten the order, are not neglected: Medusa's paralysing eye hits us from Chaos.

This function of myth, then, is one feature of mythical consciousness. We must collect some more of them. How can it be that a story about events long past can possess a function of this kind? Individual happenings and actions are divested of their individuality, and the story acquires a typical character, just like an example; in other words myth creates an unavoidable precedent. It is only then that these events and actions can (and must) be repeated. Situations, and the elements of which they are composed, are then individual, yet at the same time, general.

When any singular event takes on a general sense in this way, i.e. when it does not point to this general character but directly represents it, then we will call it a 'symbol'. I watch an event take place or am told about it; I understand what is going on. But sometimes the event has something extra to tell me. I simply take it as it appears to me and then it conveys more than it is in itself. In addition to its 'face-value' it also has 'import', and this is what it conveys to the audience. Mrs. Langer, in particular, has made this interrelation clear in excellent fashion, when she speaks of the 'symbol' as a 'sensuous object which by virtue of its structure can express vital experience. This constitutes its import.' Thus, by virtue of its being 'typical', an event in myth is capable of being repeated. And by virtue of its import the epical *motif* becomes a *motive*: it motivates life in the literal sense of the verb. With this the 'import' of the 'symbol' becomes a reality in man's own life *via* his own imitating behaviour. When myth determines the line of conduct of the audience in this way, it takes on something of a mould which gives shape to man. Thenceforth his way of living possesses a clearly recognizable pattern. And when myth determines* man's attitude to life, on a collective basis, it creates a community, maintains this community and provides it with its style of living (the 'charter' Malinowski spoke about). The words of young Nietzsche indicate this in a striking manner: 'It is only a horizon surrounded by myths which encloses a complete cultural movement and makes a unity of it'. And all these aspects of the function of myth, and in particular the rooting of this function in its peculiar relationship to time, are once more expressed in Hermann Hesse's opening sentence: 'In the Beginning was Myth'.

The myth, but there is no such thing as a single, isolated myth. Instead there is mythology, a collective term which corresponds better with the facts than the plural of 'myth', for the myths are related to one another, they represent a fantastic but nevertheless orderly coherent group, with their own logic, which brings about their unity. To this extent, the term 'mythology' is not confined to the consideration and elucidation of these tales in the study of myth.

The unity we find within any mythology, points to a unity in the world of experiences and aspirations. In addition to their mutual coherence, all these stories are united by their atmosphere. This we may call 'the mythical', to distinguish it from 'mythology'. Together, they form the literary correlative of the anthropological unity indicated by the term 'mythical consciousness'. This atmosphere is founded upon a number of constants in the style and subject matter of the narrative. These two make us aware of the constant factor in man's confrontation with experience. When, for example, K. Ph. Moritz does not tire of demonstrating that in the classical myths 'the rich, inner profusion of nature' expresses itself, that 'ein jedes dieser Wesen, in gewisser Rücksicht, die ganze Natur mit allen ihren üppigen Auswüchsen und ihrem ganzen schwellenden Überfluss in sich darstellt', with this he has hit upon the quintessence, upon 'the mythical' I have in mind here.

---

* Linked up with this fact is another meaning of subsidiary importance, where again another aspect of myth is rendered absolute. This time it is the *positive* sense of an appeal, of a summons. Yet again, it is a *narrowing* of the meaning, fashionable in left and right wing political radicalism. And this is not by accident, for here we are concerned with slogans, meant to drug the critical hesitation of followers. Georges Sorel's 'mythe de la violence' is the classical example of this misuse of the word.

Moritz speaks of this in objective, not subjective terms. How is this possible? Well, by the time we have answered this question, we can end this systematic consideration of some principles.

The unity which manifests itself in myths in the way I have just described, is one which springs from their very origin. This origin has two poles, for we are concerned here with the essence of the attitude of man under the circumstances he meets with. Consequently we may speak of a subjective and objective pole. For this reason the mythical too has a subjective and an objective aspect. 'Mythical consciousness' gives an image of reality. It does not depict reality, but neither does it produce this image out of nothing. There is something in man's practical experience which corresponds to myth; myth possesses its own peculiar truth. Yet what it precisely is, to which myth answers, cannot be defined when you try to bypass myth. Myth, μνϑοζ, fixes experience as a meeting, a communion with a partner. All speech does: I am telling you something about a subject. In myth now, this subject, viz. nature, too is understood as a partner: there is a dialogue with reality in myth. And myth does not depict this objective pole: it expresses it, it symbolizes it by theophany. It symbolizes the meeting with reality as a partner. In so far Georges Gusdorf has done well to call it 'une ontologie vécue'. This pole continues to be a supposition of myth which can never be tracked down independently. All that mythical images suggest is a mysterious realm of powers to which the mythical pattern of life of which I spoke corresponds. So powers and patterns and words belong to each other.

Nietzsche is discussing this dimension when he says of myth that it is a visible example 'einer *ins Unendliche* hineinstarrenden Allgemeinheit und Wahrheit'. And modern research confirms this by another image. Mrs. Langer puts it this way: 'The telescoping of symbols and their import, of words and world, into one metaphysical entity is the very hallmark of mythical consciousness'. This is just the phenomenon we are interested in at the moment and the more so if we stick to the image of the telescope. Thus we consider myth as a means to fetch into the present (you know: Vergegenwärtigen) all that is far off, high and sublime or deep and threatening. Here, inevitably, the objective aspect of 'the mythical' is hypostated as an entity 'an sich' far in the background, yet at the same time decisive for the here and now. But this is, unfortunately, the point where Mrs. Langer leaves off.

Where the consciousness of this 'mythical substratum' is expressed without images, we may speak of a deeply felt relation to the overwhelming mightful 'universal basis' (Weltgrund). But on the other hand we may come across poems where the abundance of mythical images makes us lose sight of the Weltgrund. These two extremes may even alternate within the works of one and the same author. If one compares the clearcut images in George's 'Freund der Fluren' (in *Teppich des Lebens*), with his conjuration of the 'unholdenhaft nicht ganz gestalte Kräfte' in *Stern des Bundes*, one becomes clearly aware of the difference referred to here. The confrontation with the fundamental forces of life, however, remains a common feature of the two poems, and in either case it is a confrontation full of sacred awe.

Full of sacred awe: here I arrive at the connexion between my subject and that of Dr. S. Prawer: 'The numinous and uncanny'. There is always a suggestion of this in poems which display 'mythical consciousness'. Yet there are countless poems which show an awareness of the numinous and yet have no mythical air. One could outline a series of gradations as follows:

(1) In three famous lines about awe and dread (das Schaudern), Goethe on one occasion (Faust, v. 6272ff) lent expression to the fundamental feeling which is cardinal to both extremes:

> Das Schaudern ist der Menschheit bestes Teil;
> Wie auch die Welt ihm das Gefühl verteure,
> Ergriffen, fühlt er tief das Ungeheure.

It was not by chance that Rudolf Otto chose these words as the quotation to his pioneer work of forty-five years ago, 'Das Heilige' ('The Idea of the Holy') in which he clarifies the numinous from so many different angles. But here, so far, we are still only concerned with the aura of the mythical.

(2) One is already on the threshold of mythical imagery when one characterizes the religious significance of an experience by hinting to some mythology or other. Thomas Mann, for instance, refers to the ominous experience of complete upheaval which, curiously enough, simultaneously offers man a strange fulfilment: in *Death in Venice* he speaks of a world which in some sacred way is completely dislocated and now 'voll panischen Lebens'. Such an expression may be seen as a seed of myth.

(3) From such a rudimentary seed a small fruit may develop, once the basic experience of such a moment is symbolized in significant images. Then 'the symbol conveys a vital experience that constitutes its import'. The following, for example, may happen. Night has fallen, one is out in the open, enjoying the silence, the all-embracing harmony. The heart is filled with a wondrous mixture of peace, quiet and longing, all endowed with a certain solemnity. In this state of quiet emotion, one identifies oneself inwardly with the birds one has just seen return to their nests. Such an identification could be limited to the rational consideration: 'Come on now, time for us to be getting home too!' But an identification of an entirely different kind, of a spiritual kind, may occur. Of course, this is not a direct analogy between the home of a human being and the nest of a bird, but a metaphysical 'getting at home' in life. The simple, familiar fact of birds flying home to their nests now becomes charged with significance due to a deeper sense of being. The spectator feels entirely pervaded by the harmony of the universe and becomes part of this harmony, without, however, losing himself. He himself flies home as it were. This, more or less, is what the grateful reader undergoes, when Eichendorff writes:

> Und meine Seele spannte
> Weit ihre Flügel aus,
> Flog durch die stillen Lande,
> Als flöge sie nach Haus.

But these moving last lines of 'Moon-night' only lightly touch on deeper associations of this kind, when they recreate the archaic symbol of the bird of the soul.

(4) The mythical imagination comes, on the other hand, into full flower when one goes a little further still. Carl Spitteler has recorded the song of Phoenix in his *Olympic Spring*. The plastic image of the bird which sings its splendid song of world-sorrow for the nymph Kaleidusa is replete with observation. The longing of the captive son of the god for his bride Aurosa (the bird relates), is eloquent in the cipher-writing of the dewdrops. The poet is not content with a delicate and simple gesture such as Eichendorff's. He gives instead a detailed description of his miraculous bird, Phoenix, resplendent at the break of day.

> Da rauschte überm morgenroten Wipfelmeer
> Der Feuervogel Phönix durch die Luft daher.
> Auf eine Tanne nebst der Blösse schwebt er nieder,
> Äugt um sich, glättete das schimmernde Gefieder,
> Dann öffnet er den Schnabel, schloss den Blick und sang
> Sein Morgenlied, volltönend gleich wie Glockenklang,
> So lautete das bilderschwere Morgenlied,
> Das Phönix mit dem Glockenmund der Welt beschied . . . . .
>
> So sang der Vogel Phönix übern Tannenhorst,
> Über der Blösse auf dem morgenroten Forst.

In these lines mythical consciousness has expressed itself to the full in a colourful play of the imagination. Thus we have, in this sense, reached the highest rung of the ladder. But now we must not forget to ask ourselves the following question: Does the presence of such richness of mythical imagery guarantee that the work is rooted in mythical consciousness? The answer must be in the negative. Lacking a numinous aura, lacking a touch of the Infinite, a glimpse of some metaphysical perspective, lacking these things, mythical consciousness is out of the question. Therefore it is in no way sufficient to note that elements of our mythical inheritance occur in a poem to justify speaking of it. For instance, classical mythology was introduced into European poetry centuries ago. The vogue even reached a height in the eighteenth century. The poetry of that period teems with gods and goddesses and their retinues, regalia and other attributes. However, there is no trace of the mythical in all these mythological ornaments. They are very cleverly handled, but the true atmosphere is lacking. One only has to compare a sweet little poem by Goetz 'Amor on the Run', with one of those forceful lines of Goethe's, which raises in our minds a picture of cosmogonic love (Faust, verse 8479), and immediately one realizes the difference in tone. Or one may compare Gleim! Such a charming bit of nothing as 'Bacchus und Cythere' is concluded by:

> Weingott, winke mich nicht länger,
> Denn ich muss erst bei dem Mädchen
> Unter deinen Trauben schlummern.

But fifty years later Hölderlin in his great serious hankering after the fountainhead of Being, will testify of the winegod:

Brod ist der Erde Frucht, doch ists vom Lichte geseegnet,
Und vom donnernden Gott kommet die Freude des Weins.
Darum denken wir auch dabei der Himmlischen, die sonst
Da gewesen und die kehren in richtiger Zeit,
Darum singen sie auch mit Ernst die Sänger den Weingott
Und nicht eitel erdacht tönet dem Alten das Lob.

In dozens of authors like Goetz and Gleim, we certainly come across a 'consciousness of myth', but this was no 'mythical consciousness'—it was rather an artistic consciousness of myth. They knew quite a lot about mythology and they used this knowledge as a tool, an implement in the handicraft of decorating their work according to an age-old recipe. Now with the tongue in their cheek, now with a rhetorical gesture, but all the time using it as a luxurious adornment, never once with a core of devotion. Oh no—But medieval art, *that* now was of a far more mythical nature. How many Annunciations, Christmas-stables and Pietas do we not find there, to testify of that closely lived-through relation to the universal basis (Weltgrund), which we have made out to be an indispensable element of mythical consciousness.* This will be the standard in this paper on modern poetry: Not all religious poetry is mythical in structure; but there can not exist genuine mythical poetry without offering a glimpse of the numinous sub-stratum.

And now I should really give examples to illustrate each point of those stages which I have developed here revealing the existence of a mythical consciousness in lyrical works with reference to modern German poetry. A line can be drawn from Neo-romanticism, through Expressionism, magischer Realismus and Surrealism up to the experimental poetry and social realism of the present day. I would have to begin with George and Rilke and take into special account separate authors. For lyrical poets such as Carossa, Däubler, Benn, Loerke, Friedrich Georg Jünger, Langgässer, Lehmann, Celan, without mentioning others, are of particular importance in this context.

However, in this paper there is only space to point out a few characteristics. I believe that it can be concluded:

(a) that a basic feeling for the numinous is still strongly represented today. On this basis, allusions to the mythological tradition are by no means rare. I would like to maintain the same with regard to the appearance of mythical tendencies of the type revealed in Eichendorff's 'Mondnacht'. Myth, when elaborated, little by little falls into the background, however, since the fading away of symbolism.

(b) As a genre, lyrical poetry in no way favours such elaboration. Moreover, the lyric in its most modern form turns away completely from such a manner of representation. Surrealism may be quoted as an exception to this.

(c) In another respect, too, myth has not received the same amount of attention

---

*In this connexion one may compare the excellent characterization of the Christmas story by Thomas Mann in *Dr. Faustus* (ch. 44).

as it did thirty years ago. There is a strong decline of interest in continuing the tradition of the myth. In the long run it is not repetitions which are important, but original creations. This is particularly the case with surrealism.

(d) Mythical consciousness is therefore given a wide and vigorous representation, but myth meanwhile slips into the background. And it was the introductory prolegomena which served the purpose of clarifying this state of affairs: there is a close relation between mythical consciousness and myth, which does not, however, turn them into Siamese twins.

(e) The following can be stated with regard to the mythical tradition in modern lyrical poetry: Classical antiquity starts off with being all-important; afterwards Christianity becomes another source of this type of lyrical poetry; it is even not uncommon to find all kinds of syncretism. It is also striking that certain mythical themes are particularly popular: thus it is for example that the Medusa-motif nowadays appears repeatedly (this theme does of course have a clear correspondence with our present situation in which we are so clearly aware of the absurdity of existence).

*   *   *

Now that we have considered the who and what, where, when and how, there still remains the question, by no means the least significant, of why? Why is it that twentieth century poetry and art in general turn so often to myth, and that it is so often leading artists who do this? I intend here to state a few points which I consider to be of decisive importance and then finally to go somewhat deeper into the question of the relations between mythical consciousness and modern art.

The determining factors are in my opinion the following:

(1) the secularization of occidental culture,

(2) the decline of aprioristic transcendentalism in systematic philosophy (not of philosophy as such),

(3) the trend towards an essentially scientific world-picture. These factors have as their natural consequence that questions about norms, aims or ideals of life, can no longer be answered with the same authoritative or logical necessity which was previously considered possible. Nevertheless, despite this, every culture requires a guiding and binding answer to these questions. In addition to this there are two further points to be raised, namely:

(4) a profound change in our relationship with Nature, and

(5) the development within society from extreme individuality to an increasing measure of collectivization.

One could easily reduce points (1) to (3) to Nietzsche's formula that 'God is dead', but for our purposes a complementary formula of Nietzsche's is even more significant: 'In the beginning was nonsense' (*Menschliches Allzumenschliches II* nr. 22). Here we find the exact opposite to that attitude which Hesse's phrase about 'Mythos' characterizes. And Hesse's phrase was like a slogan for the stream of reactions to the experience of the absurd which Nietzsche had captured so brilliantly. Both formulae, that of Nietzsche's as well as that of Hesse's, are significant variations of the famous opening lines of the Gospel according to St. John. Combined, these variations charactize about one century of spiritual crisis in Western civilization. It is no coincidence that Hesse coined his formula in the same decade in which, for instance Stefan George announced the New God. It is only in this context that such ambitious literary phenomena may make sense.

But we will now drop this relation, in order to pay some more attention to the fact that, of all things, it had to be *art*, which turned out to be the indicated medium for the revival of myth and the expression of mythical consciousness. Art, too, acquired its own autonomy in the emancipation of our culture. Just as in epistemology the view that knowledge simply depicts reality, has been overcome, (consciousness, it is understood, is an active principle), so too, prejudice regarding art as an imitation of reality, disappears. This involves, amongst other things, the sovereignty of the artistic imagination.

Modern philosophy of art elucidates the cardinal fact that 'art does not depict the visible, it renders visible', to quote the words of Paul Klee. Aesthetics explains the essence of art when giving preciser definition to this magic formula. It then becomes clear that, using its own means, art produces a reality of its own and that the work of art has a symbolic significance. If art is one of the systems of 'Symbolische Formen', and if one of the specific characteristics of this system is that it transfers feeling with the aid of concrete images, the process of artistic creation must approach very close indeed to that of mythology. And then it only actually depends on the *themes* art treats in its own way, that is to say, on the *contents* of art, whether it will be able to meet the spiritual need we have in mind. If the artist chooses his highly pregnant images, full of dedication, to make us aware of archetypes of human themes in their timeless capacity for repetition, his work will supply exactly what is wanted in our crisis. His work then embodies the fundamental vision that mythical consciousness makes possible. The work puts a pattern of life at our disposal; thereby it stands for an attitude towards reality and puts this attitude forward with an artistic spell.

Such themes, however, are not sufficient in themselves to make art—art! That is a matter of formgiving. We must make a distinction between '*fond*' and '*form*', while avoiding playing the one off against the other. Who like our dear host is captivated by *the genius of German lyric*, asks again and again after its formal *and* metaphysical values and knows that, elucidating their relation, that apparently so innocent conjunction 'and' is crucial. However admirably Mrs. Langer has analysed 'form' as 'significant form', it is exceedingly unfortunate that she should have used this result in order to deal rather highhandedly with significant motif. Mrs. Langer is indeed right when she rejects the pretension of depth-psychology that it has solved the riddle of art by its theory of significant motifs. Depth-psychology affords us, after all, with only one approach, one entrance to this territory. Jung's theory of archetypes, especially, is very useful in this context, but the theory of 'Befindlichkeit' in the existential analysis is, for example, an indispensable completion, as well as Gaston Bachelard's outlook on our poetical relation to the four elements. Works of art whose manifest contents conjure up the import of such fundamental experience, contribute towards supplying an answer to the question: how is modern man to get once more a hold on life?

A number of factors especially in the history of German culture have stimulated the full awareness of the importance of mythical consciousness and of the fact how essential such tendencies in art could be. The fascinating development of European poetry under the guidance of French symbolism is, on the other hand, very important in connexion with our subject matter. Bowra's absorbing book, *The Heritage of Symbolism*, treats this influence. And in the third place the research on dream and myth, as regarded in depth-psychology, has accentuated the permanent importance of the mythical. This movement has promoted that mythical consciousness in the end boldly emancipated out of the mythology which was handed down to us by tradition and is in this respect 'prefabricated'.

If one considers the present situation, one notes that the unquestionable unity of spiritual life (despite its rich differentiation) is also clearly manifested in any profound revaluation of myth in philosophy. This phenomenon corresponds with and accompanies the trend in the arts. From Kant to Cassirer—that was already quite a big step. But from Cassirer to Gusdorf, for example, that is a big step too, yet it took only one decade to accomplish. You may judge for yourselves. In Cassirer, after all, the order of succession of symbolic forms is rendered in the following way: 'Science is the last step in man's mental development and it may be regarded as the highest and most characteristic attainment of human culture. . . . There is no second power in our modern world which may be compared to that of scientific thought. It is held to be the summit and consummation of all our human activities, the last chapter in the history of mankind and the most important subject of a philosophy of man. . .'. One can agree with all this except for the monopoly of knowledge which this view assigns to science. (This also forms the background to Mrs. Langer's exposition.)

Gusdorf, on the other hand, generously concedes the complementary significance of the consciousness which myth represents. He realizes that the rational-empirical mastery of reality loses its human character, if it fails to leave room for all those values in human life of which man is aware 'et qui sont les mêmes que celles dont vivait la conscience mythique'. It is the task of philosophy to acquaint itself with this substance of the mythical consciousness and by so doing, to reconcile science with mythical consciousness. One does indeed find that this reconcilation has been in progress for some time in philosophy, even in places where a devotee of continental philosophy, of German literature and its mythical imagery, would not, perhaps, expect to find this. You will remember how the organic relation of man to his world was a typical correlative of mythical consciousness. The individual factor was of only relative significance in the whole. What was involved was not the individual, but the typical and its collective realization. As a result now, of modern thinking, one can read e.g. in your great philosopher Alfred North Whitehead the following— and by the way, I would like to draw your attention to the age-old symbolism, taken from weaving, in this passage: 'There is no independent mode of existence; every entity is only to be understood in terms of the way in which it is interwoven with the rest of the Universe' (*Essays in Philosophy*).

The message conveyed by myth corresponds to this philosophical view. Its symbols ruled the emotional life of the community familiar with it and convinced by it that man forms part of a significant whole. A solemn feeling for this living cosmic unity is exactly the thing which the Dutch philosopher H. J. Oldewelt eloquently sketched as one of the most important objectives in education. But today we shall have to resist the temptation to further develop the philosophical context and background in the work of other great contemporary thinkers like Heidegger and Jaspers. Suffice it to mention these indications.

* * *

To give a prognosis is always a precarious undertaking. One might ask oneself however, which trend in mythical consciousness will ultimately prevail. For there were in the beginning indeed typically anti-Christian tendencies. In our time, however, the picture has become far more complicated. Which pattern of mythical consciousness will predominate in the future is a cut-and-dried matter only to partisans. To them it is always a matter of 'one thing or the other'. Yet observation teaches us that the proper formula is: 'one thing as well as the other'. And perhaps a bird's eye view of the entire process may lead to the possibility of 'neither-this-nor-that'. May I end by considering this last possibility?

In an exceptionally intelligent, yet spirit-defeating climate of increasing scientism, materialism and technology, that school of art which made of its works vehicles to convey mythical themes, acted as a most valuable tonic. These works gave plastic expression to a deeper union with reality. It helped to do away with the alienation between nature and modern civilization. In the meantime, over and above the disruption of the conventional alternatives ('diesseits' opposed to 'jenseits'; the outward opposed to the inward; matter opposed to spirit) an embryonic unity has been reached which is more original than all these alternatives. In the works of art which aim at this unity, the spiritual is contained within the natural phenomenon: 'Geist in den Sinnen behaust'. In such a vision of things, we perceive at the long last a whole, unblemished world, in which man is no stranger, but one of the family. It amounts to an awareness of integral life, whose unity with the cosmos justifies our calling it a 'religious' experience. In lyrical poetry it often leads to something resembling a song of the elements. The source of this art is the dialogue between man and reality, which sings its way through his works of art. Such poetry opens a range of vision in which reality, in its everyday guise, moves us like a miracle. Everyday life is great, one feels, if we live it greatly . . . and that means living it with a bold piety.

The interest in the ancient myths has fulfilled an important function. It helped to free art from three obstinate prejudices. The objectivism of the realistic convention was overcome in modern art, as well as the classical formalism, but so, too, was the subjectivism, which saw the emotions of the individual as the core of art. But from the moment mythical consciousness had learned to enfold itself freely once more in the arts, this consciousness got a more direct hold on experience than it obtained by linking up with traditional imagery, however venerable. This has gradually become a detour. If one chooses to follow this path, it is because one is driven by a nostalgia. But this may easily lead to self-deception. To mention only a few facts: we do not live in tribes any longer, nor in communities divided from one another by language barriers; our living has become cosmopolitan and poly-glot. The Umwelt has expanded, thanks to scientific thinking, into a universe ... and we know that this universe itself is expanding. ... The static order of an eter-nally-recurring, cyclic rhythm of life has made way for a restless dynamism which stands in an entirely different relation to time.

It is true that nothing ever really becomes past and done, mythical conscious-ness neither; but this applies a fortiori to scientific consciousness too! *After*, and that means *next to* causal-analytical consciousness, the appropriation of a meaning of life not by concepts, but by images, is coming to the fore again. This gives rise to a peculiar predicament. If myth is looked upon as a kind of primitive science, then one says, with Gottfried Benn, from the point of view of modern science: 'Die Mythe log!' But on realizing how science as such, fails to answer the questions which ask after the sense of life and its aims, many people once more hanker after a myth which does answer those questions. This very Gottfried Benn movingly expressed this longing for a reality made inhabitable by means of mythical images:

> Ach, als sich alle einer Mitte neigten
> · · · · ·
> · · · · ·
> Oh ferne, zwingende erfüllte Stunde,
> Die einst auch das verlor'ne Ich umschloss.

Hovering between these two extremes, myth as a 'lie' on the one hand, and as a 'fulfilment' on the other, modern intellectuals cannot settle down to a definite, distinct standpoint as regards myth. And yet, myth and scientific theory are not necessarily mutually exclusive. Their juxtaposition does not, in essence, mean a situation of conflict. Neo-positivism remains, by nature, an antipode of the tendencies to myth, but, properly understood, it is not an antagonist. The finest guarantee for a fruitful, progressive interplay between science and myth lies precisely in that consistent phenomenalistic and instrumental view of knowledge neo-positivism advocates. As a matter of fact it gives up every pretension that scientific theory should exclusively reveal the truth about the essence of reality. This was a bit of metaphysics in old positivism and as such it plainly contradicted its own theory of knowledge. This absurdity now has disappeared.

The complementary expression of sense, as offered by myth, however, no longer enjoys the monopoly it did hitherto. Whitehead's profundity, Oldewelt's wisdom, are striking examples of the *philosophical* consciousness, which likewise has a per-manent say in the matter. This has been the case since the Ionic philosophers of nature broke with the mythical story, instead of which they developed a metaphysical theory.

But then, the whole question of 'what is the meaning of life' has undergone a fundamental change. Modern man is no longer painstakingly concerned with ex-cluding all absurdity from that idea. On the contrary, we are joyfully learning to live our lives reconciled to the fundamental absurdity, not resigning but rather aware of our strength, as long as we wrestle with it.

There, where in close harmony with nature, art aims to interpret essential patterns of living and presents these typical situations to us with a profound and/or monumental simplification in concrete symbols, there mythical consciousness shows itself, without traditional myths, yet closely associated with the 'ever-mythical', most up-to-date. Purple passages in Faust II, pale beside *Über allen Gipfeln*. This appears to me to be a prototype of lyrical poetry as 'ontologie vécue', in the sense Gusdorf takes it. But Hölderlin provided us with other treasures and what about Mörike and many, many other great poets who saw us home in the sense of Eichendorff's 'Mondnacht'.

The modern artist presents us with these highly significant images in a less elaborate form, in flashes, and thus more abstract and perhaps even non-figurative. A single example, chosen at random, may fascinate for a moment the kind reader in the light of our previous considerations:

> Der Schnee von Morgen,
> der hier
> auf diese Erde
> fallen wird, wo jeder
> Engel seine
> festumrissene
> Ordnung hat,
> noch bindet ihn
> der Zirkelschlag
> des Monds.
> (Oliver Behnssen, *Texte und Zeichen*, nr. 12)

In such work one recognizes once more the spirit of Goethe's ultimate 'du auch' and that word 'auch' associates the human being addressed, by analogy, with the universe, the All. Devoutly imbued with a sense of his finiteness, but full of confidence, also the most recent poetry will often testify to an awareness of life, so masterfully expressed by Hermann Broch in his poem to Thomas Mann (*An die Phantasie*, 1945), with a line that evokes the ancient symbolism of the tree of life:

Aus den Wurzelzeiten rauscht es gottesgross.

Bibliography

ALER, JAN, 'De functie der literatuur in onze tijd' (1962).

ALER, JAN, 'De mythe in de hedendaagse kunst' in *Mythe en realiteit* (1963).

BACHELARD, GASTON, *L'air et les Songes* (1943).

BOWRA, C. M., *The Heritage of Symbolism* (1946).

CASSIRER, ERNST, *An Essay on Man* (1944).

CLOSS, AUGUST, *The Genius of the German Lyric*, 1962, 2nd. ed.

GUSDORF, GEORGES, *Mythe et Métaphysique* (1953).

HEIDEGGER, MARTIN, *Sein und Zeit* (1927).

HEIDEGGER, MARTIN, 'Der Ursprung des Kunstwerkes', in *Holzwege* (1950).

LANGER, SUSANNE K., *Feeling and Form* (1953).

MALINOWSKI, BRONISLAW, *Myth in Primitive Psychology* (1926).

MORITZ, K. PH., *Götterlehre* (new impression, 1948).

NIETZSCHE, FRIEDRICH, *Die Geburt der Tragödie*.

OLDEWELT, H. M. J., *Over ouders en kinderen schijnt dezelfde zon* (1959).

OTTO, RUDOLF, *Das Heilige* (1917).

ROBINSON, J., *Honest to God* (1963).

VALÉRY, PAUL, 'Petite lettre sur les mythes', in *Variété II* (1929).

WHITEHAD, A. NORTH, *Essays in Philosophy and Science* (1947).

ZIEGLER, KLAUS, 'Mythos und Dichtung', in *Reallexikon d. deutsch. Literaturgesch.* (1962).

Discussion

Closs asked if the speaker agreed with Ernst Cassirer's view that myths are energies and powers rather than statements which express meanings, and asked if modern man could live without myth.

Aler said he had tried to combine two things: the consciousness of a certain play of forces in the world of reality, and man's need to find a way of life enabling him to feel a part of this play of forces. Both Cassirer and Miss Susanne K. Langer had recognized that myths were not mere products of the imagination; they also contained factual material. But their transcendental subjectivism was a decisive obstacle to acknowledge fully the importance of myth. Myth had not been outdated by science—they were complementary.

Böckmann asked if art must be based on myth, and if myth was a special combination of imagination and reflection. He thought one should be cautious in the use of the word 'myth' and regard it as archaic to-day. He referred in this connexion to Nietzsche.

Aler replied that Nietzsche must be used indeed with discretion; the generations immediately following him had not understood him correctly. Much abuse had been made of his aphorisms. He (Aler) had tried to show how art was apt to be the vehicle by which in our time mythical consciousness was transmitted. It was only one current in modern art, but a very important one.

Factors in literary judgement

Some provisional notes

by

R. PEACOCK

THE theme of this colloquium involves discussion of the ways in which poetry is in relationship both with life and with ideas and thought of various kinds. As one thinks about these relations one is constantly aware that they are significant, but also that one is always trying to clarify the boundary line of poetry, the edge beyond which the elements it uses are reorganized in a special sort of pattern. In other words, if one talks about what poetry has to do with life, or 'reality', or thought, one has to be pretty sure what poetry is and is not. I thought it might be pertinent to make a few observations, however provisional, on the problem of judging the literary object, and evaluating it.

The subject is a large one. I shall consider only three general criteria, and even then I shall have to be too brief. They are: the idea of organic unity; a quality which I shall call philosophical awareness; and novelty, in which originality is involved. I do not think it is possible to find the nerve of literary art by pointing to a single principle, such as 'universality', or 'vision of eternal forms', or the depiction of a 'higher reality', and so on; nor, to turn to the instrumental side, is it adequate to raise such ideas as 'craft', or 'language', or 'creativeness' etc., to the function of being absolute criteria. A good work fulfils not one but several conditions simultaneously, its success arising from a very subtle balance between several features.

UNITY

With regard to the notion of unity, it is common enough to hear that a unified effect is required of a literary work. Often the term 'organic unity' is used, which suggests a unity arising from functional relationships; this is a more adequate term, since it is certainly necessary to refine in some way on the simple idea of unity. I would myself distinguish between *architectonic* and *metaphorical* unity. Unity in itself is not an exclusive criterion of art. It characterizes many things that are not art, a machine, a town, a report, a trial, and so on, and it would merely be casuistical to argue that these things 'become art', in the same sense in which a poem is art, when they show unity. The sense of order, of subordination of parts, of sequence, are to some extent aesthetic and pleasing, but they are features of many kinds of rationalization and organization, of hierarchies, institutions, and formal arrangements that are often called 'empty' or 'soulless' and are the antithesis of the animated forms of art. In fact, a very common feature of low-category literary works is an excellent architectonic plan. The most unpretentious magazine romances are well-constructed. Indeed, the craft of writing them is learned in a hard school, and we scholars who pass them by forget that often as much craft and skill goes to their 'making' as does to that of good literature. Detective novels are a good example of compositional unity. Their form is basically a riddle, the material being economically organized in strict relationship to a central mystery, which inevitably yields architectonic unity and even formal beauty.

In poetry the unity is more complex, and concerns not only different elements but a group of essential elements, which may be here summed up briefly as thought, feelings, imagery, and language. These interact so that they exist in each other and may be said to take on mutually something of each other's character. Thought becomes charged with emotion and associated with imagery. Feelings are converted into ideas through symbolization. Images become a kind of thought, and language takes on the nature of imagery. Poetic, or 'metaphorical', unity is the harmonious meaning or effect arising from the interaction and mutual modification of these diverse elements. It is within *this* unity, more subtle than architectonic unity, that metaphors and symbols are set in motion, that language ceases to be simply conceptual, and that the poetic work receives the special quality of being 'another world' separate from the real one.

The point I want to emphasize here, and which usually goes unnoticed, is that this kind of unity pertains to *texture*, and not only to total design. This feature is apparent in any section of a literary work, in a single verse, in a paragraph, in a passage of dialogue. An important consequence is that our judgement of literary quality is based in the first place on the texture, not on a work in its totality. Take the following passages:

> Warum gabst du uns die tiefen Blicke
> Unsre Zukunft ahndungsvoll zu schauen . . .

> Mit gelben Birnen hänget
> Und voll mit wilden Rosen
> Das Land in den See . . .

> When to the sessions of sweet silent thought . . .

> Tel qu'en lui-même enfin l'éternité le change . . .

> Der Abend wiegte schon die Erde . . .

These are all fragments, beginnings of poems, and uncompleted thoughts. There can be no question of judging a 'total unity', since the poem is only just starting; but the poetic mode is unmistakable. The same process appears in the other arts. We do not need a whole canvas to recognize artistic quality. We can tell it from any section of a painting, just as we can recognize quality in a pianist from the first bars he plays, without having to wait until he has played right through his piece.

It by no means follows that over-all unity does not matter; far from it. Nor that every bit of texture of every work must always be as decisive as the examples given. But it does follow that judging art, or art quality, is not the same thing as judging a work in its totality, and that the former is quite as important as the latter. Possibly more so, since the quality of the texture may easily decide whether you go on reading. On this depends, too, the judgement of fragments and unfinished work, of which the Sapphic fragments, or Hölderlin's late poetic drafts, are examples. It helps, too, with the evaluation of all the excellent and fluent, but careless poets, like Byron, who write inspired passages and jingles by turns. Or again, how many novels are really and truly unified economies, in the strictest sense of perfect inter-relationship of all the parts, with nothing superfluous and no loose ends? For every perfect novel there are a thousand perfect chapters. Still another example would be the plays of Goethe, where, in the face of sheer abundance and diversity of motifs, the strict test of essentially dramatic unity breaks down.

Conversely, the sense of texture enables us to see that a work is unsatisfactory in spite of having a good shape or compositional scheme. An example is the following poem:

ZU SPÄT

Da ich in Jugendnot und Scham
Zu dir mit leiser Bitte kam,
Hast du gelacht
Und hast aus meiner Liebe
Ein Spiel gemacht.

Nun bist du müd und spielst nicht mehr,
Mit dunklen Augen blickst du her
Aus deiner Not,
Und willst die Liebe haben,
Die ich dir damals bot.

Ach, die ist lang verglommen
Und kann nicht wiederkommen—
Einst war sie dein!
Nun kennt sie keine Namen mehr
Und will alleine sein.

This poem certainly has a unified design. It presents an emotional situation in three simple stages, each taking up a stanza: the woman's past mockery of the man's love, her present need for love as she grows old, and the man's oblivion of a love that was. The metre and stanza, the simple language and rhyme scheme, are rhymically adapted to the languid rejection of interest and the death of amorous sentiment. The poem as a whole has a pleasing linguistic and musical shape. Yet a second look at the texture discovers how thin and anaemic it is. Both situation and sentiments are commonplace. And the words also: *Jugendnot und Scham, leise Bitte, aus Liebe ein Spiel gemacht, du bist müd, dunkle Augen*—they are all clichés. No image enlivens the poem except the banal *verglommen* for love. The title, too, shares the general banality. It could also be argued that the last stanza does not make sense. We are led to conclude that the poem is promising in its general design and fails in its textural detail.

The point need not be laboured further. Judgement of quality, and of a total work, are separate aspects of evaluating literary works, though they are of course complementary. But the texture is the more important. For if the fault is architectonic and not textural we speak only of relative failure—failure to sustain the quality in a whole. But if the texture is poor no amount of abstract compositional unity can make a complete poetic reality.

Let me comment here on the view widely held today that literary works create their own basis of judgement. Wolfgang Kayser says: 'Wir fragen, was das Werk sein will und messen es an ihm selber' (*Literarische Wertung und Interpretation*, in *Die Vortragreise*, p. 50). This is not true as it stands, because it is over-simplified. The first stage of judgement, as we have just expounded, is to recognize quality. Now this we can only do by reference to a standard—that is to say, a conception of what a literary work is and looks like—and such a conception develops within our sensibility as we become familiar with good literature. When we read a work which is either quite new, or new at least for ourselves, we apply to it standards outside itself, criteria established in previous literature, both generally and in reference to specific genres or forms. In doing this we get the feeling that 'there is something in it', even though it may take us time to come to a fuller understanding. It is at the *second* stage of evaluation that we look at a work in the light of its own law. What we judge from the work itself is its individual character amongst other works. We expect it, in fact, to have an individual cast, and do not make the mistake of condemning it for being unlike other works. But we do this only after we have decided that it *is* an example of literary expression.

PHILOSOPHICAL AWARENESS

The question as to whether poets should also be philosophers, with new or interesting ideas, moral views, or a *Weltanschauung*, raises a number of difficulties. It is customary nowadays in poetics to play down heavily the thought-content of poems; nevertheless some kinds of didactic poetry in the past set out deliberately to embody ideas, and if the latter are extracted from such work what is left can be very exiguous. In the ode form 'thoughts', 'sentences', and near-discursive statements are everywhere in evidence. In the eighteenth century, again, a common attitude was to compose a philosophical poem in which a common stock of 'ideas' were presented in 'poetic form', or 'adorned by poetry', and presumably the ideas were felt to be part of the value for money, or of the 'total experience', as we should probably say now. Didactic poetry has to be appreciated as such, and not as though it were romantic *Erlebnislyrik* or a bit of Mallarmean symbolism.

In a way, of course, it is a pointless question. The fact is that in genius, as in nature and human character, everything is possible, any and every combination of interests and gifts. The result is that when a man with the gift of verse- (or drama-, or fiction-) making is also interested in philosophical ideas, he inevitably runs the two together and philosophical poetry emerges; and we can add that his ideas can be either his own, or derivative, or a mixture of both. This is what all philosophical poetry is. It is an amalgam, but a unity, an indivisible kind, that we must accept; all attempts to put the significance into the 'poetic', or aesthetic, component alone are beside the point.

Philosophical poems are, however, only one field in which this problem appears. Plays and novels are just as frequently a medium for ideas and creeds. But the question should be put in its sharpest form: must a work (poem, play, or novel) *always* embody thought, beliefs, or a view of life, either as something original or as something embraced with conviction?

Two extreme views, juxtaposed, are illuminating. The first was held by Bernard Shaw, who took up a very simple position. Writers and artists only attracted his interest if they had a philosophy, as for instance Michelangelo, John Bunyan, Goethe, Wagner, and Ibsen had. He believed in parable, and art was most significant for him when it consisted of parables. His own plays belong to this category, and we remember how he disparaged Shakespeare for having no philosophy but merely expressing commonplaces about life that everyone knows for himself after a few years of adult experience. This attitude is probably shared by large numbers of people—'I like a play with ideas in it' 'I like a novel that gives you something to think about'. And it may be that professional students of literature underestimate its potency and influence, and moreover its *legitimacy*, from this point of view. Literature may not be just direct moral teaching, but no one can forbid it to have relations with morals, whether of individuals or societies; or, nowadays, with scientific thought and world-views which influence culture and social institutions. It seems to me that Brecht's impact is due largely to his moral fervour. His apologists tell us vociferously that he is of course 'not only a doctrinaire but a poet'. It may be true. But quite apart from the element of doctrinaire politics Brecht has played variations on two great themes—poverty and peace, or money and war—which are central problems of world life in our age and time. Without this substance his notorious theatrical experiments would be hollow.

Mr. T. S. Eliot takes up a position opposite that of Shaw. He has a highly developed sense of the differing functions of poetry and philosophical beliefs. It appears sharply in his rejection of the claim of poetry since the romantic period to be a substitute for religion. Eliot looks for his philosophy and theology in the relevant sources. Poetry does not exist to do their job, but one of its own, for which reason alone we cultivate it. It is a mistake, he believes, to ask poetry to do more than its own task or give more than it can. Moreover, if we do not expect poetry to create philosophies or religions we shall be able to enjoy it all the more as poetry.

Creative writers argue *pro domo*; readers must find a middle way, or at least an independent, reader's view. One might put the point thus: in every serious literary work of quality we can feel a latent philosophical power, an awareness of philosophical

values, in the sense of ideas about life which are also, in different circumstances, the subject of philosophical or religious or ethical argument. Whether such
awareness remains implicit, or crystallizes into explicit statement, depends on the
style and temperament of the author; Shaw's favourites are examples of a fair
measure of the explicit mingling with the implicit. But a work of art or poetry, as
such, must present its ideas in terms of sensibility. The thought is not expressed
directly but is suspended in a context of story or feeling; captured in symbols, it is
half shrouded, half emergent. A simple example appears in Thomas Mann's early
work in connexion with his attitude to the two philosophers, Schopenhauer and
Nietzsche. These two, in philosophical argument, draw conclusions of *thought* about
the primacy of mind or of 'life', and are opposed to each other. Mann, as a novelist,
gives a picture of life and temperament which expresses the conflict between the
Schopenhauerian and the Nietzschean ideas as a matter of attitudes, as something
experienced in his feelings and apprehended in his sensibility. Similarly, Chekhov's
plays are impregnated with social analysis, but it is expressed in pictures and in
terms of feelings. He shows us through his persons the malaise experienced by Russian
bourgeois society at the beginning of this century.

To illustrate a further, very subtle and difficult, aspect of the relation between
thought and poetic forms, let us put a line of poetry side by side with one of the
Pensées, in prose, of Pascal. One of the sections, or strophes, of Hölderlin's *Der
Rhein* begins thus:

> Ein Rätsel ist Reinentsprungenes—

I think even a fanatic of the 'poetic' as against the 'discursive' must admit that these
words, whatever else they mean or do, contain an abstract idea. I would in fact
maintain that one's *first* reaction to this line is to the thought as such. In prose it
would run: things, or beings, whose origin is immaculate are a mystery. But Hölderlin has nevertheless expressed the idea in such a way that it has a resonance deriving
from more than abstract thought. He touches our deepest feelings of piety and our
belief in the mysteries of divine being. The sound-pattern in the words has strict
unity: with one exception the vowels are all front sounds, the consonants are predominantly liquids or continuants, and repetitions give assonance. The rhythmic
sequence, with the syntactical inversion, is also highly significant. This musical
form, which here is incredibly concentrated, implementing the wonderfully inspired
compound formation *Reinentsprungenes*, transforms conceptual statement into a verbal
expression in which feeling and thought cannot be separated, as we are drawn into
a region of religious sentiment.

Let us now look at the *pensée* from Pascal, in which a similar process occurs though
prose is the medium. 'Le silence éternel de ces espaces infinies m'effraie'. It is the
sort of passage which strikes us, as we come across it in a prose writer, as being
'poetic' without the help of conventional metre or rhyme. It is, in the first place, a
prose statement, and we can divide it into two parts. One refers to a fact: the infinite
spaces are silent and have always been so throughout time. The other describes an
emotional reaction: that fills me with fear. But the *pensée* as a whole strikes us with

the force of poetry. The statement about silence is enormously impressive. Mr. T. S. Eliot has pointed out that Pascal was not disturbed or impressed by the 'infinite spaces'; anyone can feel that. But by their silence; there lies the imaginative power of the idea. In this short piece of prose, then, we have something profoundly and startlingly observed, then imaginatively presented, and accompanied by an emotional outburst. By these three elements it is lifted out of conceptual or factual statement and transformed into an utterance near to poetry.

NOVELTY

Whether works must be 'original' in ideas and form, whether they must show striking novelty, is another of the most frequently posed questions and the most often misunderstood.

One answer could be perfectly simple. It is that there must be something new of some kind, because a work that has nothing novel is a repetition, or imitation. A work that uses again ideas previously used, and past language or forms, is superfluous. In fact a very large number of works (especially poems) can quickly be shown to be *unconscious* imitations, as, for example, epigon poetry, or the common-places of the merely fashionable, or work that is just banal in subject, feeling, and form. For the banal in art is the known masquerading as new creation. We always understand such works quite easily; we are used to them and know what is in them. By contrast, every genuine work should at its first appearance look a little strange, and invite us to contest with it for its secret.

One aspect of this problem in particular leads to confused discussion and judgement. People often link the idea of the new with the idea of a predominant new contemporary feeling and style common to a number of writers of the same generation; they show a change of 'consciousness', as we say, which characterizes the new present as against preceding phases of style. Such changes, seen in a somewhat simplified perspective, are the materials of historical interpretation, being distinguished as significant 'periods'. The fact that such changes do occur, and the habit of historical interpretation, dispose critics and others very easily to adopt the view that a writer who is any good at all '*ought* to express his time', as one says; or, in other words, he ought to be writing in such a way that later historians will be able to say that he was characteristic of what they deem to be the character of his period. Thus a factor of historical interpretation is transformed into a criterion.

This is erroneous; it is a short-circuit and a crude simplification. A 'period' is all sorts of things, and in no way just equivalent to one profiled view. There are many ways of being 'of one's age' without necessarily fitting into one profile. Art and poetry bring to consciousness new ways of thought and feeling, but many and varied ones, in currents and cross-currents, and they do so by virtue of the innocence and spontaneity in genuine artistic creation. It is the mark of the poet to be absolutely true to his feelings, intuitions, and insights, and to have the faculty of revealing them in language. It is a necessary and logical consequence that he expresses the life *he* feels and sees, which must be the life of today and not of yesterday, the life of his personal present. All good literature has this kind of contemporary authenticity; it is all of its time, and by its very nature expresses *some* aspect of its age. Being novel, and expressing some contemporary theme or feeling, does not mean that all authors at a given moment are lined up in chorus and speaking in unison. Nor that an author should feel an obligation consciously to look round, sum up for himself what the age is about, and 'express it'. You can make generalizations *ex postfacto* about the literary productions of a given period but injunctions to writers are out of place. You could conceivably tell a writer to give a picture of something that has never been expressed before, as Flaubert told Maupassant to describe people and things in a different way from any previous one; or as Yeats told Synge to go to the Western Isles and depict the peasants and fishermen there and the way they lived. But to tell a man to 'express his age', or to imply in criticism that this is what one expects, is to take hold of the wrong end of the stick. No one knows really what the age is, or rather was, until it is past or passing, and its documentation well-nigh complete. Thomas Mann has said how in his earlier years he wrote without giving much thought to others or to 'the time', and only later did he realize that in speaking for himself he had also spoken for his contemporaries, and thus had been a representative voice without knowing it.

Another important point, which has been implied in the preceding paragraphs, is that novelty is intimately connected with individual style. Every authentic style is personal and *ipso facto* a new creation; and every significant poet or writer has his authentic style. This becomes established usually in a series of works—a single one is not enough. Here we come face to face with a further cogent reason why evaluation must often go beyond the single work in order to function adequately and with security. What Henry James called 'the figure in the carpet', or Proust the 'song' that inheres in a true style, both of which are largely determined by the unconscious and are guarantees of creative integrity, are relevant to the evaluation of each of a writer's works. Many good judges, for example, have withheld, or severely qualified, their admiration for Picasso because he has had so many styles. In his cubism, constructivism, neoclassicism, surrealism, etc. he was suspected of always imitating others for want of a genuine line of his own. Amongst dramatists Cocteau has come in for the same kind of criticism. It may be mistaken or not, but it is at least symptomatic for the expectation we have that there is a close relation between new vision and authentic personal style.

The novelty of literary works may lie in the picture, or the feelings, or the language, imagery, and style. But all these things need not be equally novel in all cases; and in fact one observes often not absolute novelty but novelty by mutation, whereby certain elements of continuity and tradition are retained. Klopstock, Goethe, Hölderlin, constitute a series showing mutations and novelty in poetic expression. Mostly, of course, new vision shows itself naturally in new forms, but novelty can lie in the variation or further developing of a form as well as in a wholly new invention; blank verse, the sonnet, the German classical drama from Lessing to Hebbel, are examples. Equally, a personal variant of a general *Weltanschauung* may contain its element of originality, as is the case with Goethe's pantheism, or with the individual differences of the romantics within a framework of generally accepted beliefs.

206

CONCLUSION

In these cursory notes I have raised only three salient problems of literary evaluation. There are numerous others, as for example the question of subjectivity in judgement, of the formation of the taste, of the part played by 'beliefs' in literary works and their sympathetic reception, of permanence as a criterion, of what we mean by 'great' poetry; of the complicated nature of historical aesthetic judgements; and so on. But the three points I have discussed are quite central to evaluation; every work must be referred to these three criteria, whatever else may also be involved.

In concluding, I wish to re-affirm an observation made at the outset. It cannot be too often emphasized that in making judgements the decisive thing is not one quality or feature but a *group* of qualities, which are held in balance. The 'universal', 'reality', the hidden 'truth' of things—it may be that conceptions such as these are not irrelevant; but one thing is certain, they cannot be clues to judgement. They cannot be criteria, because they are unproved terms. Moreover, taken singly, they do not allow for the enormous variety of literary expression. Similarly, some leading ideas from aesthetics, such as Croce's 'intuition' and 'expression', or current notions of symbolization, do not provide criteria. They are generalizations about aesthetic phenomena arising *after* judgements have been made. To help the act of evaluation we have to look for a decisive pattern in which certain features and qualities are co-present, interfused, and intricate. There must be unity (or *Einstimmigkeit*, to recall the expressive German word for this phenomenon), but of the right elements, and metaphorical, not merely architectonic. There must be a worthy theme, an informing idea, some 'philosophical awareness', if banality and triviality are to be avoided; but the presentation is by image, symbol, or form, and with adherent emotion. There must be novelty, original ways of seeing and speaking being the sign of authenticity and sincerity; but not every aspect of a work need be equally new. There must, let us add, be technical power, a craft, command of an apparatus (language, imagery, myths, verse, fiction, etc.), because the use of such an apparatus is the instrument of imagination and makes the superabundance, as against the utility, of expression; but it must be dove-tailed with meanings, and not be simply empty play. Every good literary work satisfies these principal criteria, and simultaneously. In many works the conditions are only partially fulfilled; to that extent they are imperfect, but not necessarily wholly bad or without interest.

In my view the recognition of the features and qualities mentioned, and of their balance and interfusion, is an objective process, independent of purely subjective impressions or responses. It could nevertheless be maintained that the subjective does play a part, and a legitimate one (not a nefarious one calling for strictures only), in evaluation. This occurs particularly in connexion with the *function* of art and literature in the life-economy of the individual. It goes beyond mere opinion, perhaps even beyond judgement. For many people select from the mass of their reading certain authors and works according to their nature and natural taste, and these become a living part of themselves, the agents of a creative communion with literature. A few people have what is called 'catholic' taste, which, however, might be a virtue and might be a defect. Catholic taste is not fair judgement; it could be a substitute for judgement altogether. Good judgement, on the other hand, can perfectly well exist without universal appreciation. These processes have a complex psychology behind them, however, and go beyond the limits of this paper.

SEVENTH SESSION

Chairman: Professor L. C. KNIGHTS

Professor A. CLOSS: Concealment and revelation in modern German lyrical poetry.

Concealment and revelation in modern German lyrical poetry

by

A. CLOSS

The tygers of wrath are wiser than the horses of instruction.

('Proverbs of Hell', W. Blake)

Der Dichter ist, wie der Philosoph, ein Auge.

(Jean Paul)

I

THE BI-POLARITY OF LANGUAGE: THE POSSESSING AND POSSESSED POET

IN his prize-essay on the origin of language Herder says:

> Man demonstrates reflection when the force of his soul works so freely that in the ocean of sensations that flows into it from all the senses, he can, in a manner of speaking, isolate and stop One wave, and direct his attention toward this wave, conscious that he is so doing. He demonstrates reflection when, emerging from the nebulous dream of images flitting past his senses, he can concentrate upon a point of wakefulness, dwell voluntarily on One image, observe it calmly and lucidly, and distinguish characteristics proving that this and no other is the object. He demonstrates reflection when he not only knows all attributes vividly and clearly, but can *recognize* one or more distinguishing attributes: the first act of this recognition yields a clear concept; it is the soul's First judgment—and what made this recognition possible? A characteristic which he had to isolate and which came to him clearly as a characteristic of reflection. Forward! Let us cry $\epsilon\H{v}\rho\eta\kappa\alpha$! The first characteristic of reflection was the word of the soul. With it human speech was invented!
>
> Johann Gottfried HERDER '*Über den Ursprung der Sprache*' 1770, published 1772, cf. E. Cassirer's *The Philosophy of Symbolic Forms*, vol. I, translated by R. Manheim, 1953, Yale University Press.

It would be entirely consistent with Herder's and also Hamann's theories of language if one slightly altered the above last sentence: 'With it human speech was invented' to the statement: 'With it, poetry was born'. There is the ocean of emotions and sensations, and there is the poet's sovereignty to hold in his artistic vision one wave and mirror infinity in it. Language is created by man and man reveals himself in it. Lyrical expression can recapture and form the infinite landscapes of

211

man's soul; it can give artistic shape to his inmost secrets, his wildest dreams and deepest convictions, his despair and his ecstasy. It is, as stated in the Introduction to the Symposium, in the poet's power to give permanence to the fleeting moments of our life: 'Dem Augenblick Dauer verleihen' (Goethe: *Das Göttliche*, about 1783). He can harmonize the sensuous and intellectual chaos of our world, and secure the very continuity of man's spiritual existence. Hence a study of poetry concerns us all. It is by no means merely of an esoteric occupation or academic research into the secret which underlies the interrelationship between substance and artistic presentation in general and above all the limitless flux (Entgrenzung) and the process of condensation (Verdichtung) in lyrical expression.

What is poetry? When Professor E. H. Gombrich in the Introduction to his book: *The Story of Art* (1950) states: 'There really is no such thing as Art. There are artists'—one is tempted to apply the same response to the question about poetry, i.e. there really is no such thing as Poetry. There are only poets. Art and Poetry with capital A and P simply don't exist. But if we don't attach a fetish value to these terms they do mean much to us.

Poetry is essentially an artistic expression of human feeling, thought and vision; it has a law in itself, an 'inner' music; it lives on the two levels of the soul: rational and irrational, intellectual and magic. The poet is the possessor, the maker ($\pi o \eta \tau \acute{\eta} \zeta$) as well as the 'possessed' medium of inspiration, or in Herder's vocabulary: he is the revealing creator as well as the revealed creature of language.

In our time (as also in the German seventeenth-century poetry, but for different reasons) the balance between the powers of verbal constructions or word-combinations and imaginative feeling have been upset. Contemporary lyrical poetry is predominantly cerebral. Craftmanship counts above everything else. I shall, later on, refer to particular symptoms of this development.

Poetry like any other art demands *detachment* from raw actuality, from causal order, from purposiveness and physical interdependence of our material world, but it shrinks into insignificance if it becomes detached from a deeper reality. Between the latter and that of our *actual* self-centred ego, between the revealing greater Self and the individual's material existence lies the mysterious 'Veil of Maya'. The poet, through his power of imagination, creates his own universe, which is *not merely a verbal universe* or an exercise in abstractions, but a symbolic manifestation of man's visions, experiences and feelings: i.e. an artistic *semblance*, not actual feelings, *but a creative semblance of feelings*. The poet, creating from the deep recesses of his spiritual inwardness is profoundly desirous to satisfy his urge to empathy—an empathy which produces art as an equal to Nature, not an imitation of Nature. Or as Professor Srinivasa Iyengar in his recent *Adventure of Criticism* (1962) put it so subtly, 'Art is less than life, yet greater'.

Apart from Herder's above quoted prize-essay, the views of Hamann about language as the essential link with human experience are relevant here. Hamann, too, rejects arid rationalism because of its schismatic effect upon the union of Nature and Spirit in language. He believed in the bi-polar character of language: sensation *and* intuition, experience *and* reason. Goethe understood this well when he wrote in his autobiography:

The principle to which all Hamann's utterances can be reduced is this: 'Everything that man undertakes to perform, whether by deed, or word, or otherwise, must arise from all his powers united together; everything in isolation is worthless'. A splendid maxim, but difficult to follow. In life and art it may well apply; on the other hand, in every deliverance by speech, which is not quite poetic, there is a great difficulty, for words must be detached and individualized in order to say or signify anything. A man, when he speaks, must for the moment be one-sided. There is no communication, no instruction, without separation. But since, now, Hamann always opposed this separation, and as he felt, imagined, and thought in a unity, and wished to speak in the same manner, and demanded the same from others, he came into conflict with his own style and with all which others could produce. In order to accomplish the impossible, he reached after all elements, the deepest and most secret contemplation in which nature and spirit have hidden meetings, illuminating flashes of understanding, which shine forth from such a contact, significant images which hover in these regions, vigorous aphorisms from sacred and profane writers, and everything humorous which could be added; all this constituted the wonderful whole of his style, of his communications. [Goethe: *Poetry and Truth*, XII, translated by R. O. Moon (1932).]

Such a *unity-concept of existence* is not shared by most of our contemporary poets, to whom language is *not* the force of revelation and reason. In a recent, most penetrating study of Hamann's theory of language J. C. O'Flaherty draws the final conclusion which has, although not directly expressed, immediate bearing on our present argument:

If, as Hamann maintains, the final aim of the rationalist is to render man completely independent of objective experience, i.e., to break through 'the confines of sensory experience' to an absolutely autonomous position, he must entirely eliminate language. For linguistic symbols, whether abstract or not, 'belong with their elements to *sensation and intuition*'. (Hamann's italics, VII, 13) ... The rationalist shares with the mystic a dissatisfaction with natural language, but unlike the mystic he does not seek to dispense with language entirely in order to gain an immediate insight into the nature of reality. The rationalistic procedure involves reducing language to 'empty' or relational symbolism, which is adequate for the space and time categories of the mathematical disciplines, but which is totally inadequate for interpreting the meaning of life. [James C. O'Flaherty: 'A study in the philosophy of Johann Georg Hamann', *Unity and Language*, Chapel Hill, University of North Carolina (1952).]

According to Hamann *natural language* has the primacy over *abstract* language which mutilates and sloughs off the sensual associations, and which is *non*-imaginative, *non*-affective, and does not speak to the heart. 'The purity of a language diminishes its riches; a too strict correctness diminishes its strength and manhood' (II, 151/2). Language and thought are inseparable. J. C. O'Flaherty differentiates three groups of thinkers:

(1) the group which tries to escape from the fetters of language, as the ultimate reality must be intuited, e.g. Plato,[1] Bergson and certain contemporary Soviet linguists. [See J. Stalin: *On Several Problems of Linguistics*, tr. by J. V. Murra, New York (1951).]

(2) the group which tries to render language a tool of reason, e.g. Descartes, Leibniz, Bertrand Russell, Whitehead . . .

(3) the group which believes in the togetherness of thought and language, e.g. Hamann, K. W. von Humboldt, Cassirer . . .

Group 2 is obviously the predominant one in our own age. The word has become a dissecting instrument, a self-destroying scalpel in the hands of many a literary artifex. As Molière's remark in *Le mariage forcé*: 'La parole a été donnée à l'homme pour expliquer sa pensée' appears to have been turned upside-down in Talleyrand's celebrated statement: 'La parole a été donnée à l'homme pour déguiser sa pensée', so here in modern poetry the very function of matter and form in language is challenged by a deliberate emphasis on linguistic patterns. The ultimate divorce of reason (which asserts autonomy) from experience deprives words of their fullest and deepest response to human imagination and emotion.

Form attains an absolute priority over matter. It is very easy to be misinterpreted here. Matter and form, receptivity and spontaneity are neither in K. W. von Humboldt's nor in Schiller's view disjoined parts.

In her celebrated aesthetic philosophy and theory of art, *Feeling and Form* (London, 1953) Susanne K. Langer challenges the conventional 'content-form' dichotomy, a formula which has caused a number of misunderstandings among literary and art critics. S. K. Langer overstates this particular argument about content and form. It has, to my knowledge, not been at all realized that her view is fundamentally the same as Schiller's in his *Aesthetic Education of Man*. Poetic expression is no abstraction from the 'content', it is also no 'escape from reality', but it is as vivid an experience as reality can be. Susanne K. Langer differentiates between the *actual* (das Aktuelle) and the *virtual* (the non-actual, das Eigentliche). Art creates a semblance, or if you like to call it an illusion of greater artistic truth and greater reality than actuality can offer: thus in sculpture and architecture there is *virtual space*; in music there is *virtual time*, in poetry and literature in general there is *virtual memory*, i.e. a memory in which the merely descriptive or informative actuality has been transformed and shaped by the act of artistic imagination. But we miss in S. K. Langer's theory the principle of personal commitment. Professor L. C. Knights (cf. 'Idea and Symbol: some hints from Coleridge' p. 142, in *Metaphor and Symbol*, XII Bristol Colston Research Society Symposium, 1960) sharply censures her assertion that: 'Art . . . has no consequences' (*Philosophy in a New Key*, 1942, p. 214), and he refers us to Coleridge who assigns to imagination the power of 'a transforming energy of the mind'. Indeed those words confirm the very principle of my thesis here: It lies in the nature of all great poetry to make us feel drawn into its mystery and personally implicated. We experience a sense of being wholly involved when the poet's imagination opens up before us the depths of man's soul, an intangible Reality which is vaster and deeper than ever imagined on the ordinary level of human experience. Whether a Greek temple or a Michelangelo statue creates a similar degree of personal commitment, lies outside our discussion, we are here mainly thinking of e.g. Sophocles's *Electra* or *Ödipus*, Cervantes's *Don Quichote*, Shakespeare's *Lear, Hamlet, Macbeth,* Racine's *Phèdre,* Goethe's *Faust* or *Trilogie der Leidenschaft,* Schiller's *Wallenstein,* H. von Kleist's *Penthesilea,* the poetry of Hölderlin, Mörike, Rilke, George, Yeats, etc. only to mention a few of the greatest examples in world-literature.

II

A VERBAL AND A SYMBOLIC UNIVERSE

All these artistic creations reveal to us an individual experience through poetic vision. But the relationship between thought and language has in our own days become a problem of linguistic preoccupation against which, according to Cassirer, there is no remedy, as the organic unity (so vividly described by Herder and Hamann and Goethe), the natural balance between reflexion and sensation seems to have been lost to man. No more wholly involved, many a contemporary artist reflects our deep-rooted crisis. He lives either in a verbal or symbolical universe:

> ... Yet there is no remedy against this reversal of the natural order. Man cannot escape from his own achievement. He cannot but adopt the conditions of his own life. No longer in a merely physical universe, man lives in a symbolic universe. Language, myth, art, and religion are parts of this universe. They are the varied threads which weave the symbolic net, the tangled web of human experience. All human progress in thought and experience refines upon and strengthens this net. No longer can man confront reality immediately; he cannot see it, as it were, face to face. Physical reality seems to recede in proportion as man's symbolic activity advances. Instead of dealing with the things themselves man is in a sense constantly conversing with himself. He has so enveloped himself in linguistic forms, in artistic images, in mythical symbols or religious rites that he cannot see or know anything except by the interposition of this artificial medium. His situation is the same in the theoretical as in the practical sphere. Even here man does not live in a world of hard facts, or according to his immediate needs and desires. He lives rather in the midst of imaginary emotions, in hopes and fears, in illusions and disillusions, in his fantasies and dreams. 'What disturbs and alarms man', said Epictetus, 'are not the things, but his opinions and fancies about the things'. [Ernst Cassirer, 'An introduction to a philosophy of human culture', *An Essay on Man,* Yale University Press (1944).]

I have already referred to the contemporary predicament which is also confirmed by Jacques Maritain in his *Creative Intuition in Art and Poetry* (New York, Pantheon Books, 1953): Our contemporary poetry makes the great mistake 'to put the instrumental and secondary before the principal and primary, and to search for an escape through the discovery of a new external approach and new technical revolutions, instead of passing first through the creative source, and thus taking a risk, but having a chance to find a real solution. . . . Another mistake, connected with the first, has been to conceive of forward movement only in terms of flight from Naturalism, as if it were enough to run farther and farther away from an error to get at the truth'.

Thus the natural landscapes are superseded by verbal landscapes of intellectual complexity which in their best representations reflect inventive power and structural force. Their language is that of the intellect concealing the unity of our dual existence. This turning-away from the appearances of things and the common emotional experiences of man towards abstractions is the key-note of contemporary Western poetry which aiming at freedom from imitation of Nature at *any* price, discards Nature itself [i.e. Nature the reality which surrounds us and in which we live and of which we ourselves are a part] and thus paralyses the very source of art.

Moreover, the plunge into abstractions destroys our total feeling towards life and its sense of mystery, as soon as cold science has thrown its searching light into the vast silences of Nature. But the poet, being part of Nature himself, does not 'imitate' her, but he goes to her for his world of images. She gives him everything. Nature *is* transfigured and recreated by the poet's volution and intuition. What else *could* he achieve! But it is a deeper reality, a creative vision. Poetry is, according to T. S. Eliot's *The Sacred Wood* (1920), not a turning loose of emotion . . . but 'an escape from personality'. . . Is this an entirely new approach to our problem?

There is, according to Jacques Martain (l.c.) really *no* essential contradiction between the two apparently opposed statements, made by the prophets of contemporary French poetry;

> Rimbaud: 'Je est un autre' (I is another),
> Lautréamont: 'Si j'existe, je ne suis pas un autre'.

In a similar way one could say: He (the poet) is a human being, he is some other being and yet he is a human being. The 'possessed' poet is, so to say, outside himself, concealing his empirical self by revealing his deeper Self; cf. also Friedrich Nietzsche's *Birth of Tragedy* (1871) . . . 'this self is not the same as that of the waking, empirically real man, but the only verily existent and self-resting at the basis of things' . . . (cf. *Medusa's Mirror*, 1957, p. 12).

Here is an example of the revelation of a deeper Self in a modern work of art. H. von Hofmannsthal in a poetic prose-passage of his in *Andreas* (translated by Mary Hottinger, *Selected Prose*, introduction by H. Broch, London, 1952) reveals to us the secret powers of Nature in an age which seems to have lost its totality of existence. If, as he himself in the *Book of Friends* maintains, the weakness of our age lies in the fact that we treat the situations 'analytically, and in so doing dissolve the magic', his description of Andreas's departure from the Finazzer Valley and the farm, the village and above all from the mysteriously lovable, young girl Romana, raises the situation to a symbolic revelation of the forces of Nature in and around us. There is no question of a Romantic abandonment. The worlds within and without are one:

... Nature came home to Andreas as never before. It was as if the whole scene had risen from his own being at one stroke—that power, that uprising and its crowning purity. That majestic bird was still wheeling above, alone in the light; with widespread wings it swept slow circles. From where it hovered, it could see everything—the Finazzer valley and the farm ... Andreas's soul enfolded the bird—he soared towards it in ecstasy. This time he felt no impulse to lose himself in it; he only felt its supreme power and gift flowing into him. Every shadow, every clog, fell away from him. It was borne in upon him that, seen from high enough, the parted are united, and loneliness is an illusion. He possessed Romana wherever he was—he could take her into him whenever he would. That mountain, rising before him and towering to the skies, was a brother and more than a brother. As it took the tender fawn to its breast in its mighty spaces, covering it with cool shade and hiding it from the pursuer with blue gloom, so Romana lived in him ... Circles dissolved in circles. He prayed with her, and when he looked, he knew that the mountain was simply his prayer. An unutterable certainty came home to him. It was the happiest moment of his life.

Here the poet's vision is rooted in very mysteries of the total human soul. Nature reveals to him the ultimate significance of the scene. The division between the inward and outward situations becomes non-existent, as both are identical. Such art is far more than the product of cerebral craftsmanship. It is rooted in the language of poetic intuition, a language revealing the unity concept of existence, mentioned above. Rilke's last great poem on the threshold of his death is in contemporary German poetry another rare example of the depth of man's physical and spiritual experience:

> 'Come, then, my last and latest acceptation,
> pain in this fleshly web beyond all cure:
> as once in mind, see now my conflagration
> in you; the wood no longer can abjure
> agreement with that flame which you're outthrowing;
> I feed you now and burn in you as well ...
> ... O living, living: being outside.
> And I in flame. And no one knowing me.'

> tr. by J. B. Leishman: *Rainer Maria Rilke*, 1906–1926,
> pp. 353–4; London 1957.

III

THE MERE LOGIC OF LANGUAGE

In the aesthetic phenomenon of the artist lies, as we shall see, the key to some puzzling images in contemporary German poetry, but a great number of obscurities can be traced to quite different reasons. Above all, contemporary European poetry as a whole betrays a marked loss of individual characteristics. The mere language of logic is quite unable to evoke H. von Hofmannsthal's or Rilke's vision, as it can never become the key to poetic revelations. It remains the product of the analytic mind; it tends to become levelled out and repetitive whilst the language of poetry grows out of a synthesis of the unconscious and conscious in the creative individual. Thus the poet's utterance is original as well as universal, at the same time endowed with power of concealment and revelation as Leibniz's individual monads. All great poets have their own characteristic style. Through them language undergoes an essentially individual transformation.

> . . . Here we meet with a sort of metamorphosis of all our common words. Every verse of Shakespeare, every stanza of Dante or Ariosto, every lyrical poem of Goethe has its peculiar sound. Lessing said that it is just as impossible to steal a verse of Shakespeare as to steal the club of Hercules. And what is even more astounding is the fact that a great poet never repeats himself. Shakespeare spoke a language that had never been heard before—and every Shakespearean character speaks his own incomparable and unmistakable language. In Lear and Macbeth, in Brutus or Hamlet, in Rosalind or Beatrice we hear this personal language which is the mirror of an individual soul. In this manner alone poetry is able to express all those innumerable nuances, those delicate shades of feeling, that are impossible in other modes of expression. If language in its development is in need of constant renovation there is no better and deeper source for this than poetry. Great poetry always makes a sharp incision, a definite caesura, in the history of language. [Ernst Cassirer: 'An introduction to a philosophy of human culture', *An Essay on Man*, Yale University Press (1944).]

Contemporary poetry, however, shows a striking affinity between various modern representatives in spite of all obvious differences: there are expressions reminiscent of surrealism, dadaism, montage technique, political satire and commitment, e.g. the intellectual experiments of Paul Celan (born 1920) remind one of surrealism, the satirical absurdities of Günter Grass (born 1927) recall Dadaism. Whilst Eugen Gomringer (born 1925) and Helmut Heissenbüttel (born 1921) revel in feats of mechanical engineering technique, Hans Magnus Enzensberger (born 1929) does not conceal his Ego as one of the most uncompromising European poets of 'committed' verse ('la littérature engagée') in a scientific age.

The difference between the scientific and the emotive language has been expounded in Dr. I. A. Richard's theory. Dr. D. G. James in *Metaphor and Symbol* (l.c. p. 97ff.) objects to such a distinction between the two expressions: scientific and poetic. It is, of course, the imagination, 'the vision of the poet, not his feelings, which in the first place engages us . . . but our emotions will be part and parcel of a pattern of perception . . . vividly apprehended by the poet's imagination and then by us also'. The actual argument in question is always the power of imagination in man (whether poet or scientist)—an intuition which in both cases breaks into and through the area of the empirical surface of facts, and moves about in spheres not realized. Yet, 'the proper terrain of science itself is the limited one of understanding' (l.c. 103) natural, physical phenomena. The poet's vision can move freely beyond those boundaries.

Wladimir Weidle's lament about the split in modern lyrical poetry into analytical intellectualism and an avowed surrender to the unconscious is most symptomatic of a general European situation. In his book *Les abeilles d'Aristée* (1954) [*Die Sterblichkeit der Musen* (1958)] the author prophesies the 'Götterdämmerung' of our civilization which has allowed literature to sink to the level of documentary pastiche and montage, and which is threatened by the destructive forces of a technical science and mass-conscience. The poet [in contrast to Goethe's *Harzreise im Winter* (... 'Dem Geier gleich ... schwebe mein Lied' ...) or Schiller's *Die Künstler* or to Novalis's revelation of the soul] emerges as a de-humanizing faber technicus who as in the case of Gottfried Benn can achieve verses of perfect artistry at the price of almost total personal concealment.

A. A. Scholl (born 1926) differentiates between cold 'abstrakte Struktur-Lyrik' and suggestive 'gegenständliche Lyrik'. In his *Poesie* we have an extreme example of a so-called structural, abstract poem in which an individual content seems completely disguised, concealed, even eliminated by the contrapuntal framework of majuscules and minuscules without punctuation marks. Both parts (in big lettering and in small lettering) form a unity in themselves, at the same time both are tectonically interlocked with each other:

POETRY

begins where the contents end

THE MYSTIC ROSE BLOOMS

beyond the golden words
outside the city walls
beyond discursive forms
outside the systems of thought

IN THE BLAZE OF THE FROST
IN THE MUSTY PATTERN OF THE TAPESTRY
ON THE BACKWALL OF THE ALTARS

in the focus of that
which does not occur

THE POEM IS

a molecular model of vowels
a church window of nouns
a spider's web of memories
a prism of Utopias
a constellation of omissions

A SOLAR SYSTEM
BEYOND THE SOLAR SYSTEM

transitory	THEREFORE IMPERISHABLE
provisional	THEREFORE ULTIMATE
temporal	THEREFORE TIMELESS
fragmentary	THEREFORE PERFECT
defenceless	THEREFORE MIGHTY
imitable	THEREFORE IRREPEATABLE
alogic	THEREFORE LOGIC
irreal	THEREFORE REAL
out of reach	THEREFORE WITHIN REACH
near at hand	THEREFORE UNATTAINABLE
	FOR SPACE-SHIPS
vulnerable	THEREFORE INVULNERABLE
	FOR TACTIC AND STRATEGIC WEAPONS

It is carried
on a tiny chain
under the shirt
on the bare skin

A. A. SCHOLL

Such a composition with fixed rules reminds one of the responses in a musical counterpoint: a melody is added as an accompaniment to a given melody and those two melodies can be interchanged in position above and below one another. Similarly the two wings of the above diptych can be read in vertical or horizontal arrangements.

Intellectual over-refinement and personal concealment in art go with a return to the expression of the Primitives, particularly at a time of crisis in man's self-knowledge.

Man is, according to Ernst Cassirer's *Essay on Man*, ultimately not only an 'animal rationale' but above all an 'animal symbolicum'. Rousseau's pronouncement 'L'homme qui médite est un animal dépravé' is irrefutable, as the intellect cannot reveal the symbolic forms of the universe (cf. Cassirer l.c. p. 24/25): 'It is not an improvement but a deterioration of human nature to exceed the boundaries of organic life'.

Yet, as we have seen, there is no remedy against this reversal of the natural order. Man has now moved from his physical universe into a symbolic or a verbal universe, into a world of linguistic artistry and esoteric dreams.

Here lie the roots of many upsurgings of the unconscious through visions, dreams and ecstasies in modern lyrical poetry. Where, however, instead of a genuinely inspired symbolic language rationally contrived images are formed, they lack the universal appeal and power of persuasion of so-called 'ultimate realities'. Moreover there is a shift of stress as to what is important and unimportant: e.g. the body has been replaced by mechanical patterns, or as Ferdinand Léger (1955) (famous for his compositions of cylinders, tubes etc.), put it:

'L'objet a remplacé le sujet.'

Such so-called de-humanization of art or poetry need in itself not at all mean a loss or symptom of a disintegrating culture. It is unmistakably morbid where merely clever antics of craftsmanship conceal the artistic impotence behind a hap-hazard informality of paradoxes or empty explosions of volition. It can, however, act as a protest against convention, banality and outworn concepts and thus, with some justification, stand side by side with a masterpiece, cf. the tattered Nike bronze by the Greek sculptor Christos Capralos (born 1909) with the Nike of Paionios in Olympia or the Nike of Samothrace in the Paris Louvre[2]; moreover, the protest against profundity (Tiefsinn) leads to a rediscovery of Dada; also poets such as Christian Morgenstern (1914) and Paul Scheerbart (1914) have with all the obvious differences their counterparts in the technical word-designers of contemporary nonsense verse.

IV

THE MAGIC OF OTHERNESS:

MERRY-GO-ROUND, KALEIDOSCOPE, FISH, BIRD, TREE

Certain distinct linguistic devices which *conceal* rather than reveal reality, are common to many modern European poems, but as stated in the Preface of this book, German lyrical poetry will here serve as a test case in question. A once treasured order of things is turned topsy turvy and intentionally made to look absurd. The letter, the alphabetical symbol, becomes autonomous. In extreme cases the absence of control and reason, of moral or even aesthetic preoccupations reminds one of Breton's first Surrealist Manifesto (1924) and of some Surrealist ancestors: Baude-laire, Rimbaud, Guillaume Apollinaire etc. Moreover, a comparison of such arbi-trary fantasies with the sixteenth/seventeenth-century mannerisms of Arcimboldo, Parmigianino, Pontormo and the literary conceits of that time is not far-fetched; see also Gustav René Hocke: *Über Manierismus in Tradition und Moderne* (Merkur, 1956). Sensation is one of the main aims of such artists. They seek the merveilleux, the precious, the union of dissonant elements, and a cool, analytical craftsmanship is their ideal: cf. Paul Valéry: 'Enthusiasm is not an artist's state of mind'. They want to shock. Their attitude might be expressed in Giambattista Marino's words:

Chi non sa far stupir
vada alla striglia* . . .

Moreover, contemporary German lyrical poetry (as well as drama) shows a pre-dilection for *archaic* themes and *chimerical* concepts of a society which is haunted by

*curry-comb

anxiety, uncertainty and incongruous waking-dreams. Its hybrid art is a cross-bred expression composed of individual and fantastic extravangances. There are new horizons, new laws of time and space in an atomized complex of fragmentations with no personal centre any more. G. Benn's poems such as *Verlorenes Ich* ('Statische Gedichte'), or *Levkoienwelle* ('Trunkene Flut') are direct forerunners if not inspirers of many contemporary eccentricities: cf. *Verlorenes Ich* (Lost Ego) which has been blasted by stratospheres:

> Verlorenes Ich, zersprengt von Stratosphären
> Opfer des Ion—: Gamma-Strahlen-Lamm—,
> Teilchen und Feld—: Unendlichkeitschimären,
> auf deinem grauen Stein von Notre-Dame. . . .

Lost Ego

Identity lost, torn apart by stratosphere,
Victim of the ion—: the lamb of gamma-rays—,
Tiny particle and meadow—: Chimeras of infinity
on your grey stone of Notre-Dame.

The days drift by you without night or morning,
the years without snow and fruit
Threateningly keep infinity hidden—,
The world as a flight.

Where do you end, where do you pitch your tent.
Where do your spheres spread themselves out; loss, gain—:
A game of beasts: eternities,
You flee along their trellis.

The look of beasts: the stars seen as intestines,
the Jungle-Death as the reason for creation and existence,
Man, battles between nations, Katalaunean,
all down the abyss of beasts.

The world crumbled in thought. And so did space and time:
and what mankind wove and weighed,
Function only of infinity—
the myth has lied.

Whence, whither—no night, no morning,
No *evoë*, no requiem.
You would like to borrow for yourself a slogan,
But from whom?

> Oh, when everyone inclined towards a centre
> and even the thinkers only thought out god,
> they joined the shepherds and the lamb,
> when the blood from the chalice had made them pure,—
> and all flowed from the one wound,
> broke the bread, which everyone enjoyed:
> oh far-off compelling, fulfilled hour,
> which once enfolded even my own lost self.

or the line in Benn's *Levkoienwelle* ('Wave of gilliflowers'): Man's Self is a fraud, the intellect an (exclusive) guild—

> das Selbst is Trick, der Geist is Zunft

WAVE OF GILLIFLOWERS

> Oh behold, you wave of gilliflowers,
> whose eyes are already brimming over—
> from former times—it is the place
> where an old wound lies;
> for once again we live in days
> when everything aims towards its end,
> 'mänadisch analysis' and questioning,
> which plays around the last of the roses.
>
> One dreams, one finds one's personality
> through self-unfolding of the intellect;
> one dreamt deep; the wrong wave-length:
> the Self is false, the intellect a guild—
> unlearn yourself and every place,
> where you still see a homeland,
> give yourself up to the wave of gilliflowers,
> which flows around the last of the roses.
>
> The off-shoots of the twigs mature,
> it is a great straining of fruit,
> the lakes grow dim like streaks,
> the gardens—such a swelling glow,
> there is the Lernean region
> and a host of figures beckon,
> who mow the blood and sow the end,
> until they sink into the heart of the shadows.

(All translations are my own unless mentioned otherwise. They merely aim at simple renderings into English.)

In spite of so much Geist the scene is obscure: 'Verlerne dich und jede Stelle, wo du noch eine Heimat siehst, / ergib dich der Levkoienwelle' . . . One is here reminded of the end of Chapter IV ('The Pavilion On The Links') in the *New Arabian Nights* by Robert Louis Stevenson (1883, p. 211) which 'tells in what a startling manner I learned that I was not alone in garden sea-wood' . . . 'The darkness was intense. And, as it was blowing great guns from the sea and pouring with rain, the noises of the storm effectually concealed all others'. So also in many a modern poem the human melody is hidden from us or stifled in artifices. The repetitive tone is symptomatic of a number of rather playful, intellectual variations.

No less significant is the baffling and most significant use of certain disguises which are preferred above others in order to conjure up the magic of Otherness, but without fully disclosing its secrets: e.g. the merry-go-round, the rotating kaleidoscope tube with its ever changing coloured objects, moreover the world of the fish, the bird, the tree etc. These images have at the same time an immediate appeal to us if through them our very existence seems to be reflected and revealed as for instance in the melancholy and playful monotony of the revolving roundabout.

It is therefore no coincidence that apart from Rilke's *Das Karussell* the *merry-go-round* has become a favourite amongst writers such as Joachim Ringelnatz whose *Don Quijote* suggests in its rhythmical quality a round-about, but it appears to be a rather trite poem, and not at all as ironical in tone as it is meant to be. The intentionally commonplace statement: 'Ein Schutzmann ist keine Tante' does not spark off any new perspectives. Similarly Günter Grass's 'Atlantic-Transatlantic' roundabout: *Wie traurig sind diese Veränderungen*, a parody on the purposeless to-and-fro of the journey between the New and the Old World, takes its main life from the barren play upon the words: 'patentierte Sitzgelegenheiten—patentlose Besitzer': the patented seats and the patentless possessors. The sensation of individual boredom and indifference is, according to Erasmus Jonas's *In eigener Sache*, merely a simulated apathy concealing, behind 'a cigarette unattentively wedged between the lips', man's shattered hopes and feelings.

The present German division between East and West produced not only two Germanies of opposing ideologies but also brutally added to modern language-predicaments in our age of mass-illiteracy greedy for easy and pretentious popularization (as became manifest in G. Orwell's description of the shrinking language in his book *1984*). Uwe Johnson's two novels *Mutmassungen über Jakob* (1959) and *Das dritte Buch über Arnim* (1961) depict the irreparable injury to words such as Freiheit, Gleichheit, Brüderlichkeit, etc., behind which lie two different and irreconcilable interpretations economically, politically, philosophically according to whether you live on *this* or the *other* side of the wall.

The *kaleidscope* with its constantly changing scenes offers another chiffre through which the author e.g. Franz Mon conceals his personal experience behind a succession of colourful fragments. Human Space and Time, as e.g. in *Zuspruch* by H. Heissenbüttel have lost their meaning: . . .'The face will firmer pull its forgetfulness round the shoulders / tear-distorted lips will rise and walk away' . . . It is as if the fantastic word-designs had been seen through a broken mirror: 'Son of Man . . . you know only a heap of broken images, where the sun beats' (T. S. Eliot). The

separate pieces are joined together by arbitrary *montage* method, e.g. H. Heissenbüttel's *Combination VII*: 'The time is bitter / But the green stone of transformation
burns in the cloud-hole ... The landscape of words displays combinations denied
to invention ... Fragments of a text into which other fragments keep on being
interpolated' ... The so-called 'überscharfe Realistik' (Günter Grass) owes much
to such 'automatic', unconsciously or subconsciously framed texts.

The emphasis lies on construction of a word-world in which the author conceals
himself behind his mask which, however, opens new vistas under the disguise:
'Larvatus prodeo'. He goes below and beyond accepted horizons. He listens to the
language of the fishes (Wieland Schmied: *Die Fisher*): they reveal to him the
India of our adventurous voyage. In the realm of the dolphin ('We cast anchor
in the heart of a dolphin') the frontiers of our own existence take on deeper dimensions. Whilst the image of the *bird* to which we shall refer presently, has for centuries
propelled the enthusiastic thoughts of poets into cloudy spheres, it is now not so
much the feathered vertebrate but its primeval ancestor, the fish, which is the key
to man's unexplored spaces. The mysterious mighty dolphin (cf. *Der Delphin* by
Astrid Claes, born 1928) is the poet's lover and the chosen mask for the other world—
the true home of which people have not the haziest idea:

> ... Ihr wisst nur von meinen leichten Tagen,
> Doch die dunkeln habt ihr nicht gezählt. ...

THE DOLPHIN

Leave the requests, friends, leave the questions,
for why is it that you have chosen me?
you know only of my easy days,
yet you have not counted the dark ones.

I will journey further on the streams,
it is useless for you to torment me so—
for, many years ago,
I married a mighty Dolphin.

I never see him, for he must sleep
somewhere in the deep where he lives.
Sometimes I sing in a harbour,
because I know that it is then he raises his head.

Because I know that then he listens,
turning his large and weary eyes to the wind.
No-one shall ever be companion to me at night
until we both are finally united.

The image is most suggestive, considering the properties of the animal: the dolphin,
a small whale (cetacea, cf. κῆτοζ), particularly the fish dorado (coryphaena kip-
puris), is renowned for its colours and when it is taken out of water or is dying,

rapidly changes its hue. Above all, the dolphin exhibits ancient features which connect it with the Eocene period: the dawn ($\dot{\epsilon}\omega\zeta$) of the recent flora and fauna, when the earliest organisms are thought to have developed. Its popularity and emblematic importance is proved by its appearance in heraldry and in Christian art, representing love, zeal and swiftness; cf. Thomas Moule: *Heraldry of Fish*, London, 1842: The chief of fish, the dolphin, is the emblem of the sea; it appears on early Greek coins; it is the symbol of the seat of the Greek empire. Aldus, the printer of Greek, chose the dolphin as artistic device for his famous Aldine press. The dolphin appears in the Ancient and Romantic stories of Arion, etc.

No wonder that this sensational small whale has captured the imagination not only of the Romantics but also contemporary poets: e.g. the magic spell which the movements, the eyes, the shape and colour of this cold-blooded aquatic animal cast upon our every-day existence, is effectively caught in Günter Eich's playful verses *Wo ich wohne* which remind one of Paul Klee pictures.

Eich's poem seems to read like an illustration of Paul Klee's statement in his *Inward Vision* (1958, London): 'The visible world is merely an isolated case in relation to the universe'. Klee endeavours to present a 'reality' *beyond* all visual experience of things. Thus he opens the veil of appearances and reveals the inner world of unknown realities. But a number of other now fashionable attempts to penetrate into the dark regions of the 'Republik der Fische' degenerate to lame mannerisms. Here is G. Eich's delightful poem:

> Where I live
> As I opened the window
> fish swam into the room,
> herrings. It seemed
> as if a shoal was just passing by.
>
> They were also playing among the pear-trees.
> But most of them
> kept to the wood
> above the tree-nurseries and gravel pits.
>
> They are a nuisance. But still a greater nuisance are
> the sailors (the higher ranks, too, helmsmen and captains)
> who often come, come to the open window
> and ask for a light for their poor tobacco.
>
> I want to leave.

The image of the tree, *Du warst ein Baum*, by Anneliese Hager (born 1904) is another disguise for an inexplicable Otherness whose secret we cannot fathom:

> Du verhülltest deine Wurzeln in der Erde
>   Da ward ich trächtig von
> dem Schweigen deines Stammes und
> gebar die Antwort im Licht des Todes.

('You covered up your roots in the earth / I became pregnant with the silence of your trunk and gave birth to the answer in the light of death'.) Elsewhere the author of the above poem, like many other poets, lacks the power of original language, e.g. her poem *Paris, Juni 1951*, with the anthropomorphous and contrived metaphors: 'Haut einer verirrten Stunde', 'Unter dem blauen Haar der Nächte': 'Skin of a misguided hour', 'Under the blue hair of the nights' . . .

V

THE BITTER EDGE OF LOVE

Some of the most striking features of poetic concealment and revelation are manifested in the modern poems about Love and Nature. A parallel to the music of today will not be out of place. The discords, up to the end of the nineteenth century, were frequently dissolved. We now are more sophisticated, and our ear is accustomed to clashing sounds or images. For fear of sounding sentimental some modern authors wear a mask behind which the communication between I and Thou and between the I and the Universe is concealed. We are, in spite of obvious differences in tone and attitude, reminded of the passage in *Les Rougon-Macquart Historie naturelle et sociale d'une famille sous le Second Empire, La joie de vivre* by Émile Zola [Paris, Bibliotheque–Charpentier (1953), p. 51] where man deliberately turns away from the overwhelming sight of the starry sky which fills him with fear:

—C'est beau, les étoiles, dit-elle gravement, après un long silence.

Il laissa le silence retomber. Sa gaieté ne sonnait plus si claire, un malaise intérieur troublait ses yeux ouverts très grands. Au ciel, le fourmillement des astres croissait de minute en minute, ainsi que des pelletées de braise jetées au travers de l'infini.

—Tu n'as pas appris ça, toi, murmura-t-il enfin. Chaque étoile est un soleil, autour duquel roulent des machines comme la terre; et il y en a des milliards, d'autres encore derrière celles-ci, toujours d'autres . . .

Il se tut, il reprit d'une voix qu'un grand frisson étranglait:

—Moi, je n'aime pas les regarder . . . Ça me fait peur.

In the poetry of Stefan George (1868–1933) and Gottfried Benn (1886–1956) we already meet with the intellectual alienation and withdrawal of the modern poet from the emotional experience of love between man and woman: cf. Benn's song: 'Einsamer nie als im August. Erfüllungsstunde' . . . Against the intoxication and exchange of love the poet offers a counterforce, the intellect: . . . 'dienst du dem Gegenglück, dem Geist'.

With Günter Grass (born 1927) this counterforce displays an especially bitter edge. As Picasso deliberately distorts the human face and figure, so does Günter Grass in a consciously degrading manner. The following so-called 'love-poem', an extreme example of concealment, through the disguise of sarcasm, indicates some trends in contemporary love-poems: *Blutkörperchen*: in the state of nakedness the body's proportions are made to look repulsive: 'I don't know why you are so ugly, / why my eye cannot turn away from you' . . . yet, though she is ugly he loves her 'as far as this possible' ('ich liebe dich soweit dies möglich ist'), and he intends to think out a ballet for her little white and red blood-corpuscles. We may well quote the last line: 'Ob sich der Aufwand gelohnt hat', and turn the question against the author himself.

Such egocentric barrenness stands in sharp contrast to the Goethean principle of diastole and systole, of give and take in our physical as well as spiritual existence. In our time Hugo von Hofmannsthal seeks a similar equilibrium between the inner and the outer world, when in his *Book of Friends* he maintains:

> Man perceives in the world only what already lies within him; but to perceive what lies within him man needs the world; for this, activity and suffering are indispensable . . .

H. von Hofmannsthal, in another striking passage, demands concealment of depth. Where is it to be hidden? On the very surface: 'Die Tiefe muss man verstecken. Wo? An der Oberfläche' (*Buch der Freunde*).

But in contemporary poetry the mystery of love often remains concealed behind sneering indifference or ingenious puzzles. It is not surprising that, for instance, the poetry of Ingeborg Bachmann in *Die gestundete Zeit* (1953) and *Anrufung des grossen Bären* (1956) and of Paul Celan in *Mohn und Gedächtnis* (1954) and *Sprachgitter* (1959) etc. is marked by concettisms. It seems impossible to feel simply or to express feelings simply. These are transmitted to us through chiffres, e.g. 'schwarz' signifying guilt and crime, or 'Stein' as symbol of a loveless age: 'Es ist Zeit, dass der Stein sich zu blühen bequemt' (*Mohn und Gedächtnis*). The danger is that chiffres turn into stone themselves when creative vision (e.g. the blossom rescued from the stone, spring from death, human feeling from guilt) becomes a mannerism. Hans Carossa's saying, 'Raube das Licht aus dem Rachen der Schlange' was exposed to a similar fate. Ingeborg Bachmann's *Erklär mir, Liebe!* though in many ways an exception among modern love poems, shrinks from disclosing the soul's despair, which, however, is forcefully suggested by the startling line:

> . . . Ein Stein weiss einen andern zu erweichen . . .

Her poem, instead of giving lyrical self-expression, turns into a panegyrical enumeration of the wonders of love in Nature: the preening peacock, the amorously cooing dove, the calling drake, the wild honey, the dashing fish, the dancing scorpion, the loving insect . . .

Unwilling to reveal personal commitment the poet sings of the miracle of Eros and silences her own questioning. She sees the salamander go through every fire—without fear and without pain:

> Erklär mir nichts. Ich seh den Salamander
> durch jedes Feuer gehen.
> Kein Schauer jagt ihn, und er schmerzt ihn
> nicht.

When in 1962 the Alma–Johanna–König Literature Prize for the best German love-poem was awarded, the winner was Johannes Bobrowski (born 1917) with his poem *Im Strom*. The remarkable feature of this Prize Competition is that almost all promising poems under consideration, amongst them particularly Bobrowski's contribution, betray the present tendency of concealment ('Verschlüsselung') of the love-theme, cf. the second verse of *Im Strom*,

<table>
<tr><td>... Es lag des Täufers Haupt
auf der zerrissenen Schläfe,
in das verschnittene Haar
eine Hand mit bläulichen, losen
Nägeln gekrallt ...</td><td>The baptist's head lay
on the gashed temples,
a hand with bluish, loose
nails, clutched into the
cut-up hair ...</td></tr>
</table>

An echo of Trakl's lyrical language is unmistakable here. The lovers have come to rest. It is a sleep 'from which nobody will awaken them in their time'.

VI

ALIENATION FROM THE NATURAL SCENE

It is in German *Nature Poetry* that the contemporary powers of poetic expression are perhaps strongest. No wonder! Its roots go back to Goethe, Hölderlin, Mörike, the inexhaustible resources of the German Volkslied, and further back to Walther and Heinrich von Morungen etc. Moreover, some of the most original features of sixteenth-century German art are revealed through Nature themes: cf. Altdorfer (his 'Waldstrasse' is the first landscape picture without human staffage), Grünewald, Hans Baldung Grien, Dürer and Lucas Cranach. The vision that had inspired German Romantic Art had dawned in poetry with Tieck, Novalis, etc., in painting with Kaspar David Friedrich and Philipp Otto Runge whose work, incidentally, is too little known in England. German Romanticism was born of a pantheistic attitude towards nature that affords a parallel to Schelling's or Schleiermacher's philosophy in revolt against classicism, whilst its mysticism is reminiscent of Jakob Boehme. There is, however, a link with the present as well as with the past: P. O. Runge's colour symbolism and C. D. Friedrich's spacial concepts offer affinities with contemporary art, but they also reveal an affinity (not for the first time, cf. Grünewald's 'Isenheim Altar', the wing: 'The Two Hermits') between German and Asian ideals.[2]

In poetry it was mainly the Romantics who, by listening and abandoning themselves to the magic sounds of Nature, imagined to reveal its very soul, in a way similar to that of Michelangelo who sought the form living in the marble-block: cf. Eichendorff's *Wünschelrute* ('The Divining Rod'):

<table>
<tr><td>Schläft ein Lied in allen Dingen
Die da träumen fort und fort,
Und die Welt hebt an zu zingen,
Triffst du nur das Zauberwort.</td><td>Sunk in sleep a song is ringing
In the dreaming things around,
And the world breaks forth in singing
Once the magic word is found.</td></tr>
</table>

(tr. by Mabel Cotterell in *The Anthology of German Poetry from Hölderlin to Rilke, in English translation*, ed. by Angel Flores, 1960, New York).

Romantic Nature poetry reveals an emotionally charged or intuitively created landscape. Without forcing literary phenomena into abstract classifications we can in the German post-Romantic poetry clearly perceive the tendency towards suppression of that Romantic and personal participation in Nature's events. However, the human voice asserts itself again and again in Nature's scene. Yet the keynote in twentieth-century poetry is a de-personalization of Nature, or as Oskar Loerke (1884–1941) put it: 'Mehr Gesang der Dinge als meine Stimme'.

The whole contemporary artistic approach to Nature is, as we can see, also from international examples (for instance in Tapies's *Earth Crust*, exhibited in the Guggenheim Museum in New York a short time ago) essentially different from the Romantic attitude; cf. Kenneth Clark's remark about Sutherland in *Landscape into art* (London, 1949): 'One of the disconcerting things in Mr. Sutherland's work is the disappearance of a human scale'.

The same, of course, could be said of Paul Klee or Joan Miro, Kandinsky, Duchamp etc. Nature, to the twentieth-century artist, is either eliminated altogether or transposed; it has lost its natural order; it lacks unity; it seems too vast, too mysterious and incongruous to be grasped by the artist who in vain looks to the scientist for the meaning of the universe. In many cases the reader needs a guide to the personal imagery. When, however, the contemporary poet succeeds, without puzzling obscurity and in spite of concealing the direct vision of a natural scenery, in creating a new, spiritual relationship the alienation from the original nature-scene adds to the poem's fascination, cf. *Mein Vogel* by Ingeborg Bachmann (born 1926): in it nature is not taken literally: the bird symbolizes the poet's superior faculty: mastery over matter; poetic inspiration. The words as also the perceptions are borrowed from Nature: Vogel, Feder, Schleier, Nacht, Sterne, Warte, but they are words with overtones and figurative concepts; they are charged with a transforming meaning: flight (of inspiration), pen, veil of owl and of poetry.

> . . . Mein eisgrauer Schultergenoss, *meine Waffe,*
> mit jener *Feder* besteckt, meiner *einzigen Waffe*!
> Mein einziger Schmuck: *Schleier* und *Feder* von dir.
>
> Wenn auch im Nadeltanz unterm Baum
> die Haut mir brennt
> und der hüfthohe Strauch
> mich mit würzigen Blättern versucht,
> wenn meine Locke züngelt,
> sich wiegt und nach Feuchte verzehrt,
> stürzt mir der *Sterne* Schutt
> doch genau auf das Haar . . .
>
> (Italics are my own.)

It lies in the poet's power to throw the veil of imagination over our world of outward appearances and change it; cf. Stefan George's Seventh *Schleiergedicht* (in his *Teppich des Lebens*): 'So wie mein schleier spielt wir euer sehnen!' The poet's veil conjures up an Oriental city, an Ossian landscape, Classical serenity.

In his *Tage mit Hähern* ('Days with Jays') Günter Eich (born 1907) presents the reader with some difficulties. Its meaning, like that of Ingeborg Bachmann's 'Mein Vogel', is not a literal one, but it is hidden behind a veil of a privately metaphoric language, e.g. the name of the noisy bird Häher (= Eichelhäher) calls up the image of Eicheln ('acorns of his cries'). It is too often merely the word which is automatically suggested by its preceding expression. Thus the above poem is subjected to a typically modern process of capricious waywardness, which can lead to unaccountable results. The interpretation of Eich's verses is indicated by lines such as 'Sein Flug gleicht dem Herzschlag' . . . or 'Ein bitteres Mehl, die Speise des ganzen Tags'.

Josef Weinheber (1892–1945) in his poem *Das Kunstwerk* also suggests (as G. Eich in *Tage mit Hähern*) that the work of art arrived 'ohne mich'—but Weinheber's thoughts are still anchored in the conviction of the poet's divine imagination: 'Und plötzlich ertönt es, / wann Gott es gefällt' . . .

How strong the measure of concealment through the above alienation from natural objects can become, is evident in Gottfried Benn's *Gladiolen* poem which cuts itself off from organic life:

> Ein Strauss Gladiolen
> das ist bestimmt sehr schöpfungsdeutend,
> *fern* von Blütengeweichel mit Fruchterhoffnung—:
> langsam, haltbar, *unirritiert*,
> grosszügig, sicher der Königsträume. . . .

According to Benn's 'Phänotyp' there are two groups of writers: the Kunstträger and the Kulturträger. He sides with the Kunstträger who is a-social, loveless. His 'love' is dedicated solely to his 'royal dreams', his work of artistry which is anti-historical, stylized, static, fateless. The frigidity and sterility of the 'Phänotyp' need here not be analyzed further. It conceals rather than reveals Nature.

In contrast to it, Goethe received the veil of poetry out of the hand of truth: 'der Dichtung Schleier aus der Hand der Wahrheit'. The *Zueignung* (1784) is significant as to his relationship to life and art; he remained rooted in and dedicated to Nature and human community: 'Was fruchtbar ist, allein ist wahr'. In Goethe's or also in Schiller's or Hölderlin's view a work of art is the achievement of the human mind and as such it always remains, in the highest sense, a work of Nature. This is a truth which is fundamentally valid in spite of Benn's remark in the 'Ptolemäer' (1949): 'Die Eierstöcke sind die grössten Philosophen' (the ovaries are the greatest philosophers).

In his 'Intellektuelle Heiterkeit' the 'nature-poet' K. Krolow (born 1915–) is the spokesman of many contemporary poets when he advocates fragmentation and a chain-like continuity of themes. He defends the so-called 'porous', 'open' poems (the term obviously stems from Heinrich Wölfflin's art-categories). Such a view moves already a long way from Benn's hermetic art which aims at air-tight perfection.

Yet a sense of mystery is not lost in this age of ready-made prescriptions as to how to write modern poetry. In their best nature-poems Wilhelm Lehmann (1882–) and Elizabeth Langgässer (1899–1950) do awaken a sense of wonder which, however, in many of their poems becomes obscured by intellectual preciosity, i.e. G. Lehmann's *Unaufhörlich* which is un-intelligible without a knowledge of Wolfram's *Parzival*, VI, 282/24 ff., the story of the three blood-drops flowing from the goose which was struck by the falcon:

dô er die bluotes zeher sach	[when he saw the drops of blood
ûf dem snê (der was al wîz),	upon the snow (which was shining
dô dâhte er . . .	white) he thought . . . (of)
Kondwîrâmûrs . . .	Kondwiramur].

or Wolfram's Foreword (I. 5/6) in which the reference to the magpie colours is made:

'unverzaget mannes muot,
als agelsteren varwe tuot' . . .

[. . . a fearless man (can when overcome by despondency be)
like the magpie (white and black—heaven and hell)]

Similarly also Elizabeth Langgässer's poem: *Rose im Oktober* is charged with names, conceptions and themes from the Arthurian saga (Avalon, Kondwiramur, Grail).

VII

CONCLUSION

If these nature-poems fall short of greatness it is because they are predominantly *invented* and thus ultimately conceal the forces within the heart of the poet who suffers 'the assault of his god', as Rilke puts it in *Über den jungen Dichter*, 1913 (translated by G. Craig Houston, 1954, London, edited and introduced by J. B. Leishman)[3], revised version: 'The Young Poet. Some conjectures concerning the coming into being of poems' in *The Creative Vision. Modern European Writers on their Art*, edited by H. M. Block and H. Salinger, New York, 1960 (pp. 45–46). Here Rilke reveals the very secret of poetic creation: . . .'Even now when I must acknowledge that poems are formed, I am far from thinking them invented; it seems to me rather as if there appeared in the soul of the poetically inspired a spiritual predisposition, which was already present between us (like an undiscovered constellation)'.

This is essentially also the view of Goethe, Hölderlin, Blake and all great writers (not only the Romantics!) to whom poetry is less a matter of intellectual argument and wit than of imagination. The poet's true Self is rooted in a spiritual single-mindedness. However selfish he as a human individual may be, in the art of creating he is not a self-centred being but a disinterested personality revealing himself in and through the work and by doing so, sacrificing himself for the work with an original singleness of purpose. Moreover, in the best works there is craftsmanship as well as sheer delight, a quality often lacking in 20th century experiments.

The poet's intuition shapes a work of its own value, but at the same time he draws us into its artistic sensation. This is no paradox. There is concealment as well as revelation. Both must be balanced. The sharing of the poet's emotion, reflexion, experience and vision is to many who shrink from narrow political or moral allegiances, a manifestation of the concatenation and perpetuity of the human mind and an essential tie between men. Only a really 'possessed' poet can, quite unconsciously, forge this spiritual bond. He descends to the troubled mind like the Angel in St. John V, ... 'In a pool lay a great multitude of impotent folk, of blind, halt, withered, waiting for the moving of the water. For an angel went down at a certain season into the pool, and troubled the water: whosoever then first after the troubling of the water stepped in was made whole of whatever disease he had'.

Angelus enim descendebat praestituto tempore in piscinam, et turbabat aquam: itaque qui primus ingressus erat post aquae turbationem, sanus fiebat a quocunque detineretur morbo.

NOTES

1. Plato: 7th Epistle:

... For everything that exists there are three instruments by which the knowledge of it is necessarily imparted; fourth, there is the knowledge itself, and, as fifth, we must count the thing itself which is known and truly exists. The first is the name, the second the definition, the third the image, and the fourth the knowledge. If you wish to learn what I mean, take these in the case of one instance, and so understand them in the case of all. A circle is a thing spoken of, and its name is that very word which we have just uttered. The second thing belonging to it is its definition, made up of names and verbal forms. For that which has the name 'round', 'annular', or 'circle', might be defined as that which has the distance from its circumference to its centre everywhere equal. Third comes that which is drawn and rubbed out again, or turned on a lathe and broken up—none of which things can happen to the circle itself—to which the other things mentioned have reference; for it is something of a different order from them. Fourth comes knowledge, intelligence and right opinion about these things. Under this one head we must group everything which has its existence, not in words nor in bodily shapes, but in souls—from which it is clear that it is something different from the nature of the circle itself and from the three things mentioned before. Of these things intelligence comes closest in kinship and likeness to the fifth, and the others are farther distant.

The same applies to straight as well as to circular form, to colours, to the good, the beautiful, the just, to all bodies whether manufactured or coming into being in the course of nature, to fire, water, and all such things, to every living being, to character in souls, and to all things done and suffered. For in the case of all these no one, if he has not somehow or other got hold of the four things first mentioned, can ever be completely a partaker of knowledge of the fifth. Further, on account of the weakness of language, these (i.e. the four) attempt to show what each thing is like, not less than what each thing is. For this reason no man of intelligence will venture to express his philosophical views in language, especially not in language that is unchangeable, which is true of that which is set down in written characters. ...

The Platonic Epistles, translated by J. Harward, Cambridge University Press, 1932.

2. See the Illustrations attached here at the end of the book. They all emphasize some striking parallels between art and literature as regards the above discussed formal problems and experiments, cf. also Hannah Priebsch Closs: *German Painting in Germany. A Companion to German Studies*, J. Bithell; 5th ed., 1955, pp. 506–533.

3. As to the above Rilke reference to the spiritual predisposition: 'Geistige Prädisposition in der Seele des dichterisch Ergriffenen', I am grateful to my revered friend J. B. Leishman who shortly before his untimely, tragic death in the Swiss Alps in August 1963 sent me the full original quotation from Rilke's *Selected Works*.

I. *Nike* of Samothrace, Paris, Louvre.

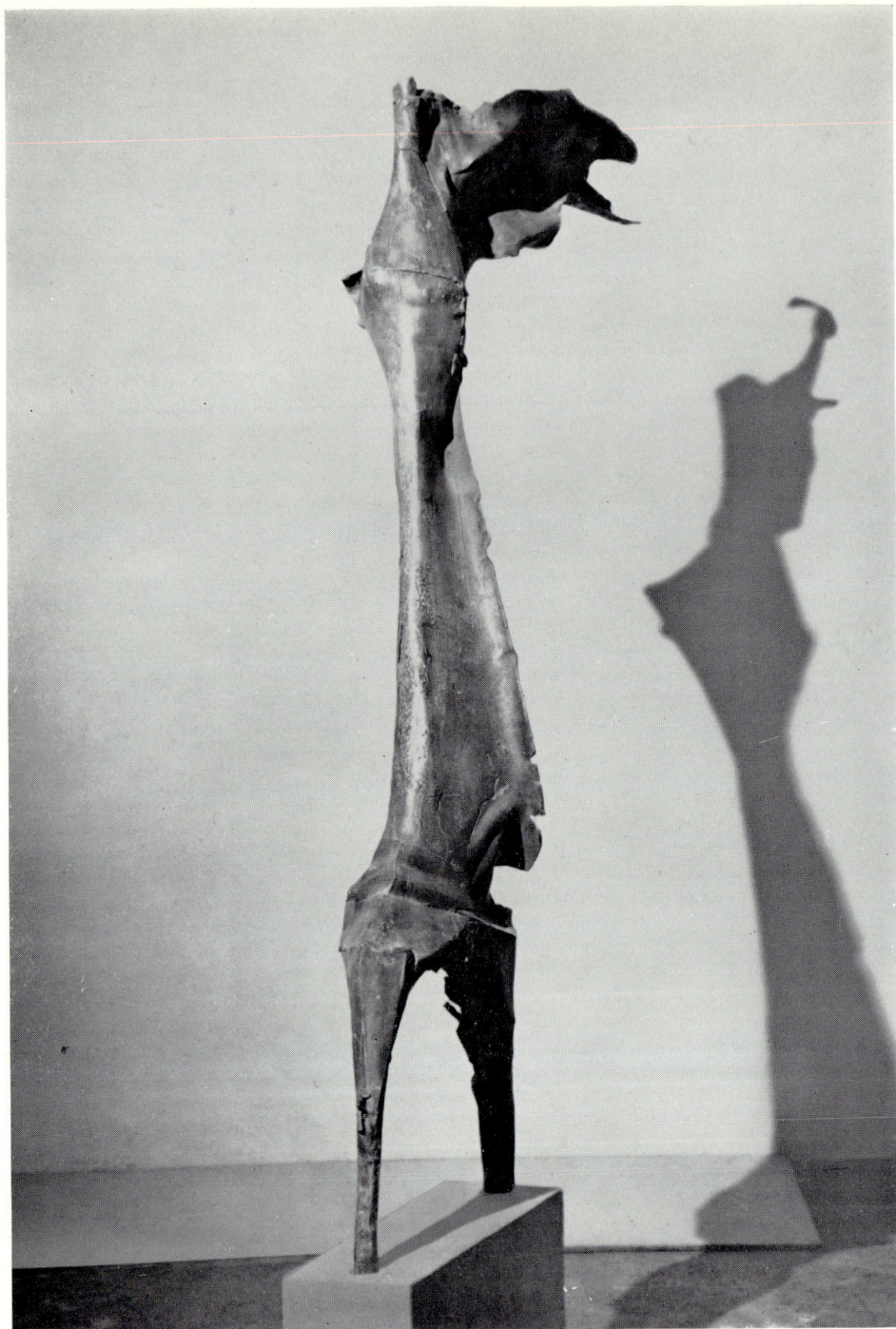

II. Christos Capralos: *Nike*. Bronze, h. 186 cm.

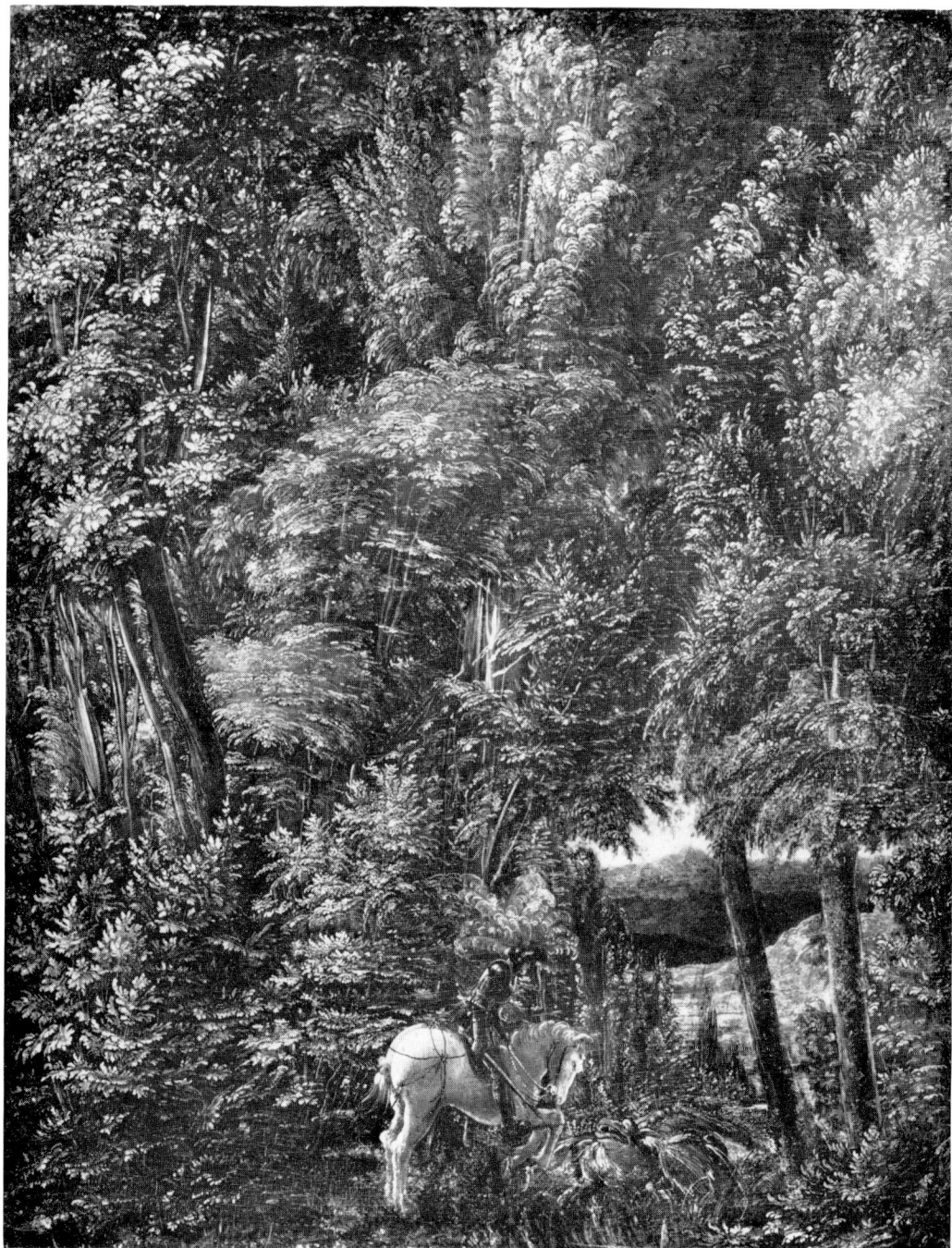

III. Albrecht Altdorfer: *St. George and the Dragon*, Alte Pinakothek, Munich.

IV. Caspar David Friedrich: *Zwei Männer in Betrachtung des Mondes*, Dresden.

V. Philipp Otto Runge: *Christus auf dem Meere*, Hamburg.

VI. Matthias Grünewald: *St. Anthony and St. Paul in the Wilderness*,
Isenheim Altar, Colmar.

VII. Paul Klee: *Sterbende Pflanzen*—Piante Morenti, 1922.

CHECKED

122184

LINKED

CHRIST'S COLLEGE LIBRARY
WOOLTON ROAD
LIVERPOOL 16

Please return this book to the Lib